# Minds & Hearts

OTHER BOOKS FROM BRIGHT LEAF

*House Stories*
*The Meanings of Home in a New England Town*
BETH LUEY

*Bricklayer Bill*
*The Untold Story of the Workingman's Boston Marathon*
PATRICK L. KENNEDY AND LAWRENCE W. KENNEDY

*Concrete Changes*
*Architecture, Politics, and the Design of Boston City Hall*
BRIAN M. SIRMAN

*Williamstown and Williams College*
*Explorations in Local History*
DUSTIN GRIFFIN

*Massachusetts Treasures*
*A Guide to Marvelous, Must-See Museums*
CHUCK D'IMPERIO

*Boston's Twentieth-Century Bicycling Renaissance*
*Cultural Change on Two Wheels*
LORENZ J. FINISON

*Went to the Devil*
*A Yankee Whaler in the Slave Trade*
ANTHONY J. CONNORS

*At Home*
*Historic Houses of Eastern Massachusetts*
BETH LUEY

*Black Lives, Native Lands, White Worlds*
*A History of Slavery in New England*
JARED ROSS HARDESTY

*At Home*
*Historic Houses of Central and Western Massachusetts*
BETH LUEY

*Flight Calls*
*Exploring Massachusetts through Birds*
JOHN R. NELSON

*Lost Wonderland*
*The Brief and Brilliant Life of Boston's Million Dollar Amusement Park*
STEPHEN R. WILK

*Legends of the Common Stream*
JOHN HANSON MITCHELL

*I Believe I'll Go Back Home*
*Roots and Revival in New England Folk Music*
THOMAS S. CURREN

# Minds & Hearts

## The Story of James Otis Jr. and Mercy Otis Warren

JEFFREY H. HACKER

BRIGHT LEAF
Amherst and Boston
An imprint of University of Massachusetts Press

*Minds and Hearts* has been supported by the Regional Books Fund, established by donors in 2019 to support the University of Massachusetts Press's Bright Leaf imprint.

Bright Leaf, an imprint of the University of Massachusetts Press, publishes accessible and entertaining books about New England. Highlighting the history, culture, diversity, and environment of the region, Bright Leaf offers readers the tools and inspiration to explore its landmarks and traditions, famous personalities, and distinctive flora and fauna.


Printed in the United States of America

ISBN 978-1-62534-574-5 (paper); 575-2 (hardcover)

Designed by Sally Nichols
Set in Adobe Baskerville
Printed and bound by Books International, Inc.

Cover design by Kristina Kachele Design, llc
Cover art: John Andrews, *Battle of the Cowpens,* 1781, Science History Images/Alamy Stock Photo; John Singleton Copley, *Portrait of Mercy Otis Warren* (1728–1914), Art Reserve/Alamy Stock Photo; Henry Blackburn, *Portrait of James Otis* (1725–1783), The Picture Art Collection/Alamy Stock Photo.

Library of Congress Cataloging-in-Publication Data

Names: Hacker, Jeffrey H., author.
Title: Minds and hearts : the story of James Otis Jr. and Mercy Otis Warren / Jeffrey H. Hacker.
Other titles: Story of James Otis Jr. and Mercy Otis Warren
Description: Amherst : Bright Leaf, an imprint of University of Massachusetts Press, [2021] | Includes bibliographical references and index.
Identifiers: LCCN 2020053350 (print) | LCCN 2020053351 (ebook) | ISBN 9781625345745 (paperback) | ISBN 9781625345752 (hardcover) | ISBN 9781613768303 (ebook) | ISBN 9781613768310 (ebook)
Subjects: LCSH: Otis, James, 1725–1783. | Warren, Mercy Otis, 1728–1814. | Otis family. | Women authors—Massachusetts—Biography. | Revolutionaries—Massachusetts—Biography. | Massachusetts—History—Revolution, 1775–1783.
Classification: LCC E302.6.O8 H33 2021 (print) | LCC E302.6.O8 (ebook) | DDC 973.3092/2 [B]—dc23
LC record available at https://lccn.loc.gov/2020053350
LC ebook record available at https://lccn.loc.gov/2020053351

British Library Cataloguing-in-Publication Data
A catalog record for this book is available from the British Library.

For JLL

Political liberty . . . is a tranquility of mind arising from the opinion each person has of his safety.

—James Otis Jr., quoting Montesquieu
*Boston Gazette,* January 11, 1763

O might I weep my weary life away,
And close mine eyes at misery at large!
Yet I could bear my griefs tenfold enhanced,
If this might heal or mitigate thy pain,
Or sooth the anguish of a brother's heart.

—Lucia, in Mercy Otis Warren,
*The Ladies of Castile,* act 3, scene 1

# Contents

# Minds & Hearts

# Introduction

In a fit of madness and self-effacement toward the end of his life, the firebrand Boston attorney and politician James Otis Jr. (1725–1783) destroyed the last of his letters, books, and papers in a giant bonfire. John Adams called him "the earliest and principal founder" of the American Revolution.[1] "I have never known a man whose love of his country was more ardent or severe," the aging former president would recall, "never one whose services for any ten years of his life were so important and essential to the cause of his country as those of Mr. Otis from 1760 to 1770."[2]

Adams may be forgiven a Massachusetts bias—rival Virginians in the early 1800s were casting Patrick Henry as the first hero of the colonial uprising—but Otis's role in arousing and articulating core grievances against British rule can scarcely be overstated.[3] While Otis receives undue credit for coining the motto "Taxation without representation is tyranny," his electrifying oratory and fierce commitment to Enlightenment ideals established that principle as the ideological cornerstone of the revolutionary movement.[4] In the groundbreaking Writs of Assistance Case of 1761, he challenged unfettered search and seizure by British customs officials. Later in that decade, with

Samuel Adams, he led colonial opposition to the Stamp Act and Townshend Acts. He was conflicted by the prospect and contours of American freedom but among the first to recognize its imperative. Of all the agitators, rabble-rousers, tax protesters, and political insurgents who took up the cause of liberty, it was Otis to whom contemporaries referred simply as "the Patriot." Why he is not counted among the nation's founders is one of the most moving but little remembered tragedies of that turbulent era.

The most ardent of Otis's admirers and molders of his reputation was his younger sister Mercy Otis Warren (1728–1814). A poet, playwright, essayist, historian, and political commentator of uncommon influence for a woman of the eighteenth century, she has earned unofficial designations as the "poet laureate," "conscience," and "first lady" of the American Revolution (the last of these shared with her great friend Abigail Adams). Warren's satiric verse dramas, featured prominently in the patriot press, were powerful weapons in the battle for public opinion in the years leading up to and during the War of Independence. She was a correspondent and respected adviser to a who's who of political leaders during the revolutionary period and early republic—from John Adams and Samuel Adams to George Washington, Thomas Jefferson, and Elbridge Gerry. Her Anti-Federalist pamphlet *Observations on the New Constitution* (1788) stirred heated debate over the proposed U.S. Constitution and helped win ratification of the Bill of Rights.

John Adams, Alexander Hamilton, and Thomas Jefferson all invoked the same superlative in extolling Mercy's writings. Adams, a longtime friend and literary mentor, found in her work "incontestable evidences of real *genius*"; on another occasion, he referred to her as "the most accomplished lady in America."[5] Hamilton was hardly less admiring, commenting on her dramatic works, "Female *genius* in the United States has outstripped the male."[6] Jefferson, within days of taking office as president, wrote to Mercy's husband, James Warren, "I have long possessed evidence of her high station in the ranks of *genius*."[7]

Mercy Otis Warren wrote in obscurity for much of her life; her most inflammatory material appeared anonymously for her physical safety and because she was a woman. It was not until 1790 that a collection of her original verse, *Poems, Dramatic and Miscellaneous,* appeared under Mrs. Warren's own name. Her three-volume *History of the Rise, Progress, and Termination of the American Revolution* (1805), based on her unique vantage point, became one of the earliest major chronicles of the quest for independence and established her as America's first female historian. The *History* was well-received among ideological allies but otherwise ignored. Like other founding mothers, Warren was all but forgotten until the twentieth century.

In the various accounts of James's and Mercy's lives, one recurring element that has called out for greater attention is the close and mutually inspiring bond between them—fraternal, political, and intellectual. Their relationship has been outlined before in parts and pieces, in the context of his life or hers, but never in its full breadth and depth, as a sustained narrative and the central point of interest. A dual biography provides the ideal vehicle for just such a focus.

Although many of the letters and other vestiges of their relationship have been lost, we know that the connections between Mercy Otis Warren and James Otis Jr. went far beyond those of ordinary sister and brother in colonial New England. Born and raised in the West Parish of Barnstable, Cape Cod, they had much in common from a young age—a love of learning, a fascination with politics, and onerous roles in their immediate family, just to begin with. Three and a half years her senior, James took Mercy under his wing as a household ally, study partner, and trusted companion. She looked up to him as a role model, mentor, and leader of seaside adventures.

Their childhood bond solidified in young adulthood, laying the groundwork of a mature intellectual affinity, profound mutual admiration, and lifelong attachment. They cherished one another and would stay the best of friends. Well into middle age, they would sign their letters "your affectionate brother" and "your affectionate sister."

When an incident at a Boston watering hole removed James from the front lines of the patriot campaign, Mercy took on her brother's cause as a kind of surrogate, agitating for individual liberties and national independence through the written word. She calmed and comforted him as no one else could. She defended his reputation and perpetuated his friendships. James's larger-than-life persona made an appearance in several of her plays; she lionized him in her history of the Revolution. Above all, she made advancing his ideals her life's work, and in doing so she established a voice, a stature, and a legacy entirely her own.

Their relationship was, all in all, a powerful and enduring motivation for James and for Mercy alike. Their story is worth telling in its own right—one of family pride, personal trauma, sibling devotion, and commitment to principle at the swirling center of the nation's founding. This book places the Otises squarely in the spotlight *together,* amid the rush of events and competing ideologies of eighteenth-century America.

In James's case, the destruction of personal documents created a permanent obstacle to any full-scale, comprehensive biography. Aside from five political pamphlets, a handful of newspaper articles, a smattering of letters to clients, and some legislative records, there has been little documentation with which to reconstruct his day-to-day life and endeavors. Mercy, on the other hand, left an extensive body of published works and private correspondence from which biographers, historians, and literary critics have produced rich accounts of her life, times, activities, and place in American letters. Those accounts are relatively recent, however, with a natural emphasis on correcting history's gender bias and giving Mercy her separate due.

The most in-depth secondary source on James remains *The Life of James Otis, of Massachusetts* (1823), by the Boston historian and literary editor William Tudor. The son of one of John Adams's law clerks, Tudor agreed to take on the project at the request of the former president more than three decades after Otis's death. Tudor presented a vivid portrait and colorful narrative, along with fragments of correspondence and a few official documents, but Adams himself may have been less than pleased with Tudor's standard of objectivity. Adams had urged Tudor "to honor merit, but not to adore it," but the *Life* was unapologetically reverential.[8] It held back little in relating Otis's outbursts of temper and irrational behavior, yet it resisted the terms "madness" and "insanity" in accounting for them. "The chief fault of Otis," Tudor concluded tamely, "was his irascibility." Had Otis not incinerated so much of the evidence, it might have been easier to make the case that he was, as Adams believed and Tudor pronounced, "the most learned, the most eloquent, the most ardent, and the most influential man of his time."[9]

Shorter treatments in the two centuries since Tudor's hagiography have both perpetuated myth and corroborated fact. Francis Bowen's *Life of James Otis* (1844) and John Clark Ridpath's *James Otis: The Pre-Revolutionist* (1898) brought to bear some new material and a healthy dose of patriotism but remained limited in depth and less than historically detached. Among more recent portrayals, Clifford K. Shipton's biographical sketch in *Sibley's Harvard Graduates,* John Waters's *The Otis Family in Provincial and Revolutionary Massachusetts* (1968), and John R. Galvin's *Three Men of Boston* (1976, about Otis, Samuel Adams, and Thomas Hutchinson) stand out for their impartiality and exacting research if not their scope. And while the essays of Bernard Bailyn, Ellen Elizabeth Brennan, Richard A. Samuelson, and James R. Ferguson, among others, offer rigorous analyses of Otis's writings, a definitive biography continues to defy scholars.[10]

The literature on Mercy Otis Warren remained sparse for more than a century after her passing. Even historians in the latter 1900s, seeking proper recognition for the role of women in America's past, tended to overlook her contributions. For despite an education generally reserved for young men and despite her successes in the male domains of writing and revolution, she was less a proto-feminist than a smart, strong-willed, exceptionally talented woman of her time. While she recognized and resisted the second-class status of her gender, she never advocated openly for women's rights and regarded her duties in the "domestic sphere" as a religious and civic calling. If Abigail Adams achieved prominence as a founding mother for her appeal to "remember the ladies," Mrs. Warren kept her sights set and pen trained on the ideals of individual liberty and popular sovereignty.

Foremost among secondary sources on Mercy Otis Warren—and invaluable to the study at hand—are three highly accessible scholarly works: Rosemarie Zagarri's *Woman's Dilemma: Mercy Otis Warren and the American Revolution* (1995); Nancy Rubin Stuart's *The Muse of the Revolution: The Secret Pen of Mercy Otis Warren and the Founding of a Nation* (2008); and Jeffrey H. Richards's *Mercy Otis Warren* (1995). These studies corroborate, complement, and significantly expand on Elizabeth Ellet's early profile in *The Women of the American Revolution* (1848); Alice Brown's first full-length biography, *Mercy Otis Warren* (1896); and Katharine Susan Anthony's ever insightful *First Lady of the Revolution: The Life of Mercy Otis Warren* (1958).

Indispensable to biographers, and engaging to any interested reader, is *Mercy Otis Warren: Selected Letters* (2009), edited by Jeffrey H. Richards and Sharon M. Harris. Other salient correspondence and primary source materials may be found in the Mercy Otis Warren Papers and Otis Family Papers at the Massachusetts History Society (MHS), Boston; the Otis Family Papers and Guy-Otis Family Papers at Columbia University, New York; and two collections published by the MHS: *Warren-Adams*

*Letters* (2 vols., 1917 and 1925) and *Correspondence between John Adams and Mercy Warren* (1878).

Scholarship on the Otises and their times owes much as well to two family histories—William Augustus Otis's voluminous *Genealogical and Historical Memoir of the Otis Family in America* (1924) and Waters's aforementioned *Otis Family in Provincial and Revolutionary Massachusetts*—though neither one, it must be said, gives Mercy her due.

Careful examination of the historical record has turned up few letters, diary entries, business records, or other documents not cited in previous Otis and Warren biographies. That said, the aggregate of known primary and secondary materials, pieced together from a dual perspective, with an eye on social conditions and local history, tells a poignant story of overlooked import. For further background on period events and developments, readers may look to any number of authoritative outside sources.

In the interest of clarity for modern readers, I have made minor alterations to original texts where appropriate, including the deletion of extraneous commas and the lowercasing of initial capital letters for common nouns (a standard eighteenth-century practice).

Finally, apologies in advance for any bewilderment or vexation caused by the profusion of Otises and Warrens named "James" who appear in these pages. There are ten. To distinguish them I have relied heavily on generational identifiers (Jr., Sr., and III, or the "elder" and "the younger"), as well as documented honorifics, nicknames, and pet names ("the Colonel," "the Patriot," and Jemmy or Jem).

## CHAPTER 1

# Flame of Fire, Calm Retreat

The Great Boston Fire of 1760 broke out in the early morning of May 20 near the stately brick Town House on Cornhill (now Washington Street), headquarters and nerve center of British colonial authority. A stiff northeasterly wind bellowed the flames through narrow, winding lanes, igniting shops and houses in the central market area and then down King, Water, and Milk Streets toward the waterfront. Bucket brigades worked valiantly but to little avail. Waves of sparks floated onto the wharves and into rigging and sailcloth, turning several docked merchant ships into massive floating pyres. A royal magazine of munitions and gunpowder exploded in the morning sky. By noon, with dark smoke engulfing the city and harbor, a reported 349 houses, shops, and warehouses lay in ash and ember. No lives were lost, but hundreds of families went homeless. It was the most destructive fire in colonial America to that time.[1]

Despite its proximity to the flashpoint, the two-story Georgian landmark known today as the Old State House emerged unscathed from the 1760 firestorm, spared only by the direction of the wind. Fortune had not always been so kind. The first Town House, located on the same site, had been incinerated with a hundred other clapboard structures in an out-of-control blaze in October 1711. The rebuilt Town House—featuring a giant lion and unicorn, symbols of British royalty, on the facade—sustained extensive interior damage in a December 1747 conflagration. When the smoke finally cleared from the great fire of 1760, however, Bostonians found the British stronghold fully intact. It seemed, if anything, even more formidable.

Census takers in 1760 put the population of Boston at 15,631. Philadelphia and New York both had outgrown it, yet the City on a Hill remained a teeming hub of maritime commerce, higher education, and feisty resistance to British mercantilism. The French and Indian War, part of the larger Seven Years' War among European powers, was putting a squeeze on royal coffers, and London looked to stricter enforcement of colonial trade duties as a boost to revenue. Smuggling in Boston Harbor was rampant.

The death of King George II and accession of twenty-two-year-old George III, announced from the front balcony of the Town House in late December 1760, raised hopes among many Bostonians for more tranquil relations with the crown and Parliament. Instead, the sequence of events in ensuing years would lead to the Boston Massacre on the square just below, the eventual reading of the Declaration of Independence from the same balcony, and, with that, the public burning of the lion and unicorn.

On the morning of February 24, 1761, the Council Chamber on the second floor of the Town House filled with spectators. The hall was the site of judicial hearings and policy consultations between the royal governor and his legislative council. Like much of the interior of the building, the chamber had been heavily renovated and elegantly reappointed after the fire of 1747. With no public gallery in which to sit, observers filed into the superior court and jostled for standing room. Gilt-framed oil portraits of the Stuart kings Charles II and James II, symbols of royal absolutism, gazed down on the scene. Flames licked at fresh logs in the fireplace.[2]

The much-anticipated occasion was a hearing to consider new writs of assistance for royal customs officials. This was no arcane legal formality in the minds of colonial merchants. The writs were general warrants that authorized customs agents, accompanied by a sheriff or constable, to enter shops, warehouses, ships at harbor, and even private residences in search of smuggled goods. The court had granted such blanket orders several times in recent years, but the death of the king meant they had to be reissued. Sixty-three Massachusetts Bay traders, resentful of British duties and anticipating a crackdown on contraband, joined in opposition.

To argue their case, the merchants hired two highly respected Boston attorneys, Oxenbridge Thacher and James Otis Jr., both Harvard graduates. Otis, age thirty-six, would be an especially compelling figure in the pleadings; his very agreement to take the case was something of a coup for the merchants. A devoted subject of the crown from backwater Cape Cod, he had climbed rapidly in the legal profession and the elite social circles of Boston. In recognition of his legal ability and political allegiance, the governor had named him advocate general in the Vice-Admiralty (maritime) Court. The position carried prestige, an annual salary of two hundred pounds, and responsibility for, among other things, prosecuting smugglers.[3] Otis, who regarded the writs as unjust and felt conflicted about enforcing them, chose to resign his post, give up the handsome salary, and risk reproach from his High Tory wife by accepting the merchants' case. And he took it pro bono.

Arguing crown interests before the court would be the eminent Jeremiah Gridley, a founder of the Boston bar, former representative to the General Court (Massachusetts's legislature), and future attorney general of the province. Gridley had trained both Otis and Thacher in the law, preparing them for the bar in his august downtown offices.

With the lawyers, onlookers, and a table of barristers all in place, the five justices of Massachusetts's highest tribunal entered the chamber in scarlet broadcloth robes, starched neck bands, and full judicial wigs—trappings newly adopted to evoke the pomp and dignity of the English courts.[4] Leading the succession, and taking center seat on the bench, was the haughty chief justice, Thomas Hutchinson. A Boston-born loyalist who had been appointed to the province's highest judicial post by Governor Francis Bernard just months before, Hutchinson was serving simultaneously as lieutenant governor of the colony and a member of the Governor's Council (upper house of the provincial legislature). Governor Bernard was eager to enforce the Navigation Acts, a series of mercantilist laws passed by Parliament to restrict colonial trade outside the empire. While it was his duty to implement crown policy, the governor was entitled to one-third of the proceeds from any ship caught in violation; the customs agent in charge of the search was entitled to another third. Moving quickly, the Bernard administration requested reissuance of the writs of assistance in the first weeks of 1761.

Lending further drama to the court proceeding was a backstory that turned on matters of personal conflict and family pride. The family pride was that of the Otises. Hutchinson's role as the presiding judicial authority was a source of simmering outrage for James Otis Jr., whose father had been promised the position of chief justice by two previous governors. Colonel James Otis Sr. was the pater familias of a clan whose roots on Cape Cod went back to the Puritan settlers and that still exerted a powerful influence on the area's commercial and civic affairs. Despite little formal education, Colonel Otis had attained prominence as a lawyer, judge, and politician, serving as a longtime member of the legislature. Yet he felt excluded from polite society and the uppermost reaches of colonial officialdom because of his provincial background.

Hutchinson claimed that he never wanted the job of chief justice—he didn't even have legal training—and purportedly cautioned Bernard that his appointment to another high-ranking position might cause grumbling. Bernard ignored the warning, and the choice of Hutchinson indeed opened a hornet's nest. James Sr., who had waited ten years for the job, felt betrayed.[5] James Jr. was furious, allegedly swearing revenge.[6] "From this day forward," Hutchinson later wrote, "the Otises were at the head of every measure in opposition, not merely in those points which concerned the governor in his administration, but in such as concerned the authority of parliament, the opposition to which first began in this colony and was moved and conducted by one of them, both in the assembly and the town of Boston. From so small a spark a great fire seems to have been kindled."[7]

Only Hutchinson and his minions ever suggested that the younger Otis had quit his vice-admiralty job and taken the Writs Case purely out of injured family pride and a desire for revenge. Otis's sense of justice and his commitment to fellow citizens were largely beyond reproach, at least at this early date. But whatever the mix of high purpose and bad blood in James's heart, two outcomes are clear in retrospect: the Otises would spearhead colonial opposition to the British administration, and Hutchinson himself would cast a dark, Machiavellian shadow in the lore and literature of the Otis family.

The undercurrents of personal animus were lost on few in attendance as Chief Justice Hutchinson called the Council Chamber to order on that cold February morning in 1761. The matter before the court was listed on the docket as the "Petition of Lechmere," referring to the application for new writs of assistance by the surveyor general of customs. No official transcripts or other records of the case have survived. Historical accounts of the three-day proceedings are based primarily on the notes of a young lawyer named John Adams, scribbling away at the barristers' table, and on his recollections more than a half-century later.

Jeremiah Gridley, his thin gray hair peeking out from a powdered wig, took the floor first in defense of the writs. His argument, according to Adams's reconstruction, addressed two basic points of law: Was the practice of search and seizure as sanctioned by the English Court of Exchequer legal or illegal? And if it was legal, was the Massachusetts Superior Court warranted in the same practice? Gridley affirmed that the searches were legal on the strength of multiple parliamentary statutes and case precedents. The writs, he went on, were valid instruments of the provincial court because they were vital to the collection of revenues and, therefore, to the preservation of the state. Hence, Gridley concluded, "The necessity of having public taxes effectually and speedily collected is of infinitely greater moment to the whole than the liberty of any individual."[8]

Thacher, arguing on behalf of the merchants, spoke with "a very easy and musical eloquence," according to Adams.[9] The sum and substance of his pleading was a response to Gridley's argument on the narrow point of jurisdiction. No, Thacher contended, the Massachusetts Superior Court was not warranted in granting writs under English judicial authority, since provincial customs agents, unlike their counterparts in the mother country, were not directly answerable to that body. The power of customs officers could not go unchecked.

Otis was next to address the court. He bowed curtly in the direction of the judges and cleared his throat. His posture was rigid, his eyes dark and intense. A portrait by Joseph Blackburn, painted at the time of Otis's marriage in 1755, had depicted a rosy-cheeked thirty-year-old, verging on portly, with a vaguely mischievous grin that reminded family and friends of his quirky, impetuous disposition as a youth.[10] Now his bearing was resolute, his lips pursed, face in full flush. While Gridley held a reputation for his knowledge of the law and general erudition, Otis had gained notice for his oratory skills and presence at the bar.

Skipping over the technicalities, he launched directly into an attack on the evils of the writs and the authority that issued them. "May it please your honors," he began,

> I take this opportunity to declare, that whether under a fee or not (for in such a cause as this I despise a fee), I will to my dying day oppose with all the powers and faculties God has given me, all such instruments of slavery on the one hand, and villainy on the other, as this writ of assistance is. It appears to me . . . the worst instrument of arbitrary power, the most destructive of English liberty and the fundamental principles of law that ever was found in an English law-book.[11]

With these opening fireworks, Otis held forth for nearly five hours on the illegality and rank injustice of the writs of assistance. Opposing them was a matter of principle, he declared; his personal reputation was of no consequence. Having renounced his position as advocate general to argue the case, he would "cheerfully submit . . . to every odious name for conscience sake."[12]

Notwithstanding the supporting statutes and precedents, Otis maintained that all general writs were illegal because they inherently threatened the liberties of British subjects. In at least four respects, he contended, they were too broad to preclude officials from abusing power and abridging the rights of colonists: (1) they could be issued to any revenue or customs officer, who in turn could delegate authority to any other official, elected or not; (2) they did not expire and could be employed forever without accountability to a judge or magistrate; (3) they were not limited to a specific property and could be exercised at will, without cause; and (4) they allowed not only deputies but "their menial servants" to enter a private residence whenever they pleased, with impunity. This, Otis thundered, violated a fundamental individual right:

FIGURE 1. James Otis Jr., engraving after an oil portrait by Joseph Blackburn, 1755. Otis was thirty and recently married at the time of the portrait.

—Courtesy Prints & Photographs Division, Library of Congress, LC-USZ62-102561

> Now one of the most essential branches of English liberty is the freedom of one's house. A man's house is his castle; and while he is quiet, he is as well guarded as a prince in his castle. This writ, if it should be declared legal, would totally annihilate this privilege.[13]

Having demonstrated how general writs threatened the rights of royal subjects, Otis argued further that they were not only illegal but unconstitutional (contravening common law principles). Here was a radical contention with far-reaching consequences, as he then called for the outright nullification of certain parliamentary acts. "All precedents are under the control of the principle of the law," Otis argued. "An act against the constitution is void; an act against natural equity is void."[14] On that basis, he insisted, the court was compelled to consider all constitutional imperatives—including individual rights and privileges—in interpreting parliamentary statutes. In other words, he concluded, the endangerment of personal freedom left the judges no choice but to reject the application for new writs of assistance.

The implication of these pronouncements was profound, if not entirely fathomed in the moment. Here Otis was challenging the absolute sovereignty of Parliament and the king. If natural rights and constitutional principles superseded statutory mandate, which he insisted they did, colonists across the empire might begin to question parliamentary authority, their own obligation to uphold the law, and their very allegiance to the crown. Thus, Otis taunted, "if the king of Great Britain in person were encamped on Boston Common, at the head of 20,000 men, with all his navy on our coast, he would not be able to execute these laws. They would be resisted or eluded."[15]

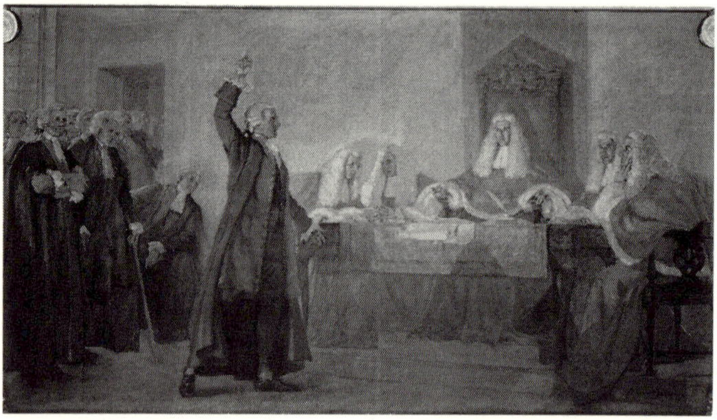

FIGURE 2. *James Otis Arguing the Writs of Assistance in the Old Towne House,* mural by Robert Reid, 1901. The oil-on-canvas depiction hangs above Nurses Hall on the second floor of the Old State House in Boston.

—Courtesy Commonwealth of Massachusetts, State House Art Commission

At the heart of the argument were Enlightenment principles that would lay the foundation of democratic government. Otis, as Adams reported, gave a "dissertation on the rights of man in a state of nature. He asserted that every man was an independent sovereign. . . . His right to his life, his liberty, no created being could rightfully contest. . . . He asserted that these rights were inherent and inalienable. That they never could be surrendered or alienated but by idiots or madmen, and all the acts of idiots and lunatics were void."[16]

Events of the next decade would cast Otis's allusion to madmen in an ironic light. On that day in 1761, however, his oration before the superior court galvanized all who witnessed it. As Adams later wrote, "Every man of an immense crowded audience appeared to me to go away, as I did, ready to take arms against writs of assistance."[17]

Hutchinson and the four other judges were obvious exceptions. The court delayed its ruling until after consulting with other judicial authorities and holding a pro forma second hearing in November. Then it delivered the inevitable and unanimous decision: the writs of assistance were perfectly legal, fully supported by English statute, precedent, and practice. Customs agents began receiving the new documents in early December 1761.

The court's determination did little to diminish the impact of Otis's performance. He became an instant hero with restive Bostonians. Nineteenth-century historians consecrated the Writs Case in the national origin myth, venerating Otis as a founder among founders. Yet it was the firsthand account of John Adams, who fell in the thrall of the firebrand attorney, that established the import of the proceedings and the reputation of the man:

> Otis was a flame of fire! With a promptitude of classical allusions, a depth of research, a rapid summary of historical events and dates, a profusion of legal authorities, a prophetic glance of his eyes into futurity, and a rapid torrent of impetuous eloquence he hurried away all before him.

> American independence was then and there born. The seeds of patriots and heroes were then and there sown.[18]

At the time of her brother's tour de force in the Writs of Assistance Case, Mercy Otis Warren was a housewife with two infant children, two homes, and a husband preoccupied with business and civic duties. Growing up in the Otis home had exposed her to the ins and outs of Massachusetts Bay politics, and she had read history and political philosophy from a young age. She had followed her brother James's career closely; she knew how he thought and grasped the full import of his position against the crown. Yet this was an idyllic time in her life, far removed from the clamor of Boston. She was happily married and raising a family with all the freedom and security she ever could have hoped for.

Mercy felt most at peace with husband James in their one-and-a-half-story, Cape-style cottage some three miles from the center of Plymouth. The forty-acre parcel had been granted to James's great-grandfather Richard Warren, an original *Mayflower* passenger, in 1627. The simple frame house, surrounded by rolling pastures, fields of rye, and abundant fruit orchards, stood on a low ridge along the Eel River a few hundred paces from Plymouth Bay, close to the site of old Plimoth Plantation. Mercy had her own name for the Warren homestead: Clifford Farm.[19]

She had met her husband-to-be before turning fifteen, likely introduced by her brother James at his Harvard graduation. Warren's intelligence, wit, and relaxed manner attracted Mercy instantly; the reassuring calm behind his warm blue eyes and his ready smile contrasted sharply with the volatility of the Otis men. Eleven years later, Mercy became his wife and the mistress of his family estate. As newlyweds in November 1754, the couple moved into the cottage with James's widowed father and unwed sister, Sarah, who married and left the following winter. Mercy was never happier than in those early years at Clifford. She reveled in the beauty and tranquility of the natural landscape, the changes of season, the bounty of her vegetable and flower gardens.

FIGURE 3. The Warren family homestead, located between Plymouth Bay and the Eel River near the original Plimoth Plantation site, was Mercy's beloved sanctuary beginning in the early days of her marriage. She dubbed it Clifford Farm. The Cape-style house, dating to 1695, was listed on the National Register of Historic Places in 1980.

—Courtesy of the author

A woman of Puritan stock and orthodox Congregational faith, Mercy expressed gratitude every day for the advantages God had granted her. Among the other blessings she counted were a husband who supported her intellectual curiosity and passion for learning. Since childhood she had surrounded and occupied herself with books, which both set her apart from most females raised in the Puritan tradition and shaped the rest of her life. James Warren, like Mercy's older brother, admired her powers of intellect and urged her to pursue her literary interests.

Not least among God's blessings in Mercy's eyes was a large, happy family. The prospect of motherhood, with all its risks and trials, was a source of excitement from the time she married. Her preparations included a range of books on childrearing, about which—like many things—she came to hold strong opinions. As James Warren oversaw the estate and partnered in his father's mercantile business, Mercy immersed herself in reading, needlework, soap- and candle-making, gardening, and, with the help of a servant named Ann, household chores. While full of energy and expectation during those long months of nesting, Mercy felt much at peace in the "little circle of domestic life . . . that Providence has widely assigned our sex."[20]

In the meantime, just as her brother James was rising in Boston legal circles, her husband was taking on new responsibilities in Plymouth. In 1756, the year Otis was appointed to the Vice-Admiralty Court, Warren assumed the position of county sheriff from his ailing father. When James Warren Sr. died the following July, Warren Jr. inherited the estate, the mercantile business, and all the boats, facilities, and operational duties that came with them.[21]

By mid-1757, Mercy was pregnant with their first child and James was spending much of his time away from the farm. The couple bought a home in the bustling center of Plymouth, at the corner of Main and North Streets, where it would be easier for her to manage a household and closer for him to the shipping docks and courthouse. Mercy hated to leave the bright airy spaces of Clifford, but they kept the family homestead and continued to spend summers there.

The Warrens would raise five boys in the Main Street house, beginning with James Jr. (what else?) that October. It was also where Mercy would do most of her writing. She had begun composing verse in her youth, under the nurturing eyes of a tutor and a doting older brother. In early 1759, while awaiting the birth of second son Winslow, she took up her pen to explore a more mature poetic style. Brother James, who visited when passing through on court business, and husband James were ever encouraging, but Mercy lacked no will or inspiration of her own. Confined to town life and long winter nights at home, she pined for the open spaces of Clifford Farm and the coming of spring. Her earliest known poem, dated January 1759, captures a fascination with the sublime and a yearning for divine redemption—contrasts of dark and light—that were to become hallmarks of her writing.[22]

On Winter

Dread Winter sits on every brow
And every aspect's pale
The sprightly lark has left the hills
To seek the warmer dale. . . .

The hov'ring snows exclude the light,
And hide the beams of day,
While stormy winds, and dark'ning clouds,
Prevent each gladsome ray. . . .

Though Winter whistles from the North
And roughen'd tempests blow
We'll not forget returning Spring
Which sinks the hills of snow. . . .

Through every season, every clime
His goodness crowns the year,
The Spring returns, or Winter frown
Yet still let man revere.

Let him admire great nature's charms
Both beauteous and sublime,
But only nature's God adore
Who lends those charms to time.[23]

However simple in structure and stilted to the modern ear, Warren's early poetry provides insight into the innermost feelings of a highly literate, strong-minded woman of faith. They reveal a steadfast belief in the will of God and a love of the natural world, while elevating reason and acknowledging flickers of doubt. About two dozen of these poems and fragments appear in archives, of which seventeen were published for the first time in 1981.[24] During her lifetime, Mercy had circulated them only among family and friends. Many date from the peak years of her homemaking and childrearing, from the late 1750s to the early 1770s. The early poems are conspicuously apolitical, disregarding or expressly renouncing the realm of public affairs. As biographer Nancy Rubin Stuart puts it, Mercy "tended more domestic fires."[25]

The Warrens traveled to Boston in 1763 for sittings at the Beacon Hill studio of up-and-coming portrait artist John Singleton Copley. Mercy was about thirty-five, James thirty-seven. Their third child, Charles, was a year old, and business was thriving. Copley painted the couple separately, in standing poses slightly facing each other. James is every bit the gentleman farmer and well-to-do merchant, donned in bob wig and waistcoat, walking stick in hand, complexion ruddy from brisk walks about the estate.[26]

Mercy, in an elegant blue satin dress with white lace trim, faces the viewer in a direct, penetrating gaze. It is a poised, confident expression, a hint of smile in the resolute line of her mouth. Her slight frame and pallid complexion, rouged in the cheek, belie her energy and resilience. A natural landscape of trees, rock, and sky fall away behind her, as if she were standing on a hill. She is tending a vine of flowers; the turn in her body suggests she has been interrupted. She is animated but serene, at home in nature, nurturing in spirit. The flowers are nasturtiums, symbols of abundance, maternal love, and patriotism.[27]

In the months that followed, the safe circle of Mercy's domestic life began to shrink. The Otises had made an enemy of the powerful Thomas Hutchinson, and the rift between colonists loyal to the administration and those who challenged it was starting to widen. Few on either side expected that the Treaty of Paris, ending the Seven Years' War in February 1763, would create the chasm in colonial-British relations that it did in the years that followed. But London's decisions to keep ten thousand troops in North America and pass along the costs of its far-flung militarism lit a fuse among colonials. The Sugar Act of 1764, whose duties on imported molasses were expressly designated for a standing army, and the notorious Stamp Act of 1765, which imposed direct taxes on colonial paper goods and printed documents of

FIGURE 4. Mercy Otis Warren and her husband, James Warren, sat for oil portraits by the rising young artist John Singleton Copley in 1763. She was about thirty-five and raising three of the Warrens' five sons at the time.
—Courtesy ART Collection/Alamy Stock Photo

all kinds, triggered the first seismic shifts in colonial sentiment against British rule.

Mercy shared the outrage of her brother, father, and husband, but she worried as much as she fumed. The Stamp Act, she later wrote in her *History of the Rise, Progress, and Termination of the American Revolution,* "gave a general alarm throughout the continent."[28] Otis Jr., recognizing the threat that taxation without consent posed to colonial autonomy, leaped to the front lines of the resistance alongside Samuel Adams and the clandestine Sons of Liberty. James Warren, for his part, ran for the legislative assembly and won.

The faith of Mercy Otis Warren, raising four young sons and carrying a fifth, was tested all at once in the spring of 1766 by the deaths of her sisters Eliza and Abigail, and by the rush of events that swept up the three important men in her life. Resisting the pull of politics and civic duty, she wrote a poem that urged her husband to set aside worldly matters and the "endless strife" of Boston for the natural beauty and "calm retreat" of Clifford Farm—her domestic counterpart to the City on a Hill.

To J Warren Esqr
*An invitation to retirement.*

1. Come leave the noisy smoky town
   Where vice and folly reign,
 The vain pursuits of busy men
   We wisely will disdain.

2. True happiness and lasting peace
   We ne'er in Courts can find
 Ambitious views and sordid hopes
   By turns distract the mind.

3. But in the peaceful calm retreat
   Amidst the beautious plains,
 Where innocence with cheerful health
   With love and virtue reign;

4. There free from envy, free from pride,
   And all the dismal train
 Of warring passions, endless strife,
   The blackest source of pain

5. Like the first pair on Eden's banks
   Before the raging fiend
 With bold elusive arts deceiv'd
   The mother of mankind;

6. We'll neither wish for wealth or fame
Nor court the praise of men
Whole pride, in spite of conscious truth
Expects applause again.

7. The solemn shades, the sylvan scene
All natures bright array
Secure and guard the wandering mind
From errors baneful way,

8. Subdue each passion, calm the soul
And teach the heavenly art
Death to defy, and life enjoy
With self approving heart.
—Clifford Farm 1766[29]

With all the tumultuous events and personal transformations still to come, there was prescience in Mercy's poetry during that spring of 1766. Parliament finally repealed the Stamp Act, but the turmoil in Boston continued to mount as the British moved to reassert authority. "This country must soon be at rest," her brother James wrote to her ominously on April 11, "or may be engaged in contests that will require neither the pen nor the tongue of a lawyer."[30]

While Mercy prayed that her brother, like her husband, might escape the warring passions of politics, James Otis Jr. did not feel free to leave Boston—neither to visit her in Plymouth nor to attend his sisters' funerals in Barnstable. "I dare not leave the town," he wrote in the same letter, "as men's minds are in such a situation that every nerve is requisite to keep things from running to some irregularity or imprudence." James's own nerves were fraying in the skirmishes over politics and personal reputation, yet he mustered the composure to reassure a concerned sibling:

> This you may depend on, no man ever loved a sister better, and among all my conflicts I never forget that I am endeavoring to serve you and yours.[31]

James never took part in the revolution he helped to spark. His nerves did not hold in the midst of rising tensions on both sides. By the time shots were fired at Lexington and Concord, he and Mercy essentially had reversed roles: his was the place of remove and repose; hers was the fervid voice of colonial opposition and the cause of liberty. The one constant was the love between them.

# CHAPTER 2

# Root and Fiber

On the "bared and bended arm" of Cape Cod, as Henry David Thoreau described the peninsula, flexed and curling into the Atlantic Ocean, the villages of Barnstable and West Barnstable are located at the biceps.[1] Barnstable Harbor opens onto the blue expanse of Cape Cod Bay, whose calm, temperate waters—sheltered from the open sea by the rounded forearm of the lower and outer Cape—the Pilgrims crossed west to their settling place in 1620. The two Barnstable villages lie snug between the barrier dunes of Sandy Neck across the harbor and a line of small hills, covered with oaks and pines, inland to the south. Fringing the shoreline just to the west, covering four thousand acres, stretches the area's most dramatic natural feature and first economic attraction: the Great Marsh.

Flooded in spring tides and storm surges, the watery meadows of cordgrass grow higher and finer through summer and fall, until harvest time in early winter. The dried product, salt hay, was valuable to English settlers as livestock fodder, garden mulch, roof thatch, and insulation. Stalks of the plant up to six feet tall were cut, dried, and stored for common use, year upon year. It was the profusion of marsh grass and the fertile onshore soil, combined with

God's bounty in the bay—shellfish, cod, striped bass, bluefish—that lured Reverend John Lothrop and his Puritan congregation south from Scituate in October 1639. Some two dozen families joined Lothrop in establishing a parish at the location that Native peoples called Mattakeese (or Mattacheese). Its incorporation later that year made Barnstable one of the first chartered towns on Cape Cod and in the entire Plymouth Colony.[2]

Barnstable lay some seventy miles south of Boston, a rugged two days away on horseback. The town of Plymouth provided a convenient layover at about the midpoint. Roads were rough and bridges makeshift, leaving rivers and streams to be forged en route. Sailing up the coast by packet boat was the faster and more comfortable mode of travel, though there was no scheduled service until the early nineteenth century. Regular mail deliveries between Boston and Barnstable were nearly as long in coming. For a century and a half, the conveyance of letters depended on the pace, frequency, and reliability—or lack thereof—of paid couriers and private travelers.[3]

Chroniclers of colonial Massachusetts and the Otis family have described this backwater area of the Cape in uniformly conservative, provincial terms. One modern historian characterizes old Barnstable as a "little self-contained world of unshifting values."[4] Another describes it as "a safe, predictable place where the outside world did not much intrude."[5] Alice Brown, an early biographer of Mercy Otis Warren, paints a similar picture in shades of old Yankee stoicism: "Barnstable . . . has always held herself in self-respecting quiet, ready to meet public questions, or content to be of the happy nations that have no history, save of industry and thrift."[6] This is hyperbole, of course. Barnstable has plenty of history; it just seems to move slowly there.

For Mercy Otis Warren, the confined, insular world of her childhood home found an idealized counterpart in the Edenic peace of Clifford Farm. For James Otis Jr., boyhood explorations of the salt marsh, seacoast, open fields, and piney knolls surrounding the family homestead—often with his sister—afforded a myriad of enduring memories and an easy escape from the stresses of adult life. So while he settled in Boston and moved beyond the Great Marsh in terms of professional success, social standing, and political influence, he remained a child of the Cape no less than Mercy or his other siblings who stayed behind. For men like James Otis, "the Cape colors him all his life, the root and fiber of him. He may get beyond but he never gets over the Cape. . . . He will feel in odd hours to his life's end, the creek tide on which he floated ashore as a boy, the hunger of the salt marsh in haying time, the cold splash of the sea spray at the harbor's mouth."[7]

Reverend Lothrop, like the *Mayflower* Pilgrims, was a separatist Puritan who broke from the Church of England. He spent two years in London's Clink Prison for refusing to take an oath of loyalty and, upon arriving in Plymouth Colony in 1634, established an independent Congregational community. In the area that would become Barnstable, Mashpee Wampanoag Natives greeted the first white settlers, from Weymouth, in the spring of 1639; that party moved farther down the Cape in short order. Lothrop and his Scituate congregation accepted a separate land grant from the Plymouth General Court in October, and they stayed for good. A monument called Sacrament Rock, located along modern-day Route 6A in Barnstable, marks the site of their first communion at the settlement.

In true Puritan tradition, Lothrop's congregation maintained a strict system of personal ethics and communal living. Local self-government, to the exclusion of any centralized church authority, promoted the common good in town meetings and working committees. Barnstable's first meetinghouse, used for religious worship as well as civic gatherings, went up in 1646 and welcomed a steady stream of new congregants as the community prospered. Livestock, farming, fishing, and shore whaling were economic mainstays from the outset. Corn, rye, flax, potatoes, and roots sustained early farm families and grew into cash crops. Local sheep, fed by endless wagonloads of salt hay, became a prized commodity. And early attempts at salt production—first by boiling down seawater, later through evaporation—gave promise for the future.[8]

Among Massachusetts settlers attracted to prospects in Barnstable early on was John Otis III of Scituate. His father, John Otis II, who arrived in Plymouth Colony as a boy, had bought a plot of land overlooking the marshes on Barnstable Bay.[9] Twenty-one-year-old John III moved to the property in 1678, nailed together what would become the family residence, and began building the Otis reputation for industry, integrity, and public service. His trading establishment became the busiest in Barnstable. His respect in the community earned him the gavel in town meetings and command of the local militia. Setting a precedent for future generations, he held a seat in the provincial assembly for nine years and in the Governor's Council for twenty-one, in addition to stints as chief justice of the Court of Common Pleas (private claims) and judge of probate for the county. His portrayal in one family chronicle bears striking resemblance to later descriptions of grandson James Otis Jr.: "The successful discharge of such varied employments is an evidence of his capacity and integrity, which, joined to his wit and affability, secured him great influence. . . . He had fine talents for conversation; his pleasantness and affability made him agreeable; his wit and humor often enlivened the company."[10]

Barnstable grew so rapidly that by 1717, the congregation made plans to divide into two parishes, east and west. Work immediately began on a meetinghouse for the West Parish, constructed on high ground with pine and oak from nearby woods. The white clapboard building, featuring a sixty-foot bell tower, hosted its first service two years later on Thanksgiving Day.[11] The presiding pastor was Reverend Jonathan Russell, who had been given his choice of which parish to lead and opted for the west because of family ties with the Otises. He was married to John III's youngest daughter, named Mercy.

FIGURE 5. The 1717 West Parish Meetinghouse, restored to early colonial style in the 1950s, is the oldest active Congregational church in the United States today. In 2016, the parish celebrated its four hundredth anniversary, dating to the founding of a separatist congregation in Southwark, England. James Otis Sr. bequeathed funds for a half-ton bell.

—Courtesy Prints & Photographs Division, Library of Congress, HABS MASS,1-BAR,6—1

Reverend Russell is portrayed in church annals as a strictly conservative minister who had received his training at Yale, a bastion of Congregational orthodoxy. Although the West Parish was stalwartly traditional in religious belief and practice, it had, over time, loosened its Puritan strictures and embraced members of other faiths in civic affairs. The congregation stayed firmly committed to the precepts of self-government, the family covenant, and responsibility for the needy while welcoming participation by the community's lay constituents.

Isolated, self-contained, and tradition-bound, West Barnstable would be largely unfazed by the evangelical fervor of the Great Awakening that swept the American colonies in the 1730s and

1740s. As New Light Congregationalists left their churches and joined the revivalist movement in all its zeal, Old Light Congregationalists like Reverend Russell and his parishioners were suspicious of traveling evangelists, their fevered preaching, and their challenges to tradition. Russell was a man of letters, reputed to own a library of more than two hundred volumes, and sided with the Old Lights in seeking a brand of Christian faith compatible with the Age of Reason. The high-minded pastor and his West Parish congregation hewed to old norms of family, community, and charity, but theirs was no hidebound piety. They espoused a devout but enlightened belief system in which a providential God revealed himself through reason and nature no less than the Bible. It was the kind of sober, rational project of faith that Russell would nurture in his two most accomplished students, Mercy and James Otis Jr.[12]

John Otis III died in 1727 as the preeminent citizen of Barnstable and one of the richest and most respected men in the so-called Old Colony of Plymouth.[13] Still, it took the success of his children in business, marriage, and political office to cement the influence and prestige of the Otis clan. Since the early decades of settlement, life in the area had been dominated by a handful of families—Lothrops, Hinckleys, Bacons, Gorhams, and so on.[14] They owned large tracts of land, dominated civic and church affairs, and strengthened their connections through commerce and marriage. The concentration of wealth among a few select families preserved the status quo and slowed the pace of change from generation to generation. John Otis III, by contrast, was a self-made man. So while he earned the admiration of his peers, a head seat in the parish meetinghouse, and all the assets he was able to pass on, it was the next generation of Otises that truly secured the family's status.

In the colonies at large, the coming of the Great Awakening posed a challenge to the wealthy class and social elite as much as it did to church tradition. The revivalist movement had emerged from the grassroots of agrarian America and offered a spiritual home for the young, the disenfranchised, and recent immigrants.

In provincial Barnstable, however, the dominance of a few Old Light clans not only protected their own political and economic interests but also served the Puritan idea of the "family covenant." This was the belief that the early New England settlers were God's chosen people and that their families were instruments of divine purpose. As both a religious mandate and a social construct, the family covenant bound spouses, children, and servants in a special contractual relationship with a shared ideal—the perfect society—and unique mutual obligations. While the Otises and other landed families were primarily secular and material in their aspirations, the covenant was a source of heightened ancestral identity within each clan. The nineteenth-century novelist Harriet Beecher Stowe, seven generations removed from her original New England forebears, wrote from experience about the importance of those blood ties: "Among the peculiarly English ideas which the Colonists brought to Massachusetts, which all the wear and tear of democracy have not been able to obliterate, was that of family. Family feeling, family pride, family hope and fear and desire, were, in my early day, strongly-marked traits. . . . 'Of a very respectable family' was a sentence so often repeated at the old fireside that its influence went in part to make up my character."[15]

All of these factors—Puritan family values, commitments to industry and public service, Old Light resistance to the new evangelicalism, and the defense of social status and economic power, all in geographic isolation—came together in a fierce sense of pride and unity among the Otises of West Barnstable, as personified by "the Colonel," James Otis Sr.[16]

Born in 1702, he was the youngest and probably the favorite of John Otis III's six children. Three older brothers followed their father into public office and the local militia, but it was James who demonstrated the kind of drive, diligence, and sense of duty that John III prized above all. James worked in his father's general store from a young age, learning the ropes of purchasing, inventory, shipping, bookkeeping, and debt collection. One older brother went to Harvard, a sure sign of arrival for the entire clan, but James demonstrated an enterprising spirit and a native intelligence that would enable him best to capitalize on the Otis legacy. His ambitions on behalf of the family business and family dynasty soon had him traveling the Old Colony and beyond in search of new trading ventures and new partners. Among the latter was a young woman from Wethersfield, Connecticut, named Mary Allyne (or Allyn).[17]

Relatively little is known about Mary's background other than the fact that an early ancestor was Edward Doty (or Dotey), a storied passenger on the *Mayflower* and signer of the Mayflower Compact. Her father, a merchant and sloop owner named Joseph Allyne, was a Plymouth native who had moved the family to Connecticut during Mary's childhood. She was raised in a strict, religious household and likely taken aback, at least at first, by the charming, outgoing young trader who came to do business with her father. James Otis and Mary Allyne were married in 1724, both age twenty-two, and he brought her back to Barnstable to settle down.

Three years later, James inherited the Otis homestead—house, barn, fruit orchards, and fields on either side of King's Highway. Like his father, he set about enhancing the property as he diversified the business and started a family. He built a large warehouse and augmented its stock of local produce—fruit, onions, butter, cheese, and wool—with more lucrative fare, such as pickled fish, pork, and West Indian rum. The profits went into new investments, new businesses, and every imaginable luxury for the household: standing beef ribs and fine European wines for the dinner table; bolts of silk, satin, and fine linen for clothing and napery; and the latest manufactured goods for everyday convenience and comfort.[18]

The family "mansion" (the term for a country house at the time) was a handsome wood-framed structure, described as a "high double house with a gambrel roof and three dormer windows,"

FIGURE 6. A stone marker and commemorative plaque identify the site of the former Otis estate on Old King's Highway in the village of West Barnstable.
—Courtesy of the author

near the West Parish center at Hinckley Lane. Already admired for its spaciousness and appointments, the residence became one of the grandest in Barnstable after Otis added two wings for his growing family and accumulation of furnishings. The house was said to be shaded in summer by "great buttonwood trees" (American sycamores) and heated in winter by giant stone fireplaces.[19]

The rapid expansion of Otis assets coincided with a coming of age of the New England economy and a new level of prosperity for many who lived there. A royal charter in 1691 had merged Plymouth and Massachusetts Bay into a single colony, which by the early eighteenth century had evolved from a collection of rugged frontier settlements into a thriving center of trade and shipbuilding. The new success gave rise to an elite class of wealthy merchants and a general appetite for material goods that would have shocked the original Puritan settlers. Change was slower to come in the conservative hinterland of Barnstable's West Parish, but even there the diversification of trade and expansion of small industry fueled the growth and well-being of the community. Its elite families indulged in luxury imports and a standard of living unimaginable only a few generations earlier. The Otis home filled with mahogany chests and cabinets befitting the family's solid standing in the community, along with ornate mirrors, fine ceramics and silver, and a tall case clock reputed to be the first in the county.

The provincialism and homogeneity of life in Barnstable did not mean that it was ethnically uniform, or that the Puritan doctrine of mutual respect was any bar to social inequality. The divide between the haves and have-nots, while widened in the commercial boom, dated to the first years of settlement and the indenture of local Mashpee as farm laborers. James Otis fashioned himself an expert on Indian affairs and assumed a kind of patrician responsibility for the well-being of the tribe. His sense of guardianship, however, did not preclude him from appropriating Mashpee land or taking on a number of Natives as fieldworkers and household servants.[20]

Slavery itself was common in the Old Colony, though less so on Cape Cod because it had fewer large estates.[21] James Otis Jr. would become the first prominent Cape Codder to speak out publicly against human bondage, and Mercy was an early advocate of abolition as well, but historical documentation indicates that they grew up with at least a few slaves on the Otis homestead. Town records list the marriages of "Amaritta and Primus, servants to Col. Otis" in 1748 and of "London, servant to James Otis Esqr, and Bathsheba Towardy, an Indian" in 1760.[22] James Otis Sr. oversaw a dozen or more laborers and attendants, including enslaved and indentured African Americans and Native Americans.

With the farm managed by a foreman and the estate staffed by fieldworkers and domestics, the ever-ambitious James Sr. was free to pursue new endeavors—including the practice of law. According to family lore, he entered the field by accident and excelled by virtue of his native intelligence and sense of fairness. (Lawyers at the time required no special training or license.) The story goes that Otis was passing time at the Barnstable Courthouse, sharing news and stories with other locals, when a neighbor with a case on the docket but no counsel on hand asked for his help. Otis agreed and won the case, garnering praise from the judge and encouragement from friends in the aftermath. He was still just twenty-eight when he launched his new career.

Riding the judicial circuit from village to town, much like Abe Lincoln on the Illinois prairie, Otis built a lucrative law practice, a devoted clientele, and the respect of an ever-widening network of contacts. Those connections opened new business opportunities and, over time, greased the wheels of his rise in politics. Otis entered public service in 1739 as the local "hogreeve," charged with preventing and appraising damage by stray pigs (a chronic problem in New England towns). Chosen as a selectman in 1744, he served on multiple working committees, managed funds for the West Parish Church, and eventually led the county militia—thereby earning the honorific "Colonel." Like his father, he would come to preside as chief justice of the Court of Common Pleas and judge of probate for Barnstable County.[23]

Barnstable's seventy-odd voters elected James to the Massachusetts House of Representatives in 1745, restoring an Otis to the colonial legislature for the first time since the end of his father's tenure.[24] On the strength of devoted support for Governor William Shirley, dutiful work in committee, and adroit political maneuvering, Colonel Otis emerged as a force to be reckoned with in provincial government. He was elected attorney general in 1748 and Speaker of the House in 1760, missing no opportunity for personal profit along the way. Capitalizing on his legislative connections and military standing during the French and Indian War, he acquired every whaleboat he could find on Cape Cod, bought timber and hired boat builders to assemble more, and sold them to the British for a series of lake battles in New York.[25]

The Colonel would follow in his father's footsteps once again as a member of the prestigious Governor's Council in 1762. By this time, however, newly installed Governor Francis Bernard had spurned Otis for the position of chief justice. Broken promises aside, the rejection pressed a particular button in James's psyche: feelings of inadequacy over his meager education. "Mr. Otis," as one family historian described him, "was a man of superior genius, but more indebted to the native energy of his mind than to a regular education."[26] John Adams, who once rode the legal circuit with him, concurred: "he is vastly good-humored and sociable and sensible, [but] learned he is not."[27] Otis eschewed book learning yet was embarrassed by his lack of it.

The governor's snub, especially in favor of a privileged, blue-blooded Bostonian like Thomas Hutchinson, struck another nerve as well. Bernard and Hutchinson had always disdained Otis's backcountry origins. They looked down on him, and Otis knew it. The abrupt halt to his rise in provincial power circles told the Colonel that he was, and would always remain, just a big fish in the small pond of Cape Cod. So while he would return to the political and personal intrigues of the Massachusetts legislature intermittently into the 1770s—with his eldest son at his side for much of it—the rebuff and insult reminded him that he was still a son of Barnstable at heart: conservative, pragmatic, proud of the ways the village and Cape had colored his life.

In the end, for all his wealth, stature, and service to colonial government, the Colonel harbored an independent yeoman spirit that went back to the first Otises in America and that took root in the Great Marsh. Notwithstanding a century of change and his own secular ambitions, the way of life he cherished in the West Parish embodied a version of the "civil body politic" as envisioned in the Mayflower Compact: orderly, principled, family-centered. It was a community that valued self-government and shared responsibility among equal citizens (albeit white and male), resisting outside authority. Like salt grass in spring tide, the principle of freedom by which they lived would rise again in the next generation.

# CHAPTER 3
# *Childhood Bonds*

The "borning room" in colonial American homes was a place of lively female bonding and, in many cases, mortal fear. The physical space, rarely a dedicated room at all, was typically a small chamber set up behind the central chimney for warmth in winter and shielded from common living areas for privacy. In larger homes, the expectant mother might retire to the master bedroom in the last stage of pregnancy. Whatever the arrangement, the arrival of a new family member was no private matter. In the practice of "social childbirth," followed throughout the colonies during the eighteenth century, close female friends and relatives assisted a trained midwife in delivery and postpartum recovery. Doctors seldom attended.[1]

Large families were not out of the ordinary, as many couples were eager to establish and grow a clan. Puritans considered it a blessing, farmers a working necessity. Couples in prerevolutionary New England raised seven to eight children on average, with wives giving birth every sixteen to twenty months over periods of fifteen years or more.[2] Stillbirth, infant mortality, and disease—smallpox, measles, typhoid, scarlet fever—could mean the loss of several children in a family, sometimes all at once. While deaths in birth and infancy were not regularly reported, estimates of child mortality run as low as 10 percent for the first months of life and as high as 25 percent up to the age of six.[3] In areas where Puritan orthodoxy still prevailed, trepidation over childbirth itself was exacerbated by the belief that infant death or deformity, not to mention the death of a mother in parturition, was a sign of God's judgment or the devil's will.[4] In places like the West Parish of Barnstable, Massachusetts, the joy of pregnancy often mixed with dread.

Even by the standards of her time, Mary Otis endured more than her share of exertion in the borning room and more than her share of heartbreak. Married at twenty-two, the norm for contemporary women, she bore a total of thirteen children in less than twenty years—an average of one every seventeen or eighteen months into her forties. Five of her brood, four girls and one boy, died in birth or infancy. Given the several weeks of rest and recuperation ("lying in") needed after each delivery, and given the natural decline in fertility during breastfeeding (all but universal at the time), the rate and regularity of Mary's childbearing over so long a span was out of the ordinary even then. The physical and emotional toll, leaving aside her child-rearing and other household responsibilities, must have been literally staggering.

The first child was James Otis Jr., born barely a year after his parents' marriage, on February 5, 1725; they nicknamed him "Jemmy" to distinguish him from James Sr. Joseph, the second of four sons who would survive infancy, followed Jemmy by exactly thirteen months. Mercy, the eldest of three daughters who lived to adulthood, entered the world on September 14, 1728.

The Otis children may have been raised in comfort, but they lived simply and pulled their weight in the kitchen and barn. Mercy, as the first daughter, bore an extra burden from the time she could swing a broom and reach the cupboard. Servants tended the garden, butchered the sheep, boiled the linens, and washed the floors, but Mercy took over more and more of her mother's tasks—mending clothes, preparing meals, and changing the diapers of her younger siblings. Soon she was directing staff. "She passed her youth," one biographer observed, "in the midst of those duties and employments to which as the eldest daughter . . . she was called."[5]

Mercy never wrote much about her mother and left few clues about their relationship.* Aside from household training, Mary schooled her in the "domestic arts"—spinning and weaving wool, dressmaking, embroidery, soap-making, and candle-making. Surviving samples of Mercy's needlework attest to her love of that craft and the level of skill she attained in it.[6] Yet despite the time they spent together and the devotion with which Mercy accepted her role, there is little evidence of particular closeness or affection between mother and daughter. Mary was a woman of traditional faith and values, aptly depicted in a 1760 portrait by John Singleton Copley clutching a Bible on her lap.[7] Mercy would recall that her mother always had some "instructive precept" to dispense, "ever ready to draw from the pure fountain of religion."[8] Mary casts a dour, aloof figure in the Copley portrait, stalwart and virtuous but bone-tired after two decades of childbearing and the loss of five infants. Mercy, while bred on her mother's Old World Calvinism and unsparing moral precepts, inherited her father's vigor. Wiry and wired, she had energy, yearning, and curiosity to burn.

Jemmy, Joseph, and their younger brothers, Samuel Allyne and Nathaniel, grew up under the firm hand of Colonel Otis. The structure and dynamics of the family followed social conventions for the American colonies, with the father exercising unquestioned authority and the parents together enforcing strict discipline. In the household as in church and local government, the

* Mary Otis's death in December 1767, for example, goes unmentioned in her daughter's correspondence, nor did Mercy compose for Mary the kind of memorial poem she did for other family members.

elder male ruled. Disobedience was a form of heresy or treason; no rod was spared in teaching the ways of the righteous.[9] Mercy recoiled at the harshness of it, later disavowing her parents' "irksome methods of severity."[10]

For the Otis sons, the stature of the family and the aspirations of James Sr. intensified the pressure of what their sister later called his "patriarchship."[11] There was an estate for the boys to take over, a business to grow, a political legacy to claim—not to mention their father's lack of education to make up for. The Colonel, moreover, for all his sociability and ease of manner in public life, could be brusque and overbearing in business and family matters. This lent a particular tension to his relationships with the Otis sons, who shrank from interaction with him and often quarreled among themselves. "The elder Otis gave them the tools to achieve and the motivation to succeed," a family historian observed, "while at the same time bequeathing to them a feeling of personal inadequacy."[12]

The gendered family dynamics of eighteenth-century America typically separated brothers and sisters at or before adolescence. While it was common for younger siblings to sleep, eat, and play together, the division of roles and responsibilities sent preteen boys to the barn, workshop, or field while relegating their sisters to the kitchen, garden, or laundry.[13] Mercy and her two older brothers, spared no job or chore, saw little of each other during the long workday.

Education was another element of colonial society that divided sisters and brothers. Reading was considered an exercise of devotion among the Puritans, who mandated that all church members be able to read the Bible. Literacy was part of the cultural heritage in Massachusetts, Rhode Island, and Connecticut, well exceeding the rates in other colonies: as high as 90 percent for men in the period before the Revolution. For women, deemed "weaker vessels" and cut off from many aspects of church and community, the rate was about 50–60 percent.[14] Although the female literacy rate was significantly higher than anywhere else in North America, educational opportunities for girls in New England were generally limited to small, private "dame schools" (taught by women, usually housewives and widows) for just a few grades. No avenues of higher education were open to girls; they had little exposure to history or secular literature. In the Congregational tradition, they learned to read from their mothers as part of a customary education in the Bible and domestic arts. Mercy Otis was probably no exception, though she took to reading more naturally and at a younger age than her peers.

For Jemmy and Joseph, education was the gravest of obligations to their father, the Otis name, and the community at large. Under Puritan law dating to the Massachusetts Bay Colony, Barnstable paid a schoolmaster and funded a grammar school for boys, though instruction was confined to private residences and teaching materials were at a premium.[15] This would hardly suffice for the sons of Colonel James Otis, who enlisted the tutoring services of the most educated man in the parish: their uncle Reverend Jonathan Russell. Beginning at age seven or eight, the two boys would walk out the front gate of the Otis house and make their way up Hinckley Lane to the church parsonage. Their younger sister, already an avid reader, was said to have watched with envy as they disappeared down the path day after day.

Obedient and uncomplaining in her menial routine, Mercy may have resigned herself at first to limited educational prospects, a lifetime of reading psalms, and the sheer injustice of her brothers' advantage. Girls in colonial America had no legal entitlements outside the home, least of all to an education. They were not raised to want any more. In the case of young Mercy Otis, however, it is easier to imagine her pining and pleading for the very kind of book learning her brothers were getting. By all accounts she was not only a precocious reader but broadly curious and hungry for knowledge. And, given the native sense of justice and equality reflected in her life's work, she had to have understood the patent unfairness of her lot as a girl—providence notwithstanding.

Big brother Jemmy recognized her burning curiosity from a young age. He saw the excitement in her eyes when they visited their uncle's book-lined study and the longing in her expression when he and Joseph left her behind each morning. Jemmy shared his books and lessons with her in the evening, and at some point joined in imploring their father to let her take part in the tutoring.

How that unlikely decision came to be made has been variously explained in family lore. By most accounts, Joseph was unsuited or ill-disposed to classroom study (probably both) and quit at the age of about ten to work in his father's store. The pleas for Mercy's attendance grew more and more persistent as it became evident that she was the more fitting student. The self-taught Colonel, who doted on his eldest daughter, finally let her take Joseph's place. Like other successful merchants in New England during the 1730s and 1740s, James Otis wanted every advantage for his children. How could he say no to a formal education for any of them, even a girl?

The bond between Jemmy and Mercy was forged in the children's room of the Otis home, in the woods and pastures along King's Highway, and in the long hours writing out lessons and poring over books in Reverend Russell's study. Their joint tutoring sessions brought them together in a way few brothers and sisters of their time experienced.

Disciplined and passionate, Mercy no doubt was the more diligent student despite lagging him in age and preparation. Jemmy, who displayed the gregariousness, energy, and good humor of his grandfather, was more easily distracted. He remained a free-spirited son of the Cape, drawn to its breezy, salt-sprayed expanses while squirming under the weight of his father's expectations. Jemmy inherited the Colonel's intelligence and craving for recognition, but, as one nineteenth-century biographer put it, "his activities were marked with a reckless audacity, which . . . did not distinguish him much from the other promising New England boys of his age."[16] Another author described him as "brilliant, erratic . . . a creature of mental impulse."[17] Then and in years to come, the Allyne side of the family saw signs in him of their irascible ancestor Edward Doty, whose argumentative nature, flares of temper, and litany of misdemeanors landed him repeatedly in trouble with the Pilgrim fathers.

Mercy was every bit as bright as her brother but more focused. His acumen and breadth of knowledge were an inspiration to her, yet more often than not it was she who snapped him back to attention with a sisterly glare or kick to the shins. Under her uncle's guidance and buoyed by Jemmy's support, Mercy learned to write, to love literature and history, to be comfortable in the world of ideas, to feel confident in herself and her gender, to express herself openly, perhaps even to imagine a place for herself outside the domestic sphere. Even though she and Jemmy were separated by three years and seven months, they became intellectual partners. He treated her like an equal. They grew inseparable.

The hundreds of leather-bound volumes crammed onto Pastor Russell's shelves ran the gamut from English literary classics—Alexander Pope, John Dryden, John Milton, and William Shakespeare—to the great works of Western history, philosophy, and religion. Russell designed his curriculum to prepare Jemmy for Harvard, which required a command of Latin and Greek as well as mathematics, rhetoric, and a host of subjects not taught in free school. Mercy, who would be no more eligible for higher education than she would be for the clergy, was excluded from instruction in the classical languages. Not to be deterred, she read Homer and Virgil in translation by Pope and Dryden, while Jemmy slogged through the originals. Sir Walter Raleigh's *Historie of the World* (1614), a moral narrative from Creation to ancient Rome, is said to have been one of Mercy's favorites, providing a kind of model for her chronicle of the American

Revolution as a mature woman. She was just ten when she started reading Raleigh's tomes.

Reverend Russell was no Cotton Mather or Jonathan Edwards. There was presumably little fire and brimstone in his sermons, which, given his erudition and Old Light traditionalism, would have emphasized exposition over emotionalism. For Mercy Otis, Russell's enlightened brand of Christian faith had to have been eye-opening, a liberation from the strict biblical precepts handed down from her mother. Her uncle's homilies in the West Parish Church on Sunday mornings provided an enthralling weekly lesson in rational discourse and elegant prose style.[18] Her own later writings—in verse, correspondence, satirical drama, and history—emphasized classical over biblical allusions, reason over sentimentality, and a studied formality of style. There is a heavy moralizing and didactic quality in her work; integrity and character are held in especially high esteem. Providence is a recurring theme, yet the retributive God of the Old Testament makes scant appearance. Russell's influence is unmistakable.

Among the Puritan precepts that Mercy carried into the pastor's study on her first day was that there is salvation in gratitude. His teachings came as an unexpected boon, a revelation every day, and she knew to be thankful. At the same time, as historian Ray Raphael astutely observes, the rigorous lessons challenged and changed her in profound ways: "She learned early on that her supreme duty, and the supreme duty of all women, was to submit to the will of God. But try as she must to submit, two things challenged her resolve: education and politics."[19]

Jemmy twitched and fidgeted even more in a church pew than he did behind a school desk; he had little patience for hymns and sermons. Academic training with his learned uncle was not as life-altering for him as it was for his younger sister, but it was readying him for Harvard and assuaging his father. As with previous generations of firstborn Otis men, Jemmy's interest in church affairs extended little beyond the practical concerns of parish administration. If his supreme duty was to submit to the will and aspirations of his father, then politics no less than book learning was *his* providence.

That education came at home, and Mercy took part there as avidly as she did at the parsonage. The founder of the Otis political dynasty, John III, had died before Jemmy could walk and before Mercy was born. James Sr. was cutting his teeth as a lawyer while the Otis children were growing up, but the up-and-coming generation heard endless tales of their important grandfather. As the Colonel gained positions of increasing influence in the church, town committees, and courts, the Otis mansion became a place where members of the community gathered to discuss and debate the issues of the day. Around the hearth and dining room table, Jemmy and Mercy gained firsthand exposure to the ins and outs of political horse-trading at the local, then provincial levels.

One can easily imagine an exasperated Mary Otis summoning away her daughter to Bible study or sewing, with Mercy ignoring her pleas. Mary would hardly be the last person to tell Mercy that "politics is not for women," but how could she be excluded? Politics was the pride of the family.

James Otis Sr. espoused a staunch Old Whig ideology, supporting the power of Parliament over the monarch and aristocracy, religious tolerance over the power of the church, and the principles of popular sovereignty and natural rights. At the heart of Whig philosophy was a love of country but a hatred of arbitrary power and the wanton exercise of it. A direct English forebear of American republicanism, Whiggism advanced some of the core tenets of the patriot movement, the Declaration of Independence, and the U.S. Constitution.[20] Colonel Otis was a devoted British subject and far from a revolutionary, but Whig ideals—passed on through his eldest son, his eldest daughter, and others of their generation—established a direct link between seventeenth-century Puritan separatism and the birth of American democracy. For Jemmy and Mercy, it was another lasting bond. They would share a political life as rich as their intellectual life, but with greater consequence.

In her classic biography *Mercy Otis Warren* (1896), Alice Brown likens the childhood relationship between Mercy and James to that of Maggie Tulliver and her older brother Tom in George Eliot's Victorian coming-of-age novel *The Mill on the Floss* (1860). In Brown's book, Mercy and Jemmy ramble the sand dunes and sheep meadows of Barnstable's West Parish with the same joy and innocence that Maggie and Tom explore the East Midlands countryside. "As Maggie trotted about after Tom, adoring, worshipful, glad of a glance," Brown imagines, "so the little Cape girl followed and imitated her big brother."[21]

Young Mercy Otis may have held Jemmy in similar awe—or perhaps not. Of greater certainty is Brown's observation that they were, from the beginning, "more or less alike in temperament—ardent, mobile, brilliant." And their affinities became more pronounced as they grew older. A few months together in Reverend Russell's study revealed a shared aptitude for book learning and a recognition that may have startled them both: "Mercy was entirely [Jemmy's] equal, so far as the ardor of intellectual life was concerned."[22] Their fascination with practical politics and Enlightenment philosophy brought them closer still and, in the end, cast them together on the stage of history.

Whatever the actual parallels with Maggie and Tom Tulliver, Brown arrives at the critical insight about Mercy and James Otis: their closeness was "not only the kinship of blood; it was an intimacy of soul."[23] Their bond ran deeper and stronger than anything forged in seaside adventures, classroom studies, or farmyard chores—any experience, in fact, that Brown herself directly addresses. The intimacy between Mercy and Jemmy was rooted in the burdens and traumas they endured within the Otis household from a young age.

There had been much to confide in each other, to commiserate over, to cry about. They had faced the stinging discipline and grim piety of loving but rigid parents. As the eldest son, free-spirited Jemmy bore the deadweight of his father's ambitions—and he teetered. His impulsive behavior was a reflection of inner turmoil and insecurity as much as the wit and whimsy ascribed to him in family histories.

Mercy, for her part, became a kind of surrogate parent for her younger siblings and matron of the estate during her mother's absences—a burden beyond her years. She found out there was a higher wisdom than her mother's stern Calvinism and more that mattered in the world than the crispness of pressed linens, yet wider horizons seemed forever out of reach. With the help of an older brother, however, Mercy's dreams of higher learning came true.

When Jemmy left home for college in 1739, he was fourteen years old (standard for matriculating students at the time); Mercy was a few months shy of her eleventh birthday. By those tender ages, they had experienced the shock and grief of four lost siblings in childbirth or infancy, with another yet to come. The tragedies of the borning room were not the parents' alone to suffer.

With everything they went through, Mercy and Jemmy Otis grew up fast and neared adulthood as kindred spirits. For the rest of their lives, they would remain as devoted to each other as anyone else they knew and anything else they believed in.

CHAPTER 4

# Prospects, Possibilities, and Contagious Enthusiasms

Harvard was just over a century old when Jemmy arrived in June 1739. The college was markedly more secular but unchanged in many ways since its founding in 1636 as a Puritan institution of "Godly learning" and clergy training.[1] Classrooms, offices, and lodgings fit into three brick buildings around the Old Yard.[2] Many students entered the ministry or academia upon graduating, though not at the rate of their seventeenth-century predecessors. Well-to-do merchant families now sent their sons to Cambridge for an exacting education and easy entrée into politics, commerce, and elite New England society. As had been the case from the beginning, however, Harvard's curriculum followed the English university system, and college life reflected traditional norms of order.[3] Behavior conformed to strict rules and penalties (a fine of two pennies for lateness, five shillings for drinking, one pound for card playing).[4] A student's class rank depended on the social standing of his family.[5]

Jemmy's entry into Harvard pleased the Colonel, vicariously realizing his ambitions in education and politics. Cambridge would open "fine prospects," James Sr. later wrote, making his eldest son "useful to himself and family and the world."[6] Otis Sr., the savviest of businessmen, could not have imagined a better investment in the future, yet he charged the cost of Harvard to Jemmy's inheritance.[7]

While the Colonel was busting buttons, Mercy was disconsolate over her brother's departure. She was duty-bound to her parents and reconciled to God's will, but she had lost her best friend, confidante, and moral support in family life and education. As evidenced by the breadth of book learning she would achieve, the tutoring sessions with Reverend Russell may well have continued after Jemmy left home. Yet even assuming Russell's ongoing attention, the absence of her brother's camaraderie and encouragement must have left an aching hole in her young life. Aside from reading, she devoted her time to chores, crafts, and assisting her mother in the nursery. Mary delivered three more daughters and two more sons while Jemmy was away at school; one of those daughters died in infancy. Mercy, at home without her adored eldest brother, shared the Colonel's vicarious pleasure in Jemmy's possibilities.

James Otis Jr. placed thirteenth among forty-one students in the Harvard class of 1743; James Sr.'s position as justice of the peace of Barnstable County ranked lower in the social hierarchy than the judgeships held by the fathers of several classmates. Jemmy roomed in Massachusetts Hall and Stoughton College with Lothrop Russell, a cousin from Barnstable.[8] Lothrop, whose quiet reserve complemented Jemmy's sociability and exuberance, was his closest companion at Harvard.[9]

Just as he lagged his younger sister in academic diligence back in Pastor Russell's study, so James got off to a slow start at Harvard. He was well-prepared for the classes in Latin, Greek, rhetoric, logic, ethics, politics, arithmetic, and geometry, but he was on his own now, without moorings.[10] He was young, fun-loving, and charismatic, always attracting new friends. A tendency to mock the serious and poke fun at authority distracted him all the more from proper dedication to studying. And still there was the quirkiness, the excess energy and odd behavior, the "queerness" that many had observed in him since childhood.[11]

On one visit home around this time, friends visiting the Otis estate persuaded Jemmy to play a "country dance" on his fiddle. Space was cleared, the dancing began; suddenly he stopped playing. Holding the instrument and bow over his head, Jemmy declared, "So Orpheus fiddled, and so danced the brutes!"* Then, tossing the fiddle aside, he ran off through the garden, the puzzled revelers chasing behind. He never played the fiddle again.[12]

A turning point for young James came in the fall of 1740 with the arrival in Boston of evangelist preacher George Whitefield, the thundering voice of the Great Awakening. After sparking Christian revivals throughout the South and Mid-Atlantic, the itinerant English cleric electrified crowds in villages and towns across Massachusetts during September and October. A throng of up to thirty thousand—a figure greater than the city's population—poured into the Boston Common to hear him preach.[13] Next, holding forth in Cambridge, Whitefield took aim at the Harvard community for its creeping impiety and lapses in godliness. "Tutors neglect to pray with and examine the hearts of their pupils," he bellowed. "Discipline is at too low an ebb. Bad books are become fashionable."[14]

* Jemmy's declaration alluded to the Greek myth of Orpheus, the god of music and poetry who attempted to rescue his deceased wife, Eurydice, from the underworld. Orpheus's skill on the lyre and the sweetness of his singing could charm wild animals, coax brutes and rocks to dance, and tame the dog-monster Cerberus at the gates of hell. Edward Bulwer-Lytton's famous comment about Orpheus is especially apropos of James Otis Jr.: "*Nothing is as contagious as enthusiasm.* It is the real allegory of the myth of Orpheus—it moves stones, it charms brutes. Enthusiasm is the genius of sincerity, and truth accomplishes no victories without it." Equally apropos of Otis, however, is a lesson implicit in the myth about impulsiveness: in escaping the underworld with Eurydice, Orpheus forgets the command of Hades and Persephone and turns to look for his wife. She vanishes instantly and forever. Edward Bulwer-Lytton, *The Last Days of Pompeii* (London: Richard Bentley, 1834), 1:145; emphasis added.

Whitefield's fireworks triggered a surge of soul-searching on campus—a revival of sorts among students and faculty.[15] James and his friend Lothrop reportedly took part in group prayers, psalm singing, and religious discussions late into the night.[16] Something changed in Otis Jr. after that. Exactly what inspired him is hard to know for sure. Despite his mother's strict Calvinism and Reverend Russell's more enlightened exhortations, James never officially joined any church or held family prayer sessions; that was more Mercy's way.[17] Maybe it was the rhetoric of freedom in the revivalist appeal, or the message of social equality. The revolt against orthodoxy and privilege, at least, would have been a rebuke to his father's Old Light, patrician values.

In any event, the Great Awakening at Harvard lit a spark in Jemmy Otis. He applied himself to academics with a new seriousness and focus, as if his uncle were glaring down at him or Mercy were kicking him under the table. Making up for lost time, he buried himself in books. The love of scholarship would burn in him from then on, and he would be every bit the orator in the courtroom and legislature that George Whitefield was at the pulpit.

Once James got serious as a student, political philosophy, the classics, history, and logic became areas of particular interest. One transformative discovery was the *Two Treatises of Government* (1689) by John Locke, whom he referred to thereafter as "the immortal" or "the great."[18] The second of Locke's treatises became the foundation of Otis's political creed in its assertions that all men are born in "a state of perfect freedom to order their actions" and that they are entitled to all "the rights and privileges of the law of nature."[19]

In accordance with those principles, Otis subscribed to the Whig view of history—that the course of events follows a natural path, determined by reason, individual rights, political and religious freedom, and constitutional government. Any obstacle or deviation on that path is a step toward tyranny; any sovereign who violates the "social contract" (a tacit agreement by which individuals sacrifice some of their freedoms to the state in exchange for protection) must be resisted. Hence, Jemmy's heroes in history included the Roman senator Brutus, who conspired against Julius Caesar's autocracy, and the English parliamentarians who led the Civil War and Glorious Revolution against Stuart kings.

In the same antiauthoritarian spirit, Otis during his senior year took the side of a Harvard instructor named Nathan Prince who had been dismissed for intemperance, slandering colleagues, and stirring up strife on campus.[20] Prince contended that the Board of Overseers had no authority to fire him, and Jemmy concurred vehemently. The Harvard administration, he exploded in a letter home, was a "miserable, despicable and arbitrary government."[21] In tone and substance, the pronouncement was a taste of things to come.

James's burgeoning interest in political philosophy also opened a new chapter in his relationship with Mercy. While his letters to the family, addressed to the Colonel, were deferential in style and businesslike in content—mainly accounts of his spending, signed "your dutiful son"—any direct correspondence with his sister would have been affectionate and full of excitement over his latest academic discoveries. On visits home from Cambridge, Jemmy shared his knowledge with Mercy just as he had before she joined Reverend Russell's tutoring sessions. Only now he was as earnest in his studies as she was. After immersing himself in reading for days on end, he would sit down with his eager sister to dissect, thrash out, and kick around the text at hand, then move on to another. She became his one-on-one student of political philosophy; her thinking evolved right beside his and the immortal John Locke's.

James's graduation from Harvard in July 1743 was perhaps more momentous in Mercy's life than it was in his own. She would turn fifteen in two months, and her world had never extended beyond the safe, insular confines of Barnstable County. Books had carried her off to ancient Greece and Rome, and she had dreamed of Boston and Cambridge since Jemmy left home. Now, with a sunbonnet on her head and a fine silk dress in her luggage, she set out with her family on a hired boat to Boston and then by carriage to Cambridge. Harvard commencement was celebrated like a provincial holiday in the 1740s, bringing out families, school officials, and dignitaries for the solemn conferral of degrees and lavish, sun-drenched picnics.[22] Jemmy took part in an honorary class "disputation" and made the rounds of classmates and their families. For Mercy, the days' events brought to life everything she had imagined and envied in her brother's world.

Most memorable of all, it was at Harvard graduation that she met her future husband. James Warren was two years behind Jemmy, the son of a successful merchant-farmer and high sheriff from Plymouth. Warren's father (also James and also called "the Colonel") had witnessed legal papers for Otis Sr. on the county circuit; the two traders had also done business together. If Mercy Otis and James Warren Jr. had ever met before Jemmy introduced them at a commencement party, it was that afternoon when they first got acquainted. And if her thoughts had never turned to romance and the prospect of marriage before that day, now she was smitten by her brother's attentive, sandy-haired friend. He was open and easygoing; conversation between them came easily. He was taken by her maturity and intelligence, she by his sense of humor and the grownup way he spoke to her. Warren, she would write in retrospect, was "a powerful magnet, the center of my early wishes and the star which attracts my attention."[23]

Jemmy moved back to Barnstable after graduation and began two years of study toward a graduate degree. He worked mostly at home, following his passions in classical languages and literature. He was never more in his element, free to read what he wanted and to indulge the side of him that craved the order and harmony of the Greco-Roman world. Left to his own devices, Otis Jr. might well have chosen a life of scholarship.[24] But the Colonel had long since determined that his eldest son should become a lawyer. Years later, the younger Otis wrote his father that he regretted not taking time "for more general inquiries in the arts and sciences." He considered them "indispensably necessary" to the study of law, a moral education, and personal happiness.[25]

For Mercy, Jemmy's time in Barnstable was another boon to her academic training. She kept up with his readings, challenged his opinions, and pursued interests of her own in literature and history. Her studies with him were as close to higher education as any young woman in colonial America could dare to imagine. Mercy may have lacked her brother's Harvard training, but quietly and modestly, without drawing attention to herself, she was no less gifted or hungry for knowledge. Their intellectual partnership continued to grow.

James Jr. and James Sr. both moved to downtown Boston in 1745. The elder Otis began his tenure in the General Court as an elected representative from Barnstable. The younger Otis, still only twenty, began his legal apprenticeship with Jeremiah Gridley, a family friend and the acknowledged dean of Massachusetts lawyers. Jemmy's grief over the death of college friend Lothrop Russell that July precipitated a period of despondency which devolved into prolonged depression and emotional detachment.[26] His acquiescence to the Colonel's bidding—the abrupt shift from academics to professional training—was likely a contributing factor.

James Jr. brought a scholar's approach to the study of law, poring over the "black letter" common-law tomes on Gridley's shelves and delving deep into parliamentary statutes, court procedures, and the preparation of filings.[27] The noted attorney and judge Richard Dana later vouched that he had "never known a student in law so punctual, so steady, so constant and persevering."[28] At the same time, Jemmy was looking out for the family business, reporting any lucrative deals he came across during his father's absences. Younger brother Joseph, who had married and taken over the family store after cutting short his education, assumed broader responsibilities as James Sr. became more involved in politics. Mercy, as a young colonial woman, took no part in such matters. In the long silences and open spaces of the West Parish, she occupied herself as ever with household affairs, needlework, church groups, and her life of letters as best she could sustain it alone.

After two years of intensive study with Gridley, Otis Jr. passed the bar in 1748 and, at his father's urging, opened an office on Main Street in Plymouth. The Colonel, still riding the Plymouth County circuit, could keep tabs on his son en route between Cape Cod and Boston; he wasn't certain Jemmy was ready for big-city practice. The young attorney had been devoting endless hours to private study, cultivating his knowledge of legal theory along with political philosophy and classical literature. Moreover, the range of cases in Plymouth was limited, and James seemed less interested in soliciting new clients or collecting fees than in arguing points of law—the more esoteric the better.

Despite the colonel's help and advice, Jemmy's practice struggled. Almost unavoidably, however, the self-educated father and his Harvard-educated son came to oppose each other in court. It happened twice, in 1748. The younger Otis prevailed both times, but he was showing signs of anxiety.[29] "I think he is excitable," brother Joseph wrote to the family a few months later. "He has taken so close to his studies that he scarcely allows himself time to eat decently or sleep."[30]

Mercy, meanwhile, was thrilled to have Jemmy nearby in Plymouth. It was a chance to see him more often and to continue their studies together. Even more exciting was the prospect of seeing his old college friend—the "center of her wishes," James Warren. After graduation, Warren had moved back to Plymouth to help on the family farm and learn his father's business. In Mercy's eyes, the opportunity for them to get to know one another must have seemed nothing less than providential. As one of her biographers plausibly suggests, "What more natural than that Warren should sometimes ride down with Otis to Barnstable, to be made a welcome guest in Colonel Otis's hospitable home?"[31]

James Otis Sr. ascended quickly in the Massachusetts legislature, rising on the strength of his support for Governor William Shirley.[32] From the first bill he advanced in the assembly—placing a bounty on the scalp or capture of Native Americans—the Colonel burnished a reputation for his staunch militarism and "expertise" in Indian affairs. In the fall of 1749, he joined a delegation headed by Thomas Hutchinson, newly appointed to the Governor's Council, that traveled to Maine (then part of Massachusetts) to negotiate a treaty with northern tribes. For the exposure to provincial government and a chance to meet other commission members, James Sr. brought his wayward lawyer son. During the long hours on horseback, the rough-hewn Otises of backwater Cape Cod established an unlikely rapport with the urbane, well-bred Hutchinson of Boston's North End.[33]

By early 1750, his practice moribund after two years, James Jr. decided to close the Plymouth office and move to Boston. He was ready to begin his own rise in the profession, to make a name for himself outside the Colonel's shadow. During his apprenticeship with Jeremiah Gridley, the younger Otis had gained distinction for his breadth of knowledge and command of legal details. Now, as he began winning cases and building a clientele from the burgeoning merchant class, he extended that reputation with his legal acumen, charisma as a speaker, and personal character.

Maybe he needed the bigger pond of Boston in order to meet his potential. His Harvard ties could not have hurt either; nor could his connections with the leading families of Plymouth and the Cape, with their far-flung trading partners. In any event, Otis Jr. became known for taking only cases he believed in and for declining retainers if the outcome was in any doubt.[34] He represented the Hancocks, Vassals, Halls, and other leading Massachusetts Bay families.[35] He traveled to Halifax, Nova Scotia, to defend three merchants under arrest for piracy and returned home with the highest fee ever paid to a Massachusetts attorney to that time.[36]

Still in his late twenties, James Otis Jr. joined the ranks of the most prominent lawyers in Boston. He became, according to fellow attorney James Putnam, "by far the most able, manly, and commanding character of his age at the bar." That view, John Adams later confirmed, was "the unanimous opinion of judges, lawyers, and the public."[37] Even Thomas Hutchinson, before the political estrangement and misunderstanding that ignited their feud, attested to Otis's skill and integrity as a lawyer: "He never knew fairer or more noble conduct in a pleader, than in Otis; that he always disdained to take advantage of any clerical error . . . and defended his causes solely on their broad and substantial foundations."[38]

Boarding with his mother's family, the Allynes, James was a young man about town, forging friendships and business relationships among the titans, blue bloods, and power brokers of colonial Boston. "Naturally and constitutionally inclined to social pleasures," as he once described himself, the up-and-coming attorney exchanged toasts and pleasantries in drawing rooms his father never laid eyes on.[39] Jeremiah Gridley, the grand master of Boston Freemasons, sponsored James Jr.'s membership in the St. John's Lodge.[40] Jemmy's engagement to Ruth Cunningham, the daughter and heiress of one of the richest merchants in Boston, extended his network and reinforced his social standing even further.[41]

The web of connections served Otis family interests as well, with the Colonel now looking to his eldest son as his trade attorney, purchasing agent, and stand-in overseer of Boston operations. Never one to miss an opportunity for profits, James Sr. had taken full advantage of the patronage system in colonial government and ran several trading ships that sailed to and from the West Indies carrying molasses and sugar, whalebone and fish, salt, rice, rum, and cloth.[42] James Jr., with his ties in the mercantile world and his expertise in trade and admiralty law, was a valued collaborator.

The younger Otis, however, brought greater enthusiasm to his off-hour academic pursuits than he did to his father's business. Gridley, who had edited a literary magazine for several years, welcomed James Jr. into his circle as a serious scholar.[43] Even as Otis built a law practice, he continued to read voraciously in legal theory and political philosophy. If nothing else, he considered knowledge in these fields critical to his professional success. "A lawyer," he would tell students and young colleagues, "ought never to be without a volume of natural or public law, or moral philosophy, on his table or in his pocket."[44]

For Mercy, now farther removed from her older brother than ever before, bookish interests paled momentarily against the glow of her impending marriage to James Warren. It had been eleven years since they had met at Jemmy's graduation, and their initial attraction had grown stronger over time. Perhaps James waited to propose until establishing himself in business, or perhaps Mercy's responsibilities in managing the household and raising siblings left her unavailable. Either way, the courtship no doubt was formal and proper: chaperoned walks around the Otis estate, church attendance together, a visit by the entire Warren family. Finally, in accordance with English custom, marriage banns (proclamations) would have been posted on the West Parish Church.

Mercy and James Warren wed on November 14, 1754, before a modest gathering of family and friends at the Otis mansion. Because marriage was a civil contract rather than a religious sacrament in Puritan tradition, a magistrate rather than a clergyman administered the vows. Household staff served a simple dinner with the customary bridal cakes and cups of sack posset—a rich, custard-like pudding that combined eggs, sugar, cinnamon, hot cream, and fortified white wine (sack) or sherry. The "celebration" afterward was brief and strictly decorous: no dancing, minimal drinking, the singing of a psalm, and early goodnights to the wedding couple.[45]

Mercy was twenty-six and James twenty-eight when they married, in both cases older than the norm in Congregational New England. Their relationship combined traditional and newer concepts of marriage, based as it was on similar social and economic backgrounds, close family ties, shared religious and political views, *and* a close romantic bond.[46] Mercy's advanced education and intellect, a most unladylike trait in that day and age, was not the impediment to James's attraction that it would have been to other men. To the contrary, he admired her talents and encouraged her life of letters. Moreover, James lent a patience and equanimity to their day-to-day life that stood in sharp contrast to the tensions in the Otis home. All in all, Mercy and James Warren were partners in a way that few married couples of their time enjoyed. They even had a common ancestor: Edward Doty of the *Mayflower* and Plimoth Plantation.

Jemmy, missing his sister and closest companion, married less than six months later, in March 1755. He was thirty, she twenty-five. Ruth Cunningham, universally described as beautiful and wealthy, was rigidly conservative in politics, placid in temperament, and coolly formal in manner—most unlike her new husband.[47] If James had hoped to find a new best friend in marriage, as Mercy had, he was disappointed in short order. The couple bought a home on School Street in Boston, not far from the newly renovated Town House on Cornhill, and had the first of their three children, a son named James, before year's end. But the differences between them, from money to religion to politics, soon became apparent.

Nathaniel Cunningham, Ruth's father, had died in 1748 and left her a fortune valued at £10,000.[48] James, who gained control of the money upon marriage, treated it like a willed estate for their children, separating the funds from his own earnings and refusing to spend or invest a penny of it.[49] Ruth looked down on his handling of the wealth as evidence of his lower pedigree. In matters of faith, Ruth entered communion and took full membership at the Old South Church; James never did so.[50] In politics, the gulf between her Tory conservatism and his Whig liberalism would only widen in the turbulent years ahead.

Among the many ironies and contradictions of his conflicted life, the man who would lay the groundwork for the Fourth Amendment to the U.S. Constitution by arguing that "a man's house is his castle" found little peace in his own home. He spent spare time at the elite Boston Latin School (for which their street was named) in conversation with faculty.[51] And out of studious habit, passion for the subject, or sheer need of escape—probably all three—he stole hours on end from his professional and domestic duties to continue his work in the classics. In the late 1750s, he researched and wrote a linguistic treatise titled *The Rudiments of Latin Prosody,* which Harvard adopted as a course text. He followed that with a volume on Greek prosody that languished in manuscript (which he ultimately destroyed) because Greek type was unavailable.[52]

As for his marriage, biographer Katharine Susan Anthony aptly summarizes James's error in judgment: "In his haste to replace his sister, Otis had wandered as far afield as a sadly mistaken man can wander."[53] And so, while Mercy and James Warren were comfortably ensconced in Clifford Farm—she reveling in nature and writing poetry, he learning the ropes of his father's business—Jemmy in Boston came to be at odds with himself in this new way. He was attached and loyal to his beautiful socialite wife, his "Ruthy," but he knew deep down how incompatible they were.[54] Feeling ever more respected in public life and ever less so at home, he turned his considerable energies to politics.

Until Benedict Arnold turned on his country late in the Revolutionary War, Thomas Hutchinson was the most despised and vilified man in America. A fifth-generation Bostonian (his great-great grandmother was the religious dissident Anne Hutchinson), he was a lightning rod of colonial disaffection as the highest-ranking native-born official in provincial government. Born to wealth, privilege, and a tacit sense of entitlement, he was proudly elitist in his belief that power should devolve to the educated upper class. And while he felt an abiding loyalty to his Massachusetts "ancestors" and "countrymen," whom he served for three decades and memorialized in a comprehensive history, he believed fundamentally that the province "cannot subsist without the protection of our mother country."[55] This made him an increasingly polarizing figure in his roles as legislator, chief justice, lieutenant governor, and finally governor. "He was passionately loyal to his community," remarked biographer Bernard Bailyn, "and he ended up the worst villain in the whole American revolutionary history."[56] Hutchinson was especially villainous in the eyes of the Otis family, as evidenced by Mercy's starkly Gothic depiction in her chronicle of the period:

> He was dark, intriguing, insinuating, haughty, and ambitious, while the extreme of avarice marked every feature of his character. . . . [He] diligently studied the intricacies of Machiavelian policy and never failed to recommend the Italian master as a model to his adherents.[57]

The accumulation of assets and a record of public service on the part of previous generations placed expectations on young Thomas Hutchinson not unlike those faced by James Otis Jr., only on a larger stage. Hutchinson's father had donated the grammar school building where he learned Latin and Greek; the Hutchinson coat of arms appeared on the lintel above the main entrance. Thomas was studious as a boy, more attentive to his schoolwork and happier to spend hours indoors than Jemmy ever was; he was as introverted and withdrawn as Otis was outgoing and fun-loving. Hutchinson began Harvard at age twelve, in the class of 1727. On the strength of his family's status, he ranked third in his class.

After the requisite years of apprenticeship and management in his father's shipping and dry goods business, Hutchinson entered politics in 1739 as a Boston selectman; shortly thereafter he was elected to the Massachusetts legislature. Well-bred, well-educated, and well-connected, he represented the interests of Boston's governing class and the British crown in a spirit of patrician honor and duty. He was "tall, slender, fair-complexioned, fair-spoken" and aristocratic in bearing—a gentleman politician who expected deference and respect from ordinary working people in gratitude for his sagacious leadership.[58] Common people and the press derided him as "Tommy Skin and Bones" or simply "the Tall Man."[59]

Hutchinson earned his place in the upper echelons of provincial government—and the animosity of ordinary Bostonians—for his role in the dominant provincial issue of the 1740s: the depreciation of the currency, or inflation. The problem became one of wealth and class, as debtors (struggling farmers, tradesmen, and shopkeepers) called for the issuance of more paper money, or greater depreciation, while creditors (rich investors and estate owners), fearing repayment of their debts in devalued cash, advocated a "hard currency" based on silver. Under a paper-money venture called the Land Bank, debtors got relief in the form of cheaper currency based on new mortgages. Well-heeled merchants, large landowners, and the British authorities stood firmly against this scheme—drawing the lines of a fierce political battle.[60]

Wealth and power prevailed in the end, as Parliament stepped in to suppress the Land Bank and Hutchinson engineered the retirement of paper money with loans of British silver. The Tall Man's political career and status in the administration flourished in the aftermath, but his countrymen hurled threats and insults in the streets of Boston. His unbending support for the crown and the ruling class—loyalties he now symbolized—created long-simmering resentment among ordinary colonials. Referring to himself in the third person, as was his habit, Hutchinson later recalled that "nothing made him more obnoxious to a great part of the people than his stand with paper money."[61] Parliament's intervention left even deeper scars, turning the issue into one of British sovereignty. For the first time in the minds of many Bostonians, the question was whether to defy the crown or not.

As he rose in office and as political factions coalesced in the 1750s, the Thomas Hutchinson who had rubbed elbows with the Otises on the trip to Maine and who had praised the integrity of James Jr. as an attorney became the family's chief rival and behind-the-scenes antagonist. James Sr., representing the change-averse views of his Barnstable constituents, actually opposed the Land Bank and drove Hutchinson's hard-money plan through the legislature. Hutchinson, however, after rising from Speaker of the House to member of the Governor's Council, consolidated power in an alliance of politicians—the court party—that supported the governor and Boston elites unfailingly.[62] And while Hutchinson had always been ambitious, the death of his wife from childbirth complications in 1754 left him deeply bereaved, lonely, and all the more devoted to his career.[63]

James Otis Sr., no less aggressive when it came to seeking office, won reelection to the House reliably every two years, played a key role in numerous committees, and headed a group of rural interests called the popular, or country, party. That pitted him in direct opposition to Hutchinson. The former legislative allies and colleagues of convenience thus became adversaries.

With their sharply contrasting backgrounds and temperaments, the political rivalry quickly devolved into personal acrimony. Hutchinson, the haughty, blue-blooded elitist, neither respected nor trusted the poorly educated, status-grabbing outsider from the boondocks and maneuvered in 1757 to block him from a seat on the Governor's Council. In words that eventually got back to the Colonel, Hutchinson told voting members of the assembly that Otis had accomplished little on his own merits and had risen "only by doing little low dirty things for Governor Shirley."[64] Otis lost the vote.

James Jr., meanwhile, had become increasingly involved in the Boston Town Meeting and several of its working committees. The more involved he grew, the more interested he became in the everyday issues and concerns of fellow townspeople. Family allegiance and the draw of politics eventually landed him at his father's side, and at a propitious time. As a political assistant and liaison for the Colonel, the younger Otis won an appointment from Governor Shirley as justice of the peace for Suffolk County (including Boston) in 1756.[65]

Thomas Pownall, who took over as governor the following year, proved even more positively disposed toward the Otises and more wary of Hutchinson. James Jr., who became friends with the new governor, smoothed over a squabble between Pownall and his father concerning the sale of whaleboats.[66] The governor rewarded Otis Jr. with the position of advocate general of the Vice-Admiralty Court, a job perfectly suited to his background in trade and maritime law. Governor Pownall also renewed his predecessor's assurance to Otis Sr. that he would get the next vacant seat on the Superior Court.[67]

A man with less to prove might have recognized those promises for what they were. For James Otis Sr., expectation failed where it promised most.

The British government recalled Pownall in the summer of 1760 and replaced him two months later with hardline royalist Francis Bernard; Hutchinson served as acting governor in the interim. Bernard arrived knowing that his orders from London were to begin enforcing the long-ignored Navigation Acts, initially by collecting levies on imported molasses (used in New England to make rum). He also knew that a third of the proceeds would be his to keep. That fact alone tipped his bias in favor of the court party and Hutchinson, who reliably supported crown authority, and against the popular party and the Otises, who favored greater colonial autonomy. Bernard rightly suspected that Otis Jr. had grown disillusioned with the administration's treatment of local merchants and might be less than zealous in carrying out the new customs policies.

The death of Chief Justice Stephen Sewall in September 1760 presented Bernard with a decision within weeks of his arrival. James Otis Sr. fully expected the new governor to honor the commitments of his predecessors and appoint him to the bench. Otis Jr., after hearing rumors that Hutchinson had designs on the seat, carried a letter from his father directly to the lieutenant governor at the Town House. The letter asked for Hutchinson's help in soliciting Governor Bernard on the Colonel's behalf; James Jr. asked bluntly about Hutchinson's intentions. The lieutenant governor later claimed to have given "a general answer of . . . uncertain nature" about his own aspirations and to have offered no help in lobbying Bernard.[68] Otis Jr., however, left the Town House convinced that Hutchinson "had no thought nor desire of the office" and that he would support Colonel Otis for the seat.[69]

Evasions and obfuscations notwithstanding, Bernard's decision was a foregone conclusion. Hutchinson, despite his other offices and lack of legal training, coveted a place on the high court. Governor Bernard knew full well that enforcing the customs mandate required the backing of a new chief justice who would rule on the legality of the writs of assistance, and that Hutchinson was far more likely to be supportive than the elder Otis. More broadly, the Tories and court party were much more in line with crown policy than were the Whigs and popular party.

The announcement of Hutchinson's appointment on November 13 came as a bombshell to the Otises and an outrage to their allies. The fight was on. James Jr. promptly quit the Vice-Admiralty Court, while his enemies circulated an allegation—confirmed by the governor—that he had threatened revenge.[70] Otis denied the accusation, casting the lieutenant governor as the mastermind of a sinister, self-serving plot and as a traitor to his people.[71] Many of them agreed.

Hutchinson assumed the Superior Court bench on December 30. The writs of assistance hearing two months later was his first significant case. To the chagrin of James Otis Jr., his family's nemesis and the embodiment of every principle he despised now sat in a position of judgment. At the table adjacent to Otis's, poised to argue against him, was his former mentor and adviser, Jeremiah Gridley. Somewhere back in the recesses, pressed among the other observers, stood James's proud, tyrannical father. His High Tory wife, elegant but emotionally estranged, was at home a few blocks away with their five-year-old son and three-year-old daughter. And his cherished sister, now a mother of two, cast a wary eye on winter's "dark'ning clouds" over Plymouth Harbor.

# CHAPTER 5

# Locke Step

The elm-shaded house at the corner of North and Main Streets in Plymouth was a roomy, two-and-a-half story colonial built in 1726 by General John Winslow, James Warren's maternal uncle and a great-grandson of original Plymouth settler Edward Winslow.[1] An adjoining row of buildings included the storefront office and upstairs rooms where Jemmy Otis had started his law career and taken up quarters after passing the bar. The Plymouth County Court, where James Warren now served as high sheriff, was steps away. And a few hundred yards down the slope of North Street, at the edge Plymouth Bay, rested the ten-ton rock on which Edward Winslow, Edward Doty, and the rest of the *Mayflower* pilgrims were said to have landed in 1620.

The Warrens were approaching their third wedding anniversary when they moved into the home in July 1757. Mercy, pregnant with their first child, spent much of her time in the large salon and sitting room at the front of the house, where she could read, sew, and chat comfortably with visitors. An area behind the kitchen hearth would be set up as the borning room for the arrival of son James that October 18. Four more boys would follow over the next nine years: Winslow on March 24, 1759; Charles on April 14, 1762; Henry on March 21, 1764; and George on September 20, 1766. Mercy suffered none of her mother's travails in childbirth or early motherhood; all of her deliveries were successful, and all five sons survived childhood in the pink of health. During the course of those same nine years, however, patriot fever would make its way through the front door, plans for colonial resistance would take shape within the wainscoted walls of the sitting room, and the future muse of the American Revolution would develop a confident, highly refined literary style in the quiet recesses and haphazard moments of domestic life.

These were not perfectly carefree times for Mercy Otis Warren. Her God offered no safeguards against "the storms of life," and the political skies were darkening.[2] Yet from day to day she found bliss in motherhood and harmony in her routines as she never had before. "My children's interest and happiness," she once wrote, "are interwoven with every fiber of my heart."[3] Her

FIGURE 7. The Winslow-Warren house in downtown Plymouth, seen here in 1909, is a short walk from Plymouth Rock and Burial Hill Cemetery. The design of the house remains much like the original, with large shade trees in front.
—Courtesy of the author

marriage to James was a source of contentment and peace of mind, no matter their responsibilities apart. The burdens of managing a second home paled against the joys and inspiration of Clifford Farm, with all its natural wonder. And none of her duties as a mother, wife, or homemaker kept her from her life of letters. Reconciling study with domestic affairs was hardly new to her, but now she could set the priorities. There were plenty of books and money for more, there was time to read them with her children, and there was the freedom to write material all her own.

The immortal John Locke, along with other Enlightenment philosophers she had studied with Jemmy, was in every fiber of her mind as well as her heart. Locke's treatises in particular established an ideological common ground between sister and brother as serious, thinking adults. In poem after poem, letter after letter, Mercy revealed her depth of faith *and* her belief in reason. She found truth and strength in divine will while stubbornly questioning God's word, her own belief, and hope itself in the face of life's hardships. It was a coming to terms of intellect and religious conviction, like the projects of Enlightenment thinkers who resisted church orthodoxy but maintained a true faith. Locke, the son of fervent Puritans and himself a devout Anglican, cleaved to the doctrine that God intervenes directly in the lives of people ("special providence") yet also argued that God grants people the faculty of reason by which to discern truth, wisdom, and the principles of natural law: "Reason is natural revelation, whereby the eternal father of light and fountain of all knowledge communicates to mankind that portion of truth which he has laid within the reach of their natural faculties."[4]

Mercy Otis Warren, who shared the Puritan belief in special providence, articulates a view strikingly consonant with Locke's on the primacy of reason—the word of God and a guiding light—in such poems as "A Thought on the Inestimable Blessing of Reason" and "An Address to the Supreme Being." The former is a metaphysical statement:

What is it moves within my soul,
And as the needle to the pole
Directs me to the final cause
The central point of nature's laws?
'Tis reason, Lord, which thou has given
A ray divine, let down from Heaven,
A spark struck from effulgent light,
Transcendent, clear, divinely bright.[5]

The latter is a prayer:

Thou author of eternal truth!
Let reason be my guide,
And grant that through life's cares and pains
The lamp may bright abide.[6]

As a young mother, Mercy was especially drawn to Locke's writings on childrearing and education. Either she found a kindred thinker in the "father of liberalism" (who never married and had no children) or she came to adopt many of his views. Locke posited that the human mind at birth is a blank slate (*tabula rasa*), which attentive parents should inscribe and mold with a firm hand in infancy, rational discipline as the child grows older, and true friendship in "riper years." Parents should teach by good example and repeated practice rather than by precepts, rules, and punishments—a message that hit close to home for Mercy. A child should be taught to submit to reason from a young age, Locke believed, with truthfulness, virtue, and wisdom as the paramount goals. Paradoxically, for a man of letters, he deemed reading and writing as essential but less important elements of childrearing. Book-learning, he argued, is "subservient . . . to greater qualities." The wisdom to which Locke refers is not scholarly erudition but the wisdom to put one's faith in a rational God: "Nullum numen abest, si sit prudentia," he concludes ("Divine help will not be denied if we have wisdom").[7]

Mercy's devotion as a mother reflected her own form of enlightened wisdom. Her children were God's blessings, to be sure, but she took an active, purposeful approach to their moral and intellectual development. Letters to her husband attest to her pride in, and stamp of approval on, whatever they were reading at the time.[8] Yet this unlikely beneficiary of educational privilege did not fully take the reins of her sons' academic training; the boys attended a dame school in Plymouth from as early as age four. The values Mercy seemed to prize above all were precisely those espoused by Locke. She articulated her view in a letter to friend and confidante Abigail Adams, who had sent her a popular manual on raising and educating children.[9] Thanking her for the volume, Mercy wrote that her own priority as a mother was to "cultivate the infant minds and plant the seeds of virtue in my children." And, she went on,

> I cannot but think the love of *truth* is of much the greatest importance, more so than any single principle in the early culture of the mind. A careful attention to fix a sacred regard to veracity in the bosom of youth is the surest guard to virtue and the most powerful barrier against the sallies of vice, through every period of life.[10]

In later periods of her children's lives, the "riper years," Mercy instinctively heeded Locke's call for parental companionship. In a number of poems and letters, she referred to her grown sons as true friends. "I write with the warm emotions of maternal tenderness," she penned twenty-year-old Winslow in 1779, "strengthened by the reciprocal tie of friendship and confidence (a light in which at a certain stage I wish to view my sons)."[11]

Jemmy was more interested in Locke's political philosophy than his metaphysics or theories on childrearing, and Mercy's attention shifted to matters of liberty and natural rights in short order. She, too, had politics in her blood, and her education in colonial affairs became more practical as Jemmy became more embroiled. He kept her informed about events unfolding in

Boston and his own perspectives, changeable as they were, on the issues at hand. With the boys in school, she was able to visit from time to time and get a look in her brother's eyes. That was her best barometer of the political climate.

Despite their geographic separation, Jemmy and Mercy remained closer in adulthood than other siblings in colonial New England, many of whom shared resources, chores, family crises, and social lives as married couples and parents.[12] The Otises' devotion to each other only deepened as Mercy and James Warren waded into real-life politics alongside Jemmy. Mercy was the person who knew him best, and she grew more concerned with every passing month.

Otis's pyrotechnics in the Writs of Assistance Case awakened Bostonians outside the merchant class to abuses of authority and threats to colonial autonomy on the part of British officials. Residents expressed their appreciation by electing Otis in May 1761 as one of Boston's four representatives to the lower chamber of the General Court. James Sr., meanwhile, continued to represent Barnstable and retained his position as Speaker of the House. The elder and younger Otises made a formidable duo in the assembly, marshaling members of the popular party and ad hoc allies in opposing the administration on a host of matters.[13]

Their political strategy in the House session of 1761–62 was to win popular support and bring Governor Bernard to their side by driving a wedge between him and Lieutenant Governor Hutchinson.[14] Otis Jr. proved masterful at using the press, especially the weekly *Boston Gazette,* to criticize the administration and promote colonial rights on such issues as trade restriction, search warrants, and the currency standard. James's attacks on Hutchinson and his well-heeled friends were, at the same time, a political overture to working-class Bostonians: "I know it is the maxim of some that the common people in this town and country live too well," he wrote in a signed letter to the *Gazette,* "however I am of a quite different opinion. I do not think they live half well enough."[15]

Even more potent—and personal—was Otis's assault on Hutchinson for plural officeholding. It was not out of the ordinary for public officials in Massachusetts to hold multiple positions, whether by appointment or election. James Otis Sr. had faced his own share of criticism for wearing too many hats in Barnstable. But Thomas Hutchinson was the chief offender in terms of the numbers and levels of offices held simultaneously in the province. His concurrent service as lieutenant governor, chief justice, and member of the Governor's Council placed him at or near the top of the executive, judicial, and legislative branches of Massachusetts government. James Otis Jr., still smoldering over the slight to his father, pounced on the issue and aired his case in the pro-Whig *Gazette.* Plural officeholding, he declared, was unconstitutional and threatened tyranny.

Hutchinson gave up none of his posts, but unrelenting castigation in the press eroded his already-tarnished public image. At the same time, the Otises' maneuverings in the legislature frustrated the Tall Man's political agenda. "Two lawyers of the same name carry all before them in the House," fumed the indignant lieutenant governor.[16]

The legislative session of 1762–63 opened auspiciously for the Otises, as James Sr. finally won a place on the Governor's Council. The popular party had solidified its power in the lower chamber, and James Jr. was convinced that they had won over Bernard. But the tide turned quickly. The Colonel's elevation to the upper chamber removed his influence from the assembly, and cracks began to show in the younger Otis's leadership—not to mention his temper. More importantly, any notion that the governor would side with colonial interests over those of the crown, or that he would clip Hutchinson's wings beyond appearances, proved misguided.

The governor's veto of a pet bill that spring put Otis Jr. on notice. Then, while the House was on summer recess, Bernard billed a minor military expense to the provincial treasury. When the assembly reconvened, Otis let loose on the House floor. The governor's unauthorized expenditure, he railed, was a breach of the Massachusetts Bay charter: the power of appropriation, no matter the amount in question, was reserved to the legislature. When Bernard suspended the assembly in mid-debate, Otis replied with a fifty-three-page pamphlet titled *A Vindication of the Conduct of the House of Representatives of the Province of the Massachusetts-Bay,* published in the fall of 1762.

At the core of Otis's argument were the Lockean tenets that "God made all men naturally equal" and that all governments, including monarchies, "were made for the good of the people, and not the people for them." The powers of the executive are not unlimited; the legislature represents the natural rights of citizens (and colonists). Governor Bernard's invasion of the treasury was unconstitutional, Otis contended, because it amounted to taxation without the consent of popularly elected representatives. "It is in effect taking from the House their most darling privilege, the right of originating all taxes," he admonished. "And when once the representatives of a people give up this privilege, the government will very soon become arbitrary."[17]

Even some members of his own faction thought Otis was overreacting. Not all of them saw the usurpation of authority or the constitutional conflict he did. Was a seventy-two-pound outlay worth getting exercised about? But Otis was keenly sensitive to the principles of personal liberty and any threat, however remote, to provincial autonomy. In fact, he was prescient. *A Vindication* became one of the first and most widely read warnings of imperialism in British North America. It helped make the printed pamphlet a primary vehicle for disseminating and debating political thought in the late colonial era.[18] (John Dickinson's *Letters from a Farmer* and Thomas Paine's *Common Sense* would be notable examples in the years ahead.) Above all, *A Vindication* was one of the earliest articulations of patriot ideals and modern democratic principles. James Otis Jr. was no revolutionary, but his thinking as early as 1762 was foundational. John Adams later observed,

> Look over the declaration of rights and wrongs, issued by Congress in 1774. Look into the Declaration of Independence in 1776. . . . Look into the French constitutions of government, and to cap the climax, look into Mr. Thomas Paine's *Common Sense, Crisis,* and *Rights of Man.* What can you find that is not to be found in solid substance in this "Vindication of the House of Representatives"?[19]

Otis's sensitivity was, we know, as personal as it was ideological. He had been barraging the newspapers with snide, derogatory letters about Hutchinson since the Tall Man was named to the Superior Court. On that and other issues throughout 1762 and into 1763, he turned his sarcasm on Bernard as well. The governor and lieutenant governor, in turn, were incensed at the ad hominem nature of Otis's onslaught; in their minds, it was nothing more than the public airing of a family vendetta. Fanned by the two administrators, the whispers and innuendos about James's out-of-control temper took on a life of their own. Hutchinson's brother-in-law and political confederate Peter Oliver, who sat with him on the superior court bench, referred to Otis in the press as "Bluster."[20] And the label stuck. James's own brother Samuel Allyne called him "Esq. Bluster" in a letter to Barnstable.[21]

The vehemence of Otis's denunciations, veering into character assassination in the case of Hutchinson, touched on issues deeper and more complicated than the slight to his father and the family name—but not unrelated. The origins of James Jr.'s instability, it has been suggested, lay squarely in his relationship with the Colonel.[22] Brothers Joseph and Samuel Allyne, even as family business partners, steered clear of their controlling, high-handed father as best they could.[23] Jemmy, being the eldest, had faced more than his share of expectations and pressures. Now, having succeeded in scholarship, law, and politics where the Colonel had not, he felt the brunt of his father's resentment. The elder Otis, moreover, was hardly less ambitious or calculating in public life than Hutchinson himself, but without the polish, intellect, or social grace that James Jr.—also a Harvard graduate and esteemed member of the bar—recognized in the lieutenant governor. Thus, the fear, shame, and latent animosity that the younger Otis harbored toward his father, despite a deeply ingrained allegiance to family, were conflicting forces that left him ambivalent toward authority and unpredictable in responding to it. Hutchinson became a natural object of displacement, a convenient father figure on whom to heap his anger. In even bigger ways, as one historian put it, James's "nagging ambivalence" toward his real father "provoked rebellion in his heart."[24]

The insults and recriminations between Otis and Hutchinson escalated in tandem with the strain in colonial-British relations, and that was just beginning. With the end of the French and Indian War and the signing of the Treaty of Paris on February 23, 1763, came rumors of tighter trade restrictions from London. Otis suffered a bout of depression in the months that followed, beset by anxiety over political prospects—to which he was more sensitive than ever—and pilloried in the conservative *Boston Evening-Post.* Articles and open letters mocked his tendency to stutter when agitated; one editorial suggested he was "raving mad."[25]

The Sugar Act, passed by Parliament on April 5, 1764, came as a shock to many colonists. With the exception of the molasses duty, which American merchants had largely succeeded in evading, the Sugar Act imposed the first British tax on the colonies in their century and a half of existence. The royal treasury needed an infusion. After seven years of war, Britain had secured most North American territory east of the Mississippi River, but at a steep cost: the national debt had more than doubled, reaching £147 million. Parliament and the new prime minister, George Grenville, resolved that the colonies should help cover the shortfall and support a ten-thousand-man British security force. Some colonists wondered whether Parliament had the right to tax them at all. Didn't tax-levying power belong to the provincial legislature? Colonial assemblies in North America had always set their own taxes.

With callous disregard for American sentiment, the terms of the Sugar Act obfuscated British intentions and misled some colonists. The measure actually reduced the duty on imported molasses from six pence to three pence per gallon, while implementing measures to combat smuggling and ensure revenue collection. With the colonial economy already suffering, merchants and maritime operators in port cities like Boston would feel the sting most. The prospect of a standing redcoat army unsettled them and others.

Otis Jr. was not among those surprised by the Sugar Act, but news of the measure jolted him into action. With Samuel Adams, a brewer's son and second cousin to John Adams, Otis took the lead in alerting colonists to the infringement of their rights. He and Samuel Adams had much in common: a Harvard pedigree but populist values, initiation into public life through the Boston Town Meeting, and injured family pride. Samuel Adams Sr. had nearly lost his brewery and the entire family fortune when Parliament dissolved the Land Bank in 1741, triggering even greater hostility toward the British in his son. The passion of firebrands and a shared recognition of the threat to colonial autonomy now cast the younger Adams and the younger Otis in common cause. Adams had a way with people; he excelled at drawing them in and inspiring their passion. Otis's youthful affability had given way to a brooding intensity; he was the colonies' first great expounder of republican ideas.

In May 1764, Otis appeared before the Boston Town Meeting to urge a united response against the Sugar Act. Later that month, Adams penned a special committee report to the Massachusetts House that condemned the measure as a dangerous precedent: "For if our trade may be taxed, why not our lands?" he argued. "Why not the produce of our lands and every thing we possess or make use of?"[26] Then in July, Otis published the second and most impactful of his four major pamphlets, *The Rights of the British Colonies Asserted and Proved,* which the House adopted as a semiofficial statement of grievance to Parliament.[27]

The treatise was at once a conciliation to the king and Parliament ("We love, esteem, and reverence the mother country") and a tenacious argument against the levying of taxes on citizens who have no voice in the decision. To do so, Otis contended, is to rob them of a natural right:

> I can see no reason to doubt but the imposition of taxes, whether on trade, or on land, or houses, or ships, on real or personal, fixed or floating property, in the colonies is absolutely irreconcilable with the rights of the colonists as British subjects and as men. . . . The very act of taxing exercised over those who are not represented appears to me to be depriving them of one of their most essential rights as freemen, and if continued seems to be in effect an entire disfranchisement of every civil right.[28]

Otis may not have been directly responsible for the slogan "no taxation without representation," but here were its conceptual underpinnings. The second British shoe had yet to drop, and already the colonials had a principle to fight for. The irony of the moment was that the intricacies of his latest treatise misled some colonists no less than the details of the Sugar Act had. For in laying out his theory of government, Otis began by asserting the sovereign power of Parliament, whose acts "it is our duty to submit and patiently bear."[29]

The apparent contradiction—Parliament could do anything it wanted, but it could not tax unrepresented citizens—captured the essential conflict in Otis's thinking. Then and thereafter, he was torn between an inbred conservative commitment to civil institutions and a zealous belief in natural rights, between loyalty to country and love of liberty.[30] Colonists in the streets heard inconstancy.

If the principles of republican government as articulated by James Otis Jr. strike modern readers as timeworn or ordinary in any sense, they were nothing less than revolutionary in his time. Just as startling were two other passages in *The Rights of the British Colonies.* One was an impassioned statement against slavery and the slave trade—among the earliest in American annals and all the more groundbreaking in its reliance on natural rights, rather than Christian ethics, as a rationale:

> Does it follow that 'tis right to enslave a man because he is black? Will short curled hair like wool instead of Christian hair, as tis called by those whose hearts are as hard as the nether millstone, help the argument? Can any logical inference in favor of slavery be drawn from a flat nose, a long or a short face? Nothing better can be said in favor of a trade that is the most shocking violation of the law of nature, has a direct tendency to diminish the idea of the inestimable value of liberty, and makes every dealer in it a tyrant.[31]

Whether Otis's views on slavery had taken shape during the Great Awakening—abolition was often part of the evangelical message—or in his readings of Enlightenment philosophy, his position set him apart from many landed citizens in Massachusetts Bay. The colony's slave population in 1764–65 stood at 5,779, or about 2.5 percent of all residents.[32] Otis's antipathy to human bondage also set him apart from his father; the ranks of slaveholders in the 1760s are known to have included James Otis Sr.

The second extraordinary passage in *The Rights of the British Colonies,* at least a century ahead of its time, was a declaration of women's rights:

> Are not women born as free as men? Would it not be infamous to assert that the ladies are all slaves by nature? . . . If upon abdication [of a king] all were reduced to a state of nature, had not apple women and orange girls as good a right to give their respectable suffrages for a new king as the philosopher, courtier . . . or politician?[33]

Here the inspiration is easier to ascertain, and much closer to home. What better exemplar of feminine potential could Otis have observed than his sister Mercy? A thirty-six-year old mother and housewife with few of his educational opportunities, she had become his intellectual equal in a way that only James fully understood. It was not in Mercy's breeding or temperament to plead the case for gender parity herself. Her acuity, breadth of learning, and talent as a writer would make her a trusted friend and adviser to the most venerated men of her generation—ones who called her "genius." In this way, on the issue of women's equality, Mercy acted as a tutor to brother Jemmy and the rest of the "founding fathers."

There was no mistaking the intent or import of the Stamp Act of 1765. Passed by Parliament without debate on March 22, 1765, the legislation would impose a direct tax on the North American colonies by requiring the purchase of an official revenue stamp on all legal documents, printed materials, and other paper goods; the measure would take effect on November 1. It was the first British tax based entirely on activities within the colonies themselves, rather than on external trade. Colonists up and down the seaboard recognized the act for what it was: the most dangerous infringement of their rights and freedom to date. The targeting of printed materials such as newspapers, handbills, and pamphlets represented an especially bald attempt to control the press and quell dissent.

Historians of the American Revolution, including Mercy Otis Warren, would view the Stamp Act as a major turning point in colonial sentiment—the spark of the uprising. It was also the starting point of her three-volume *History of the Rise, Progress, and Termination of the American Revolution* (1805): The imposition of the tax "gave a general alarm throughout the continent," she wrote. "Multitudes assembled in the principal towns and cities, and the popular torrent bore down all before it."[34]

The political divide between Tories and Whigs gave way to new polarities: loyalists versus patriots, crown versus colonies.

Massachusetts led the way in organizing resistance to the Stamp Act. Once again at the forefront were James Otis Jr. and Samuel Adams. When word of the legislation reached New England, an unusually cold winter was drawing to a close and commerce was at a standstill. Adams, finding an eager rabble of resisters among idle dockworkers, small shopkeepers, and struggling artisans, formed a secret underground called the Sons of Liberty. Chapters soon sprouted in the other colonies, establishing a loose confederation of antitax radicals.

Otis, for his part, had favored joint political opposition among the colonies since passage of the Sugar Act the year before. By May 1765, however, a succession of odd proadministration votes in the House and an apparent retrenchment in his latest pamphlet left political allies scratching their heads. Parliament, he now maintained in *A Vindication of the British Colonies,* "has a just and equitable right, power, and authority to impose taxes on the colonies, internal and external, on lands as well as on trade."[35] So Parliament *could* impose taxes unilaterally. Why the reversal? Was Otis succumbing to fear of reprisal from London? Was he seeking reconciliation as a practical political matter?[36] Or was his thinking just that erratic? Whatever the explanation, Otis's reelection prospects were suddenly in doubt.

By good fortune, a vicious piece of doggerel that appeared in the *Boston Evening-Post* on May 13 saved his political skin. The anonymous author was a customs official with a reputation for drinking named Samuel Waterhouse. His over-the-top burlesque had, in the end, precisely the opposite effect he intended. The vicious attack by an administration man told Otis's constituents that he must be on their side after all. The verse was titled "Jemmibullero: Fragment of an Ode to Orpheus," alluding to a popular British song called "Lillibullero" and the strange fiddle episode in Jemmy's college days:

I

And Jemmy is a silly dog, and Jemmy is a tool,
And Jemmy is a cur, and Jemmy is a fool,
And Jemmy is a madman, and Jemmy is an ass,
And Jemmy has a leaden head, & forehead spread with brass.

II

And Jemmy is a lying dog, and Jemmy is a thief,
And Jemmy is a jury-mouther,—Jemmy spouts his brief,
And Jemmy is a grammar-smith, and Jemmy is a grub,
And Jemmy is a Cooper's vessel—Jemmy is a tub.

III

And Jemmy's a town-meeting man, & Jemmy makes a speech,
And Jemmy swears that LIBERTY and LIBERTY he'll preach,
And Jemmy's in the CAUCUS, and Jemmy's with the REPS,
And all who'd rise as Jemmy rose must tread in Jemmy's
steps. . . .

VII

And Jemmy is an envious dog, and Jemmy is ambitious,
And rage and slander, spite and dirt to Jemmy are delicious,
So Jemmy rail'd at upper folks while Jemmy's Dad was out
But Jemmy's Dad now has a place, so Jemmy's turned about.

X

And Jemmy thinks his counter-talk will render Jemmy safe;
But Jemmy is a stupid fellow—Jemmy is a calf;
Tho' Jemmy was outrageous, Sir, yet Jemmy will get clear,
For Jemmy's most contemptible where Jemmy's most severe.[37]

Otis narrowly won reelection as Boston's fourth and final representative, joking with friends that he had been saved by a drunkard.[38] But the savagery of provincial politics and the abuses by the mother country were taking their toll. Mercy must have seen it in Jemmy's anxious, haggard expression when he and the Colonel visited Plymouth later that May.

Despite the patent contradictions in his treatises, floor votes, and comments to other politicians, James Jr. clung to the idea of an intercolonial convention to marshal forces against the Stamp Act. The visiting Otises talked late into the spring night with Mercy and James Warren, who agreed enthusiastically on the need for joint action. It was time to stand up for the ideals of John Locke. The result of their discussion, according to contemporary historian William Gordon, was the idea of the Stamp Act Congress.[39] The Warren home would be the site of many more planning meetings in the decade leading up to the Revolution, with Mercy joining the men—from Sons of Liberty to future founding fathers—in active deliberation. The initial session was especially momentous. In her chronicle of America's founding, Mercy introduced her brother to readers as he proposed the Stamp Act Congress on the floor of the General Court, just days after the conversation in Plymouth:

> In this period of suspense, apprehension and anxiety, a general congress of delegates from the several provinces was proposed by the honorable James Otis, of Barnstable, in the Massachusetts. He was a gentleman of great probity, experience, and parliamentary abilities, whose religious adherence to the rights of his country had distinguished him through the long course of years, in which he had sustained some of the first offices in government. This proposal, from a man of his acknowledged judgment, discretion, and firmness, was universally pleasing. The measure was communicated to some of the principal members of the two houses of assembly, and immediately adopted, not only by the Massachusetts, but very soon after by most of the other colonies.[40]

In the meantime, the arrival of the Stamp Act text in Virginia had provoked a bold response from a first-term member of the House of Burgesses, Patrick Henry. His series of resolutions against the measure, called the Virginia Resolves, protested the tax on the now-familiar grounds that no elected colonial representatives had cast a vote for it. Published up and down the seaboard, the Virginia Resolves rallied colonials and ignited a slow burn of indignation that built through the summer. The interests of the thirteen colonies galvanized as never before. Demanding repeal, craftsmen and unskilled workers banded together with politicians, lawyers, and merchants in special town meetings, street demonstrations, and a boycott of British goods.

Samuel Adams and the Loyal Nine, the original core of the Sons of Liberty, raised the level of tension in Massachusetts with threats and acts of intimidation aimed at customs collectors, loyalist politicians, and administration officials. Hutchinson and his faction were objects of particular resentment even though he came out publicly against the Stamp Act. As chief justice and lieutenant governor, he had aligned himself consistently with crown policies, nor did he deign to defend his views.

On August 14, the antics of protesters boiled over into violence. The first object of gang wrath was newly appointed stamp commissioner Andrew Oliver, Hutchinson's close political ally and brother-in-law (also a brother of Justice Peter Oliver, coiner of the Bluster nickname). That morning, residents near Boston Common awoke to the sight of a straw effigy, tagged with the initials A.O., hanging from an ancient elm tree in Hanover Square.* By evening, an angry mob had torn down a waterfront building designated as the Stamp Office, ransacked Oliver's home, and beheaded the effigy on his front lawn. Oliver hid in a neighbor's house as a massive bonfire, fueled by wood from the two structures, rose in the night sky. He resigned his post three days later.[41]

---

* The site became a popular gathering place of Boston-area patriots. The Sons of Liberty organized annual celebrations there to commemorate the events of 1765, hanging flags, signs, and streamers from the branches of the tree. The giant elm, dubbed "the sacred Tree of Liberty," was emulated in cities and towns throughout the colonies. Loyalists and British soldiers felled the original Liberty Tree in August 1775; a wall tablet at 630 Washington Street marks the approximate location today.

Hutchinson was next. On the evening of Monday, August 26, the lieutenant governor was sitting at the dinner table with his four children when he heard shouting outside. He looked out the window and saw a mob advancing up Garden Court Street. Soon he could make out the words: "Liberty and Property! Liberty and Property!" Hutchinson ushered his children out the back door and through the yard to safety at a relative's house. The eldest, Sarah, returned for her father and refused to leave until he came along.

Her frantic plea probably saved his life. In the course of a few hours, broad axes took down the front door, flying rocks shattered every window on three stories, and the front facade fell brick by brick. Hutchinson described the all-night pillage:

> Not contented with tearing off all the wainscot and hangings and splitting the doors to pieces, they beat down the partition walls and although that alone cost them near two hours they cut down the cupola or lantern and they began to take the slate and boards from the roof and were prevented only by the approaching daylight from a total demolition of the building. . . . Besides my plate and family pictures, household furniture of every kind, my own children's and servants' apparel, they carried off about £900 sterling in money and emptied the house of everything whatsoever except a part of the kitchen furniture, not leaving a single book or paper in it.[42]

By morning, only bare walls and floors remained; broken furniture and random household debris covered the yard. "Such ruins were never seen in America," Hutchinson hyperbolized.[43] Bostonians flocked to the site and gaped in alarm. The Town Meeting passed a unanimous resolution declaring its "utter detestation of the extraordinary and violent proceedings."[44] Yet no serious investigation was ever mounted and no one came forward to identify the perpetrators. The victims received restitution more than a year after the fact, but with that decision came a grant of amnesty to anyone involved in the riots.[45]

The attacks on Oliver and Hutchinson were the first major acts of defiance against the British authority in North America. There was no mistaking the breadth and depth of colonial anger, yet the lieutenant governor and his supporters held one man accountable above all. Appearing in superior court on the morning after the attack, a disheveled and sleepless Thomas Hutchinson blamed "some designing, wicked man" for spreading the rumors and raising the suspicions that incited the riot.[46] For anyone who didn't know who the chief justice had in mind, Peter Oliver spelled it out: "The mob of Otis and his clients plundered Mr. Hutchinson's house," he charged.[47]

Otis, like many Boston patriots, may have taken glee in Hutchinson's comeuppance yet felt genuine dismay at the out-of-control behavior of the mob. He was certainly more moderate than Samuel Adams and his bully boys, still seeking ways to quell the crisis. He implored the radicals to refrain from further violence and urged the Town Meeting to issue "dutiful and loyal addresses to his Majesty and his Parliament, who alone under God can extricate the colonies from painful scenes of tumult, confusion, and stress."[48]

As Mercy and others could see, "tumult, confusion, and stress" perfectly described Jemmy's state of mind during the summer of 1765. His competing allegiances and deepening ambivalence cast him directly in the crossfire between Hutchinson-Oliver loyalists on one side and disgruntled colonists on the other. Administration supporters called him a madman, a lying dog, an inciter of riots, the "Grand Incendiary," in Hutchinson's words.[49] A growing number of radicals, meanwhile, viewed him as equivocating and unreliable, even a traitor to the cause.

The last of Otis's major treatises, *Considerations on Behalf of the Colonists,* reinforced the doubts of many liberal Bostonians. In newspaper installments during the summer and fall of 1765, he reaffirmed the "undoubted power, authority, and jurisdiction of Parliament" and hailed the British Empire as "the wonder and envy of the world." His wish, he declared, was the "beneficial union of these colonies to the realm."[50] In that context, many readers overlooked Otis's spirited condemnation of the stamp tax and his eloquent appeal for the free conduct of the colonies—the liberty to contribute to the prosperity and well-being of empire in any ways they saw fit.

As a practical matter, James took a firm but conservative position in response to the Stamp Act, favoring peaceful political measures and diplomatic overtures by the colonial assemblies. He was one of three Massachusetts representatives selected for the Stamp Act Congress, to be convened in New York on October 7. Hutchinson and Bernard got one of their own, Timothy Ruggles, elected as head of the delegation. Ruggles had succeeded James's father as Speaker of the House.

Delegates from nine colonies attended the proceedings at New York's City Hall. It was the first intercolonial gathering in North America held in opposition to British policies. Otis stood out for his bold oratory, but his reputation preceded him. The full body of delegates, apprehensive of his inconstancy and the reaction of the British to his leadership, instead elected Ruggles as chairman of the congress. So, despite his role in conceiving the event, Otis played only a minor part in the actual deliberations. In the end, delegates passed fourteen "declarations of rights and grievances," affirming their loyalty to the crown and Parliament but protesting the Stamp Act for its economic consequences and subversion of colonial rights. Ruggles, who departed before the final session on October 25, never signed the document.

With radical sentiment on the rise in Massachusetts, Ruggles faced harsh rebuke from legislators and the press when he returned home. Otis, ironically, received a hero's welcome even though he had hesitated to sign the declarations himself; he did not think they went far enough in asserting British sovereignty.

But that did not stop Governor Bernard from blaming him for the turmoil in the colony. Otis, Bernard charged, contributed "more than any one man whatsoever to bring us into the state of outlawry and confusion we are now in."[51]

Much to James's chagrin, the disorder intensified as implementation of the Stamp Act approached in the fall. Tax officials faced daily threats, if not direct assault. Royal effigies hung in trees and burned in town squares. Street protests grew larger and more raucous. The boycott of British goods picked up steam. By November 1, every tax collector and stamp distributor in Massachusetts had resigned his commission, leaving no one to enforce the new law; not a single stamp was sold. Governor Bernard shut down the courts, but business and government carried on.

Not coincidentally, Otis's influence as a natural rights philosopher and spokesman for enlightened government had passed its peak. He would continue to advocate fiercely—perhaps even more effectively—on behalf of colonial rights and freedom, but the citizens of Massachusetts had little appetite for subtlety or equivocation. Ominous realities once again had wrenched James Jr. from the airy realm of ideas in which he was most comfortable and most himself. Declarations of principle gave way to practical politics, the ongoing war of polemics, and his struggle with personal demons.

CHAPTER 6

# Anxious Wearisome Days and Nights

James Otis Jr. wrote his family in early January 1766 to reassure them, based on good authority, that "the Stamp Act will certainly be repealed."[1] Popular resistance had rendered the measure largely ineffectual in and around Boston, as opposition coalesced and British merchants, squeezed by the colonial boycott, urged Parliament to rescind. In the colonial assembly, meanwhile, the popular party held sway. Governor Francis Bernard and Lieutenant Governor Thomas Hutchinson, stunned by the vehemence of colonial protest, prepared for more unrest and feared complete loss of control. Otis was at the center of activity on the floor of the Massachusetts House and, in collaboration with Samuel Adams, kept up the pressure in the pages of the *Boston Gazette.*

James had every reason to feel effective in his role and optimistic in his cause, but the strain was showing. Mercy, keenly in tune with his emotional state, had to have been horrified at the mere sight of his January 8 letter: it was a trembling scrawl, fragile and unsteady.[2] Then, in early February, the Colonel wrote to Joseph from Boston that James had just suffered a days-long spell of "bleeding at the nose."[3]

Mercy was pregnant with the Warrens' fifth son, George, but had lost none of her energy or intellectual appetite. Even as she raised her boys and looked after two homes, she wrote poetry, corresponded with Jemmy about politics, and joined in late-night discussions at the house in Plymouth.[4] James Warren had been pulled into the fray by the outrage of the Stamp Act, introducing a formal protest at the Plymouth Town Meeting the previous October and planning his own run for the Massachusetts Assembly in the spring.[5] The Warren home, by this time, had become a haven for colonial radicals where her husband, father, and brother would welcome Samuel Adams, the Sons of Liberty, and a coterie of other patriots in regular strategy sessions into the 1770s. Rebellion was anathema to Mercy's Puritanical upbringing and serene temperament, but her aversion to the "endless strife" of politics and "the vain pursuits of busy men" gave way in the face of British oppression.[6] She was appalled at the decisions from London and fearful of what was to come, but the times had changed since her childhood in Barnstable. No longer could she sit by and listen. She became an active and valued participant in the covert deliberations, respected by those in attendance for her commitment to principle and her political savvy. Years later she reminisced with John Adams about "the Plymouth fire side, where many political plans originated and were discussed and digested."[7]

James's life outside politics, in sad contrast to that of his sister and closest allies, was in disarray. By the spring of 1766, he had all but given up his law practice for the sake of legislative work and the defense of colonial rights. He spent little time at home. Ruth was raising their three children—James (11), Elizabeth (9), and Mary (2)—in her own way; James felt at odds with her values and powerless against her will. Both Samuel Adams and John Adams had married women who shared their opinions and supported their efforts devotedly—Elizabeth (Betsy) Wells and Abigail Smith, respectively. James enjoyed no such comfort; he and Ruth quarreled incessantly. She was embarrassed by his public outbursts and humiliated by the attacks on his name. James confided about his marital problems to John Adams, who later wrote in his diary: "He mentioned his wife—said she was a good wife, too good for him—but she was a tory, a high tory. She gave him such curtain lectures."[8] Mercy and the other Otises, put off less by Ruth's politics than by her treatment of Jemmy and her upper-crust airs, did not conceal their dislike. Mercy in one letter referred to her as "a weak infatuated woman."[9]

Otis's relationship with Samuel Adams animated the early patriot movement and seemed to radicalize James's thinking for good. In a succession of weekly letters to the *Gazette* between December 1765 and January 1766, published under the pen name "John Hampden," Otis ratcheted up his criticism of administration high-handedness; called for a "union" of self-governing colonies; and reiterated his view from *The Rights of the British Colonies* that America, an economic sleeping giant with a population nearing 20 million, might someday become "a greater empire than the world has yet seen."[10] Adams had moved him off the position that Americans should be represented in Parliament and persuaded him that the colonies should rule themselves under the British constitution.

Yet the farther Otis drifted from his dream of reconciliation with the mother country and the more he championed the cause of American nationalism, the more conflicted he became. The Hampden letters, for all their fist-shaking at imperial taxes and mercantilist regulation, reaffirmed his loyalty to the crown. James Otis Jr. was a man of disparities and contradictions: powerful intellect and volatile emotion, respect for authority and rebellious spirit, Puritanical conservatism and Enlightenment aspiration, high principle and personal vendetta, rant and retraction, radical polemic and conservative defense of the status quo. He was one of the earliest and loudest critics of British colonialism and one of the first to imagine an independent America, yet he recoiled from his own vision and favored negotiation over revolt.

Otis's prediction of Stamp Act repeal came true in mid-March. The news arrived a few weeks later and touched off wild celebrations. Happy Bostonians poured into the streets; music and cannon fire reverberated from Long Wharf to Town Hall; banners and streamers hung from the Liberty Tree. "Joy was diffused throughout America," Mercy would write in her *History of the American Revolution.* "People of every description manifested the strongest desire that harmony might be reestablished between Great Britain and the colonies. Bonfires, illuminations, and all the usual expressions of popular satisfaction were displayed on this joyful occasion."[11]

But to James Otis and others who saw through British designs, the joy was illusory. Parliament, underestimating colonial unrest and missing a prime opportunity for fence-mending, appended its repeal of the Stamp Act with a blunt statement—the Declaratory Act—that affirmed its "full power and authority to make laws and statutes of sufficient force and validity to bind the colonies and people of America . . . in all cases whatsoever."[12] So the Stamp Act was rescinded but not Parliament's power to tax the colonies.

The Declaratory Act and the suspicions it confirmed about British intentions set back colonial hopes for a more tranquil future. In James's eyes, the pronouncement was a betrayal of his faith in Parliament and a rebuke to his loyalty. Otis and Samuel Adams redoubled their campaign against the administration in the runup to the May legislative elections, while keeping the presses churning. The popular party played on public opposition to the "Black Act" and the governor's decision to close the law courts in the absence of stamps. The Bernard-Hutchinson-Oliver cohort took the brunt of the Whig onslaught, even as the governor, dismayed by Parliament's error of judgment and despairing of the situation, began petitioning London for reassignment.

Bernard and Hutchinson privately expressed relief at repeal of the Stamp Act, though both viewed Boston as a powder keg with a "madman" at the fuse.

Otis, upholding the cause of the people, kept his fire in full blaze even as some in the radical camp questioned his allegiance. The Tories, after the backfire of "Jemmibullero" the year before, sought to widen that split by recalling Otis's inconsistencies and casting him as a pretender and chameleon—a "double-faced Jacobite-Whig," according to one.[13] The Grand Incendiary, his bona fides challenged, offered to settle the entire matter of colonial rights in a one-on-one duel with Prime Minister George Grenville on the floor of Parliament. Hutchinson, missing no opportunity to amplify Otis's reputation, called him "more fit for a mad house than the House of Representatives."[14]

As the election approached, James felt tired and wrung out. "For near two years," he wrote to Mercy on April 11, "I have not had it in my power to spend any time for myself." Soon, he continued, he hoped to be relieved of "the anxious wearisome days and nights which I have seen."[15] As Mercy mourned the death of their sisters Eliza at age twenty-seven and Abigail at age twenty-two, she yearned for Jemmy to be with her and the family.[16] But his letter was one of apology: tensions in Boston were running too high; he could not leave. Amid the countervailing winds of allegiance and ideology, James was buffeted in every direction yet saw himself as a moderating force. He was hardly in a position to deter a mob's advance or the administration's harsh retaliation, but he would remain in Boston in defense of peace and liberty. He sent his love to Mercy ("no man ever loved a sister better") and promised "many more" letters to come.[17]

The election was a vindication for the popular party, the Otis faction, and resistance to the Stamp Act. James Otis Jr. and Samuel Adams were reelected to their Boston seats, along with John Hancock and fellow merchant Thomas Cushing—a clean sweep for the opposition—while Barnstable returned James Otis

Sr. and Plymouth elected James Warren. The first order of business for the popular majority was to reward Otis Jr. for his campaign against imperial interference by naming him Speaker of the House, the office to which his father had risen. But Governor Bernard, who held veto power over the selection, would not grant him the satisfaction. Citing the "notoriety of Mr. Otis's treatment of all persons acting under the King's authority both British and provincial," Bernard negatived (rejected) the appointment.[18] Irate populists elected Cushing to the speakership and exacted revenge on Bernard the same day by purging the Governor's Council of proadministration court party members, including Hutchinson and the Oliver brothers.[19]

Exceling at political organizing as much as oratory, James Otis Jr. had gone a long way in unifying the opposition and establishing a dominant anti-administration alliance in the House. While he took Bernard's denial of the speakership as another affront to the family name, he had to have been satisfied by the tenor of public opinion and the change in political climate. Bernard wanted out, and Hutchinson had become the dominant force on the Tory side. Fierce political battles certainly lay ahead, but the cause of colonial rights was clearly in ascendance. By mid-1766, Otis was dating letters with the words "Anno Libertatis Primo" ("In the First Year of Liberty").[20]

Hutchinson, who had suffered a mild stroke under stresses of his own, held that the greatest single threat to peace and stability was Otis's erratic behavior.[21] "If some way could be found to destroy the influence of one man," he wrote that December, "the people of this province would recover themselves."[22] Governor Bernard sent a similar report to the cabinet secretary at year's end: "The troubles in this country take their rise from, and owe their continuance to one man. . . . This man, James Otis, Esq . . . is by nature a passionate, violent, and desperate man; which qualities sometimes work him up to an absolute frenzy."[23]

Politics in Massachusetts Bay was one thing, the relationship with Great Britain another. The year 1767 brought little change in the attitude of Parliament or King George III toward the American colonies. The empire still sagged under the weight of massive war debt, and Chancellor of the Exchequer Charles Townshend hatched a new plan for raising revenue. The centerpiece of his program, dubbed the Townshend Acts, was based on the assumption that the colonies would accept an indirect, external tax (unlike the direct, internal tax imposed by the Stamp Act). The Revenue Act of 1767, passed in June, imposed an import duty on a variety of goods that were not produced in the colonies and had to be shipped from Britain—among them glass, lead, tea, paper, and paint.

The plan was stubbornly retrograde and a direct affront to colonists. Anger over the Stamp Act had hardly subsided, and the Sugar Act was far from forgotten. Compounding the indignation of Bostonians was the fact that the Townshend revenues would be used to support British troops in the colony and to pay the salaries of crown officials; that would make Bernard, Hutchinson, and their loyalist cohort even less accountable to the people. To collect the taxes, moreover, a separate piece of legislation established the American Board of Customs Commissioners, which would be based in Boston. Blanket writs of assistance were issued to board agents, and several new Vice-Admiralty Courts were created to prosecute offenders, inviting the very kind of abuse and corruption on the part of officials that Otis had railed against in 1761. Most odious of all to colonists was the fact that they had had no say in the decision; London had bypassed the provincial assembly in levying the new tax and in establishing the enforcement and judicial apparatus. "It was not the sum, but the principle that was contested," Mercy recounted in her *History.*[24]

For many colonists not already convinced, the Townshend Acts and ensuing events made it plain that the mother country was, indeed, a greedy master whose last concern was the well-being of its citizens. James Otis, Samuel Adams, and the growing legions of resistance mobilized once again in the provincial assembly, in the taverns of Boston, and in the parlor of the Warren home. John Adams became a frequent visitor to Plymouth; Abigail did not attend but became an intimate correspondent of Mercy, the sole female presence. Colonel James Otis, whom Bernard had vetoed from the Governor's Council, was a regular at the meetings, but his rancor was as much personal as political. Samuel Adams was most interested in plans and strategies, while James Otis Jr. sought to reconcile and pacify. He believed he could speak for every faction of the colonial opposition: radicals and moderates, the merchant class and the angry mobs, Boston elites and provincial farmers.

In the tug of competing viewpoints, James found a kindred spirit in the Philadelphia solicitor and plantation owner John Dickinson, whom he had befriended at the Stamp Act Congress in New York. In response to the Townshend Acts, which took effect on November 20, 1767, Dickinson penned a series of twelve open letters that argued respectfully but vehemently against the new taxes, and dispatched them to Otis to do with as he saw fit. "The liberties of our common country appear to me to be at this moment exposed to the most imminent danger," Dickinson wrote to James on December 5. "Whenever the cause of American freedom is to be vindicated, I look towards the Province of Massachusetts Bay."[25]

Taking the kind of nuanced position that Otis had articulated, Dickinson affirmed the right of Parliament to regulate commerce but not to impose taxes on the colonies unilaterally. With mounting fervor, he urged vigilance and perseverance in the cause of liberty lest Parliament feel emboldened to impose additional levies in the future. These were audacious words to be sure, but Dickinson was as careful and measured as Otis himself in the kind of response he advocated—peaceful, legal resistance. "We have constitutional methods of seeking redress; and they are the best methods," the Pennsylvanian wrote.[26]

Otis, hearing an echo of his own thinking, immediately submitted the letters to a startup newspaper called the *Boston Chronicle,* which carried the first of them in its inaugural issue on December 21.[27] Distributed in pamphlet form throughout the colonies, Dickinson's plainspoken *Letters from a Farmer in Pennsylvania* would play a key role in uniting opinion against the Townshend Acts and promoting colonial autonomy. Historians agree that only Thomas Paine's explosive *Common Sense* (1775–76) exceeded Dickinson's publication in circulation and influence among revolutionary-era publications.

Dickinson's plea for "the cause of American freedom," a vision shared by Otis and a growing number of colonists, was no call for independence—not yet. "There were few, if any, who indulged an idea of a final separation from Britain at so early a period, or that even wished an equal participation of the privileges of the British constitution," Mercy observed in her *History.*[28] Yet resentment toward the British was clearly escalating, and the Townshend Acts aroused even greater desire for self-rule. Beyond that, every upsurge in such sentiment, from the Stamp Act to the outbreak of revolution, brought closer cooperation among the thirteen colonies.

The Massachusetts Assembly convened in late December 1767 to consider its own response to the latest acts. Otis Jr., whose instinct for intercolonial cooperation had given rise to the Stamp Act Congress, now collaborated with Samuel Adams in drafting a document distributed to the other colonies—the Massachusetts Circular Letter—which denounced the latest taxes and called on colonial legislatures to "harmonize with each other." The Townshend duties were unconstitutional, it argued on familiar grounds, because the colonies were not represented in Parliament. But the circular letter went a step further. With North America separated from Britain "by an ocean of a thousand leagues," direct colonial representation in Parliament was impractical, and the provincial legislatures should have complete autonomy in imposing and collecting taxes, as well as appointing governors, judges, and other colonial officers.[29] This was precisely the position to which Adams had won over James Otis.

Massachusetts House members approved the circular letter on February 11, 1768. Lord Hillsborough, the British secretary for North America, responded by ordering that body to rescind the document and warning the other colonial legislatures to ignore it or face a shutdown. Meanwhile, the promulgation of Townshend duties had triggered a surge in smuggling activity, a new boycott of British goods, and the harassment of customs agents and compliant merchants. Governor Bernard, condemning the circular letter as an act of sedition, dissolved the provincial assembly on March 4. With no legal outlet for their grievances, colonists took to the streets in a new round of mob violence.

As the cycle of British repression and colonial defiance gained momentum, the cracks in James's composure continued to widen. His rhetoric and personal relationships, even with Samuel Adams, grew more strained. The circular letter itself was a source of friction between the two men, as Otis claimed authorship of its vital sections and downplayed Adams's role. "I have written them all," he claimed, "and handed them to Sam to *quieuvicue* [edit] them."[30] Although Adams did not openly contradict his friend, few fellow patriots mistook the essential content and style of the letter as anyone's but his. Otis would remain active and certainly vocal in the early resistance movement, but it was Adams—the more pragmatic but boldly confrontational of the two men—who emerged from the wings as the acknowledged leader, no matter whom Bernard and Hutchinson chose to scapegoat.

Unrest over the Townshend Acts came to a head in June 1768, when one of the new customs inspectors boarded a sloop owned by John Hancock that had arrived in Boston carrying a cargo of Madeira wine. The captain of the sloop *Liberty*, unaware or unheeding of Townshend regulations, allegedly offered the inspector a bribe. When the inspector refused, the captain had him locked in the hold. According to the inspector's account, he was held captive for three hours while the wine was unloaded and warned to keep quiet about the entire episode. When word got out the next morning, British officials had the *Liberty* seized, placed under guard, and removed from Boston Harbor.[31]

The confiscation of Hancock's ship brought an angry mob to the family dock, leading to the assault of two customs agents and attacks on the homes of several officials. Four days later, on June 14, Otis presided over a town meeting at Old South Church in which he read a petition he had prepared for the king. "I hope and believe we shall, one and all, resist unto blood," he cried with raised fist.[32] The crowd cheered, but Samuel Adams and others in attendance were disappointed; they found the petition vague and overly theoretical. Bernard, to whom Otis delivered the document that afternoon, felt let off the hook by its lack of specific demands.[33]

The Grand Incendiary took to the podium in the Massachusetts House one week later, after the governor conveyed Lord Hillsborough's demand to withdraw the circular letter. Urging defiance, Otis ranted to the assembly for two hours about the ignorance and corruption of both houses of Parliament and Hillsborough himself. "Pray what are those men?" he began about the House of Lords.

> 'Tis notoriously known there are no set of people under the canopy of heaven more venal, more corrupt and debauched in their principles. Is it then for their superior learning? No, by no means—'tis true they are sent to the universities of Oxford and Cambridge—and pray what do they learn there? Why nothing at all but whoring, smoking and drinking. . . . As a finishing stroke they are finally sent to France—what do they see there? Why—the outside of a monkey. What are they when they return home again? Complete monkeys themselves.

Barely pausing for a breath, Otis then turned his wrath on the lower chamber:

> Shall we now take a view of their House of Commons—What are those mighty men that affect to give laws to the colonies? Surprising!—a parcel of button-makers, pin-makers, horse jockeys, gamesters, pensioners, pimps and whore masters.

And finally:

> We have now before us a letter from Lord Hillsborough—from the style one would conclude it to be the performance of a school boy—they are pleased in their wonderful sagacity to find fault with our Circular Letter. I defy the whole legislature of Great Britain to write one equally correct.[34]

The Massachusetts Assembly voted ninety-two to seventeen against rescission in late June. Four other colonies (Virginia, New Jersey, Rhode Island, and Connecticut) had already endorsed the Massachusetts position, and the rest came out against the Townshend Act in short order. Yet heads shook and glances were exchanged on the floor of the General Court as Otis unleashed his tirade. He was coming unhinged. Governor Bernard called the speech "the most violent, insolent, abusive, treasonable declamation that perhaps was ever delivered."[35] Otis's fellow legislators could hardly have disagreed. It was juvenile name-calling and out of control.

Lord Hillsborough, in any event, took the colonial response as an act of rebellion. Alarmed by the apparent breakdown in law and order, he had two regiments of British troops dispatched from Halifax to assist in "preservation of the public peace."[36] Bernard learned of the order when it was made in June. Colonists did not find out until the ships were at sea and 3,500 British regulars began disembarking at Long Wharf on October 1, 1768.

Stunned Bostonians watched in silence as the first redcoat battalions marched, bayonets fixed and colors flying, up King Street and past the Town House to the Common, where they mustered and drilled to the crash of musket fire. Thus began the military occupation of British North America and a whole new level of tension in crown-colony relations. In retrospect, the spiral of violence that precipitated the Boston Massacre and culminated in armed revolt appears all but inevitable from that moment on. As Mercy wrote in her *History*, "The American war may be dated from the hostile parade of this day."[37]

---

James Otis Jr. was hardly the only colonist to suffer psychologically in the years leading up to the Revolution; the heightening conflict took its toll on protagonists from both sides. Otis's close friend Reverend Jonathan Mayhew was a Boston Congregational minister who exhorted radicals in sermons against the Stamp Act and died in July 1766 of "an obstinate nervous disorder in his head."[38] John Hancock, of flamboyant signature and genteel manner, was, according to Dr. Benjamin Rush, "much influenced by frequent attacks of the gout, which gave a hypochondriacal peevishness to his temper."[39] The imperious Thomas Hutchinson suffered his mini-stroke during the same month, May 1766, as the rout of his Tory faction in legislative elections; as governor in 1770, in the aftermath of the Boston Massacre, he came close to a breakdown. John Adams, for his part, retired to his Braintree home in 1771 due to chest pains and general exhaustion after a single year in the Massachusetts Assembly.[40] Even the calm, self-possessed Samuel Adams showed the effects of adult palsy—trembling lips and quavering voice—when he was cold or tired.

Otis's disturbance was still intermittent. He continued to function, but the flameouts became more frequent and more acute as pressures on him mounted. He avoided home and the haranguing of his wife. He was known to drink, and that would set him off. While it was his nature to remain loyal and to serve—"among all my conflicts I never forget that I am endeavoring to serve you and yours," he had written Mercy—the objects of his commitment grew more and more at odds.[41] He was instinctively faithful to the English crown, shrinking repeatedly from direct confrontation at the same time that he crusaded for colonial rights and Enlightenment principles of government. He spoke out vehemently for the cause of liberty and its various factions while vowing allegiance to the British constitution and facing hostility from his own side. "The crisis of loyalty was too much for [his] disposition," wrote family historian John J. Waters in a discerning assessment. "James Otis, Jr., could not serve equally George III, Massachusetts liberty, and his own family."[42]

In moments of personal crisis, Jemmy's thoughts may well have turned to the root and fiber of his boyhood on Cape Cod—the cold splash of the Atlantic Ocean, the creek tide, the salt marsh at haying time. A Barnstable historian once observed, "In much that is formative in human character, the Cape landscape has lent itself to make the Cape man free, self-reliant, frugal, and indomitable."[43] As the showdown with Britain loomed steadily closer, it was not Otis's politics or philosophy that left him compromised. It was certainly not his hunger for freedom, his native self-reliance, or his Yankee frugality. It was his nerves.

# CHAPTER 7

# A Comet Passes

The taverns and coffeehouses of colonial Massachusetts were popular gathering places that, by the mid-eighteenth century, had largely replaced churches and meetinghouses as the focal points of social and leisure activity. Modeled after old English inns and public houses, they attracted a regular (predominantly male) clientele with hearty food and drink, boisterous conversation, and a range of activities benign and illicit.[1] Early American coffeehouses specialized in coffee, tea, and chocolate, all introduced to the colonies in the late seventeenth century. Taverns were notorious for heavy drinking, gambling, fighting, and other less than pious behavior. John Adams bemoaned "the number of idlers, thieves, sots, and consumptive patients" in the watering holes of Boston.[2] Among more well-to-do patrons, slaves were bought and sold over pints of malt ale.

Over time, a number of Boston coffeehouses appealed to a broader clientele by serving cider, ale, wine, rum, and brandy, and by lifting the ban on gambling.* Tavern licenses proliferated.

* The Massachusetts Assembly in 1712 passed a ban on the sale of distilled liquors, but most proprietors ignored the law and enforcement was lax.

In more provincial settings, the local drinking establishment—referred to as the "ordinary"—was and remained a staple of everyday social interaction and entertainment. It was a place to eat and drink, meet friends, play cards, exchange gossip, read the newspaper, post bulletins, trade livestock, take music lessons, or just get warm by the fire. The Crocker Tavern in Barnstable, as in other outlying towns, also operated as an inn for visitors, a mail depot, and eventually a stagecoach station.[3]

Like other aspects of daily life in the late 1760s, the taverns and coffeehouses of Boston became hotbeds of political partisanship. Nowhere were the lines of division between Whigs and Tories, patriots and loyalists more acute, or more closely drawn, than the busy pubs in the waterfront and Town Cove areas of the city. Notable among them were the British Coffee-House, located where Long Wharf met King Street (now 66 State Street); the Bunch-of-Grapes Tavern, steps away at the corner of King and Kilby Streets; and the Green Dragon, later dubbed "headquarters of the Revolution," a few blocks north on Union Street.

James Otis Jr. had been a regular at the Bunch-of-Grapes since his days as a young attorney, having stopped in for a quaff after court appearances or for meetings of the St. John's Masonic Lodge.[4] Otis's mercurial wit and ready laugh were equally familiar to frequenters of the British Coffee-House, where he had consulted with clients at gatherings of the elite Merchants' Club. The group had met regularly in a front room of the coffeehouse for nearly twenty years.[5]

By 1769, however, patrons of the two establishments were as polarized as Otis's own loyalties. Those who passed under the iconic tavern sign of the Bunch-of-Grapes, its ripe purple clusters hanging over the door, were Whigs and patriots, the unemployed and politically disaffected, the rowdy ranks of anti-British radicals. They were devoted readers of the *Boston Gazette,* Otis's pamphlets, and John Dickinson's *Letters from a Farmer.* The British Coffee-House, in stark contrast, was the all-but-exclusive enclave of administration officials, Tory politicians, military officers, and loyalist citizens. They got their news from the *Boston Evening-Post, Boston News-Letter,* or *Boston Chronicle,* if not from the Town House or London directly.

That winter the local press reported a nonimportation agreement among Boston merchants that resisted the Townshend Acts with a boycott of British goods beginning on January 1, 1769. Otis and Samuel Adams championed the cause in Massachusetts; importers in New York, Philadelphia, Charleston, and other major ports followed suit in the succeeding months. After the *Gazette* identified John Mein, the *Chronicle's* publisher, as one of several traders who had violated the agreement, branding him as an enemy of the people, he retaliated with a lengthy front-page list of men who had signed the document but breached its terms.[6] That, coupled with lost profits, took the wind out of the boycott's sails.

Governor Francis Bernard and Lieutenant Governor Thomas Hutchinson, in the meantime, were roundly denounced in the pages of the *Gazette* over the arrival and quartering of British militia in the heart of Boston. Bernard took the brunt of criticism for a series of letters to ministers in London, obtained by the Sons of Liberty and excerpted in the *Gazette,* in which he exaggerated colonial opposition and requested expanded power over the Governor's Council.[7] The assembly immediately demanded his removal.

That May, Bernard received word from London that he would, at long last, be returning home. Before departing he tendered a request to the General Court for the balance of his salary and expenses incurred in housing crown troops. With the Town House surrounded by British cannon and militia, the legislators convened their June session at Harvard, where Otis delivered an impassioned and prophetic speech to a joint gathering of students and legislators in the great hall:

> The times are dark and trying. We may soon be called on in turn to act or to suffer. You should study and emulate the models of patriotism. To you your country may one day look for support, and you should recollect that the

> noblest of all duties is to serve that country, and if necessary to devote your lives in her cause.[8]

Otis's speech drew cheers from the Harvard student body; the assembly declined Bernard's pay request.[9]

The summer of 1769 brought ample cause for celebration among liberty-minded colonists, if tempered in each instance by the bigger picture. Church bells pealed, cannon thundered, and tankards at the Bunch-of-Grapes met in toast as Bernard made his exit on August 1. With his departure, however, came a sobering recognition that their insufferable countryman Thomas Hutchinson would be taking the reins of power as acting governor. The ambitious plural office-seeker and enemy of the Massachusetts everyman would be rising to the highest position in the province.

The fourth anniversary of the Stamp Act riots, observed on August 14, brought even more revelry—and defiance—to the streets of Boston. The destruction of Hutchinson's mansion was fresh in the minds of disaffected colonists who crowded around the Liberty Tree at 11 o'clock that Monday morning. The elm on Hanover Square had been the site of increasingly festive observances on each anniversary since 1765, but this time the Sons of Liberty planned a special series of events to express their "opposition to illegal, oppressive, and arbitrary measures, at home and from abroad."[10] After fourteen toasts in the shade of the elm, a throng of more than three hundred protesters ambled in parade—Samuel Adams leading the way, James Otis taking up the rear—to the Liberty-Tree Tavern in Dorchester, where they feasted and drank away the afternoon.[11]

With all the merriment, however, there was a distinctly cathartic aspect to the day's events. Over the course of an unusually hot, stormy summer, the tussle over the Townshend boycott and the menacing presence of "lobsterbacks" in Boston had created a lethal atmosphere.[12] Newspapers on both sides of the divide poisoned the air even further with a steady flow of jeers, exaggerations, and accusations. For Otis, whichever tap house he was frequenting, the political and personal pressures finally reached a bursting point.

The match to the powder keg was a series of dispatches from four British customs officials to London that fell into the hands of Adams and Otis in late August. The letters were highly defamatory and clearly part of a campaign to undermine the two colonial leaders. Adams, ever spoiling for a fight, was delighted at the provocation. Otis, claiming "abusive misrepresentations of me [and] my country," was either supremely offended or mortally terrified at the insinuations of treason.[13] He would right the wrong and defend his name, come what may.

The first thing he did was place a signed advertisement in the *Gazette* that charged the customs officials with false accusations, declared his "true and faithful allegiance" to the king, and beseeched the state secretaries in London to disregard the aspersions on his loyalty. "Satisfaction has been personally demanded, due warning given," Otis wrote in the ad, "but no sufficient answer obtained."[14]

Otis and Samuel Adams had delivered their demand on Friday evening, September 1, when they met with the four commissioners at their offices in the Concert Hall. They met again early the next morning, when Otis confronted two of them at the British Coffee-House.[15] No apology or retraction was forthcoming at either parley, which stoked James's agitation even further. At the *Gazette* pressroom on Sunday afternoon, September 3, while working with Otis and other patriots on the next day's edition, John Adams grew concerned at James's rambling. His diary entry for that day reads, "Otis talks all. He grows the most talkative man alive. No other gentleman in company can find a space to put in a word. . . . He grows narrative, like an old man. Abounds with stories."[16]

James's signed advertisement ran on page 2 of the Monday edition, along with his response to another tax collector's letter. It was in the latter piece that Otis derided the four commissioners as "superlative blockheads" and singled out one of them, John Robinson, for especially harsh reprisal. "If he officially or in any other way misrepresents me," Otis announced, "I have a natural right if I can get no other satisfaction to break his head."[17] A meeting that night of the Merchants' Club was, according to Adams's diary, a "continued scene of bullying, bantering, reproaching and ridiculing" on James's part.[18]

Swaggering around town on Tuesday, September 5, Otis heard that Robinson had purchased a heavy walking stick with which to defend himself. James rushed straight to the same shop to acquire "the fellow of it."[19] That night, as Bostonians took to the streets to view a passing comet (still a portent of change in the minds of old Calvinists),* Otis made his way back to the British Coffee-House in case Robinson or any of the other commissioners were to show up.[20] Who arrived first, and in what condition, is not known for certain. In any event, Otis encountered Robinson at a table with several fellow revenue officers and military men.

Words were exchanged. Otis suggested that he and Robinson step outside or into a back room, where they might seek a "gentleman's satisfaction." By that he meant fisticuffs, since dueling was illegal. As Otis turned to leave, however, Robinson reached toward him to deliver the supremely insulting gesture to a gentleman of the time: a tweak to the nose. Exactly how the fight played out was described differently in partisan newspapers over the weeks that followed. Did Otis raise his cane to block the tweaking hand, or did he deliver the first blow? Either way, the flurry of fists and cudgels lasted several minutes. According to

* The sighting was most likely Messier's Comet, discovered by the French astronomer Charles Messier that August; it has also been called the Great Comet of 1769. Its unusually long tail was visible over Massachusetts for five nights in early September.

James's account and the story in the *Gazette,* Robinson's friends leaped into the fray and—amid cries of "Kill him! Kill him!"—assisted in beating Otis into submission.[21]

Robinson's version and other articles omitted the involvement of friends, but a passerby on the street named John Gridley (Jeremiah's nephew) reported the lone figure of James Otis under "barbarous" assault. Gridley came to his defense and endured a savage attack in his own right, sustaining a broken wrist and other injuries. Otis, according to an article in the *London Chronicle,* "received many very heavy blows to the head, and one particularly on his forehead, that instantly produced a copious discharge of blood."[22]

The doctors who treated Otis's gash concluded that it had been inflicted by "an edged weapon."[23] Robinson denied the use of swords or knives, but John Adams allegedly described the scar months later as so deep "you could lay a finger in it."[24] The emotional trauma was permanent as well.

James was sturdy enough to submit a letter to the September 11 issue of the *Gazette* in which he referred to the attack as an attempted "assassination." The editors of the paper and Samuel Adams, writing under the pen name "An Impartialist," stuck to that term in using the episode for propaganda purposes. Otis had been assaulted in a "preconcerted plan," they charged, with an intent to kill.[25] His blood had barely dried and already he was being martyred to the cause.

News of the incident reached Plymouth and Barnstable within a matter of days, but the details were spotty. The Warrens and Otises agonized over the extent of his injuries, fearing the worst. When word of his survival finally arrived on September 10, Mercy wrote Jemmy a long, heartfelt letter. She had sustained every blow right along with him, and she would never forgive the government men:

*My dear Brother,*

*You know not what I have suffered for you within the last twenty four hours—I saw you fallen—slain by the hands of merciless men. I saw your wife a widow, your children orphans, your friends weeping round you, and your country in tears for the man who had sacrificed interest, health, and peace for the public weal—but my distress was this evening alleviated by hearing that your life is now not despaired of.*

*I wish to know every circumstance of the guilty affair; is it possible that we have men among us under the guise of officers of the Crown, who have become open assassins? Have they with a band of ruffians at the heels, attacked a gentleman alone and unarmed with a design to take away his life? Thus it is reported—and are these the* conservators *of peace? We knew before that the business on which this armament was sent hither was detestable—that it was abhorred by everyone who had any remains of integrity, humanity, or any ideas of freedom. Yet though we knew their errand was to uphold villainy, and protect villains, I believe few expected they would carry their audacity so far as to stand by and [??] the miscreant, to spill the blood of citizens who criminate the designs and their measures.*

*Thanks to the unerring hand which directs and overrules every event, the blow was not fatal, or to use one of their own expressions, the vilest of them* can go no further than the length of their tether. *When public affairs are in such a situation, how happy it is for the man of public avocations to have the answer of a good conscience? This I trust you have—and though your conflicts are many and severe yet, I doubt not but in your calm moments you can retire into your own breast, and there find that principle of uprightness and benevolence which ought to actuate, and which can only support you, and bear you above all opposition. You have long and painfully struggled to promote the interest of your country, thousands are thanking you therefore, and daily praying for the preservation of your life. To theirs let me add my earnest solicitations that when you recover, you will never either give or receive a challenge from any man on earth, let his rank and character be what it may. This I urge for the sake of your lovely babes, for the sake of your worthy and venerable father, for the sake of your many tender friends, and for that of this people who stand in need of your assistance. . . .*

*With a sisterly affection I must entreat that you never let either public oppression or private wrongs, the injustice of a few in power, or the folly of the many that are out, ruffle and discompose a man whose superior abilities are such that with a calm and steady mind, he is capable of promoting the greatest good to his fellow creature—and in consequence thereof to secure himself eternal felicity.*

*You will excuse the freedom of my pen, when you consider it held by one who has your welfare more at heart, after a very few exceptions, than that of any other person in the world. I hope soon to hear that you are restored to perfect health and from your usual affection and attention. I expect this intelligence from your own hand as soon as you are able to write. I now only add my fervent prayers for the most permanent happiness to you and yours. As ever I subscribe your most affectionate*

*Sister,*
*Mercy Warren*[26]

# CHAPTER 8

# Privation to a Friend

James appeared to recover in the weeks following the beating. John Adams noted in mid-October that he "bore his part very well" at a dinner with provincial officials.[1] In mid-November, Otis moderated the Boston Town Meeting.[2] By the onset of winter, however, it was clear that he was drinking heavily and losing his grip. When a doctor named Sylvanus Gardiner asked him to try a case on his behalf, Otis replied that he was a broken man who had many regrets and feared death. "I have done more mischief to my country than can be repaired," he reportedly moaned. "I meant well but am now convinced I was mistaken. Cursed be the day I was born."[3] In January 1770, Adams observed that he "rambles and wanders like a ship without a helm. . . . I fear he is not in his perfect mind."[4]

Otis had not suffered, at least as of yet, a complete breakdown or break with reality. He still had days or weeks of lucidity and competence, followed by alarming mood swings and eruptions of violence. It was a pattern that would recur for years, as old colleagues in law and politics would welcome him back into the fold only to watch him fall apart again. He still had admirers, and attitudes toward mental illness had changed. Mid-eighteenth-century New England was not long removed from the Puritan view of insanity as spiritual failure or demonic possession, but the Age of Reason had yielded fresh insights and greater sympathy for people now referred to as "distracted." The empirical philosophy of John Locke and others, which posited sense impressions as the building blocks of knowledge and ideas, suggested that mental disorder could be understood in objective, scientific terms—as an impairment of human faculties or a medical condition susceptible to cure.[5]

The enlightened view of insanity was certainly easier to accept in the case of more moderate, episodic disturbances. Informed Massachusetts residents in the mid-1700s generally were not alarmed by distracted individuals who remained active in the community. Those who posed no danger to themselves or to others were considered the responsibility of their families. Many interacted freely in society at large and were treated with kindness and tolerance. Popular attitudes were slower to change with regard to acute, chronic, or violent disorders, which were more threatening on several levels. Almshouses, workhouses, and prisons served as repositories of the insane during the first half of the eighteenth century and in many places longer. Inmates were considered cursed, fallen, or less than human, and they were treated accordingly.[6] The first institutions in North America dedicated to the care and treatment of the mentally ill, still in isolation and shackles, did not appear until the latter part of the century.

James Otis Jr., oscillating between vacant rambling and fits of self-reproach, continued his overall decline. On February 26, 1770, John Adams recounted, "He has been, this afternoon, raving mad—raving against father, wife, brother, sister, friend, etc."[7] Ruth, his children, and any colleagues who came into contact with him during those weeks could see it plainly; they were afraid for him and for themselves. And then, as they had witnessed before, James imploded dramatically just as colonial-British relations took a turn for the worse—this one sharp.

On the night of March 5, in the cobblestone square at the foot of the Town House, a lone British sentry faced taunts and verbal abuse from a small but growing band of neighborhood men and boys. As the gathering grew larger and more menacing, eight redcoats carrying loaded muskets showed up as reinforcements. With snowballs, rocks, and spit raining down on them, one of the soldiers—and then the rest—opened fire into the crowd. Flintlock fire echoed through the square; musket balls ricocheted off brick and cobble. When the 29th Regiment and Governor Thomas Hutchinson finally succeeded in dispersing the mob, three Bostonians lay dead and two others mortally wounded. The next edition of the *Boston Gazette* carried a front-page engraving by Paul Revere that depicted the shooting under a history-making headline, "The Boston Massacre."[8]

On March 16, with Samuel Adams waging a propaganda war over the incident and John Adams lying low after agreeing to defend the soldiers in court, James Otis went on a "mad freak," as one acquaintance called it, smashing windows in the Town House.[9] Just a few weeks after that, at his nearby Court Street home, neighbors watched in dismay as Otis fired a musket wildly into the night air from an upstairs window. "Brother James is much worse," Joseph wrote to their father in Barnstable. "My heart sinks at the thought of his being lost to the world and his family."[10] At Joseph's suggestion, James's guns were confiscated. For everyone's peace of mind, he went to live with brother Samuel. That spring, no longer fit to serve, Otis lost his seat in the assembly; Samuel Adams took sole leadership of the Whig caucus and its agenda.

Mercy, alone with the Warrens' five boys in Plymouth when the legislature was in session, struggled to come to terms with the coffeehouse attack on Jemmy and the condition in which it left him. "Though the wounds did not prove mortal," she recounted later in her *History,* "the consequences were tenfold worse than death. . . . Reason was shaken from its throne."[11] In the spring and summer of 1770, with his incapacitation readily apparent, Mercy felt her faith tested as never before. As would become her habit, she took up a pen to reconcile her feelings and pay homage to her brother. In a poem dedicated unmistakably to Jemmy ("a friend of very superior talents and virtues"), with an opening line that cut deeper than bone ("What is it moves within my soul"), she turns to the lodestones of her belief system—God and reason—for a higher truth and measure of peace. There is calm conviction in her voice, but her faith in providence is as shaken as Jemmy's mental state. Ultimately the poem is a dual prayer: one to spare her brother an "endless dark, void of hope," the other to invoke its polar opposite—unwavering transcendent light.

A Thought on the Inestimable Blessing of Reason,
occasioned by its privation to a friend of very
superior talents and virtues, 1770

What is it moves within my soul,
And as the needle to the pole
Directs me to the final cause
The central point of nature's laws?
'Tis reason, Lord, which thou hast given
A ray divine, let down from Heaven,
A spark struck from effulgent light,
Transcendent, clear, divinely bright,
Thou hast bestow'd lest man should grope
In endless darkness, void of hope.

Creative being!—who reason gave
And by whose aid the powers we have
To think, to judge, to will, to know,
From whom these reasoning powers flow,
Thy name be ever magnified
That thus to Angels we're allied,
Distinguish'd thus in the great chain
Nor left the least in thy domain.

Yet should'st thou but a moment frown,
Or wink this boasted reason down
'Twould level proud imperious man
With the least worm in nature's plan.
Then humbly will I thee implore,
Whom worlds of rationals adore,
That thou this taper should preserve
From reason's laws let me ne'er swerve,
But calmly, mistress of my mind
A friend to virtue and mankind.
Oh! gently lead me on to peace
May years the heavenly gleam increase,
Nor waste beneath the frown of age,
As I tread down time's narrow stage,
But brighter burn as life decays
More fit to join the heavenly lays.
And when the tenement shall fall
When broken down this feeble wall
Then may the glad, enlighten'd soul
Freed from these clogs, this dull control
Expand her wings, shake off her load,
And rise to glorify her God.[12]

No one was in a better position to observe Jemmy's distress or its effects on Mercy than James Warren. With his brother-in-law and father-in-law now out of the picture—there were no Otises in the General Court for the first time in memory—Warren felt he had a banner to carry. He had been representing Plymouth in the assembly since 1766 and, like Mercy and others, recognized that a real fight was brewing with the British. Whereas Otis Jr. shrank from open rebellion when push came to shove, James and Mercy Warren would face it head on.

Jemmy's reversal, both psychological and political, had to have saddened his old friend almost as deeply as it did Mercy. The two Jameses went back a long way, and Otis's about-face seemed complete. By the time Otis returned to Boston after a year's rest, his guilt over the "mischief to his country" had evolved into a full embrace of Tory politics and Thomas Hutchinson. Reelected to the assembly for one final term in 1771, Otis actively opposed the radicalism of Samuel Adams, even as he got his father restored to the Governor's Council and Warren named Speaker of the House.[13] Such was the transformation of Otis Jr. Such was his sway, despite everything, with both the acting governor and the patriot party. And such was the chaos in provincial politics.

Mercy was at a pivotal moment in her own life, albeit on firmer ground. She would turn forty-three that year, and her sons were growing up fast: the eldest, James, would be fourteen; the youngest, George, was going on five. As for the brother she adored, the devastating truth was that Jemmy's light had gone out. She dismissed his current politics as a symptom of his disarray, and she could never forgive John Robinson or Thomas Hutchinson for what they had done to him; the family would do well just to keep Jemmy safe from himself. In the meantime, Mercy's evolving notions of enlightened government cast individual liberties and republican government in "a ray divine." Every action by the British that infringed on those rights—from the imposition of taxes and the installation of troops to the treatment of her father and brother—reinforced her allegiance to the patriot cause. "From reason's laws let me ne'er swerve," she had written in the poem to Jemmy. The happiness and well-being of her domestic circle always would be paramount, but something in her now longed for "expanded wings." She knew her mind, she trusted her quill, and, like her husband and Samuel Adams, she felt compelled to fill James's void.

Notwithstanding patriot propaganda, the Boston Massacre divided rather than united Massachusetts colonists. Loyalists viewed the incident as a riot or act of provocation on the part of local agitators rather than a cold-blooded murder on the part of soldiers as portrayed in the *Gazette;* many on the patriot side took pause in the face of five lost lives. By the same token, the shooting had incited the radical faction to a heightened level of passion, while developments in London added even more fuel to their fire. As all the colonies learned a few weeks later, Parliament had voted on the same day as the shooting to rescind the Townshend Acts, save for the tariff on tea. That element remained in effect for the explicit purpose of reaffirming, in the words of Prime Minister Frederick, Lord North, "the right of taxing Americans"; also remaining in place was the hated American Board of Customs Commissioners. So while the partial repeal did little to mollify patriot radicals, it put a damper on the non-importation movement and resistance in general. The Adamses and the Warrens voiced their concerns at the Plymouth fireside.

James Jr. was composed enough to pull strings in the legislature and even to argue some cases at bar but grew fatigued and short-tempered by the spring of 1771. "He will certainly soon relapse into his former condition," John Adams predicted in mid-May. "He trembles. His nerves are irritable."[14] Compounding the stress was the approach of Otis's lawsuit against John Robinson, filed in the aftermath of the coffeehouse attack.

The case came before the Suffolk Inferior Court on a stifling hot day in July 1771. Representing Otis were John Adams and two other Tory attorneys, who sought three thousand pounds in damages. Otis won a two-thousand-pound award from the jury, but he scoffed at the sum and demanded a written apology instead. Months later, with the case on appeal, he finally agreed to settle when Robinson extended regrets through his father-in-law, who paid the lawyers' fees, the court expenses, and Otis's medical bills—about two hundred pounds in all. James turned down the jury award.[15]

In no surprise to family and close colleagues, Adams was right on the mark in his prognosis. By the fall, Otis had bottomed out.

He flew off the handle at strangers, wandered and raved, jumped out of windows.[16] The family, unable to manage him any longer, had no choice but to petition the probate court for a finding of insanity and the appointment of a custodian. That would be one of several private individuals, typically with a home in the countryside, to whom the severely distracted were assigned. In accordance with town procedure, the judge of probate—none other than Thomas Hutchinson—petitioned the Boston Board of Selectman to conduct an examination of the individual in question and to assess his mental condition. In late November, the panel (which included John Hancock) returned its finding: James Otis Jr. was a "Distracted or Lunatick Person" and should be remanded to custody immediately.[17]

Hutchinson was coldly vindictive in reporting the fate of his longtime nemesis to former Governor Francis Bernard back in England: "Otis was carried off today in a post-chaise, bound hand and foot. He has been as good as his word, set the province in a flame and perished in the attempt."[18] In a letter to Mercy, a friend who attended the hearing described "the afflicted countenance of his venerable father"—James Sr., now nearing seventy—who was also on hand in court.[19]

Jemmy spent the better part of the next three years under the custodianship of Captain Daniel Souther at Nantasket (now Hull), on the South Shore between Boston and Plymouth. Souther operated a home for the distracted that was privately supported by family members and other patrons.* Establishments such as these followed the English model of care, prevalent for much of the eighteenth century.[20]

Not long after his arrival at Souther's farm in late December 1771, James received a letter from his sister Mercy. At some point during the preceding months, anguished and despairing in his

* A surviving invoice from Captain Souther to James Otis Sr., covering the period from May 30, 1773, to August 4, 1774, indicates an average of 16 shillings per week, for a total bill of 49 pounds, 5 shillings, 12 pence. Invoice, November 22, 1774, OFP.

endless cycle of collapses, recoveries, and relapses, Jemmy had looked to God for help. The only god he could trust was Mercy's, however, so he asked her to pray for him. There was no pretense or false assurance in Mercy's reply, no promise of salvation or providence. What Jemmy received instead was the truest medicine she could think of—her love, devotion, and promise to visit:

> *My unabating affection for my brother and friend is such that I can no longer forbear letting him know he is the continual subject of both my sleeping and waking thoughts. I need not tell you that could my prayers or endeavours prevail, you would soon be as happy as [a] mortal could wish. I do not imagine there is any degree of vanity in thinking it will give you some pleasure to hear from a sister whose friendship you never once doubted, but whether you will think it worthwhile to answer me or not, my inclinations will ever prompt me to write you. . . .*
>
> *Your last request, my dear brother, to me was to implore the God of Heaven (on your behalf) at whose awful name I tremble but when I approach to ask his mercies, for at no other time will he indulge his feeble creatures to invoke him. Your peace and your happiness in life is my daily and my fervent wish, but above all, that unchanging felicity which I wish for my own soul, will I pray may be the portion of yours. I have many things to say to you which I cannot write, but if I live am determined to see you as soon as possible wherever you may be. Till then be assured I remain as ever*
>
> *Your affectionate sister*[21]

Jemmy found refuge along the five-mile peninsular beaches of Nantasket, where, on summer walks at twilight, he collected flat blue stones that Souther used to pave his yard. Neighbors said that Otis's behavior was eccentric but harmless, that he was especially fond of children. He taught them to dance, organized games for them, marched military-style with them around the village. On dark winter evenings he taught school in town.[22]

His favorite student was a girl named Susanna Haswell, whom he called his "little scholar."[23] She was no more than ten or eleven years old at the time he met her, about the same age as Mercy during their last lessons together with Reverend Russell. Susanna was the daughter of a British customs official who had settled his family in Nantasket in 1767, when the girl was five. James recognized immediately that she faced the same unjust plight as his sister—an aptitude and appetite for learning but no chance at a formal education. He took the girl under his wing.

Under the married name Susanna Rowson, the little scholar went on to prominence as a novelist, playwright, poet, actress, and founder of the elite Young Ladies' Academy of Boston. Her sentimental novel of 1791, *Charlotte: A Tale of Truth* (later *Charlotte Temple*), is said to have been the bestselling work in American literature before Harriet Beecher Stowe's *Uncle Tom's Cabin* (1852). Rowson's five plays produced in Philadelphia and Boston during the mid-1790s, among the first by a woman to appear on the American professional stage, aired political views that James might have recognized as his own had he lived to hear them. Mercy, whose plays never left the printed page, may have applauded her dialogue from a live audience.[24]

# CHAPTER 9
# The Scribbler

The true American Revolution, John Adams famously remarked, took place "in the minds and hearts of the people."[1] The standard-bearers of the early patriot campaign—John Adams, Samuel Adams, James Otis Jr., and company—recognized that colonial attachments to the mother country ran deep and that the propaganda war against British authorities would need to be wide-ranging and unrelenting to turn the tide of public opinion. Nowhere in the American colonies was patriot sentiment fiercer or more pervasive than in Boston, yet even there politics divided many families; the split in James's house was not out of the ordinary. In provincial towns and villages, ever suspicious of the big city and its liberal, ungodly ways, loyalists remained prevalent into the 1770s.

In the war of ideas, the tightening of economic restrictions and escalation of military activities on the part of the British slowly but surely undermined their own interests and boosted the efforts of anti-administration agitators. As royal subjects across the colony faced test after test of their allegiance to the crown, the patriot press took aim at fence-sitters and holdouts with a steady barrage of polemics—sensationalized reporting, editorial suasion, philosophical argument, open denunciation, stinging parody, and clever satire. Every great revolution is a civil war, it has been said, and every war effort needs its propagandists.[2] In the case of the American Revolution, that war was won in the years leading up to armed conflict, 1772–75.

One of the savviest political minds in the patriot camp, to the surprise only of those who were new to it, belonged to a woman. No one in 1772 recognized the tenuousness of the movement and the need to rouse citizens more than Mercy Warren. "The colonies still stood suspended in the pacific hope," she later wrote, "that a change of ministry, or a new parliament, might operate in their favor and restore tranquility. Not yet conscious of her own strength . . . America still cherished the flattering ideas of reconciliation."[3]

With the muting of her brother's voice, Mercy took on his mantle as a full-throated crusader for republican principles. She advanced James's views with equal conviction—the intellectual affinity between them was as tight as ever—but her inclination and flair were more literary than philosophical. Her first public writings, published anonymously during those three years preceding the war, took the form of satiric verse dramas that poked fun at colonial authority, cast its leaders as traitors, and trumpeted the cause of freedom for ordinary citizens. She produced three such works during this period—*The Adulateur* (1772–73), *The Defeat* (1774), and *The Group* (1775)—and at least two overtly political poems, "The Squabble of the Sea Nymphs" and "To the Hon. J. Winthrop, Esq." (both 1774).

Whereas James's philosophical tracts had laid an ideological framework for the independence movement, Mercy's writings, all of which debuted in the popular press, reached a wider audience and exerted a greater influence than his. To say that it was rare for a woman of the time to write about politics understates the matter. It was unheard of, even under the cloak of anonymity.

The dramatic form was especially unlikely for Mrs. Warren, given the hostility to theatrical performance in Puritan New England. In the early 1770s, several colonies still had blue laws on the books that banned stage acting as profane.* A distinctive American drama did not make its appearance until after the Revolution, and it took one more generation—that of Susanna Rowson—for a work by a female playwright to reach the commercial theater. So to fault Warren's propaganda pieces for their dramatic shortcomings—some modern critics point to limitations of plot and character development—is to overlook their true purpose and effect. Her objectives were not theatrical but political: to expose the corruption of Tory leaders, stir up resistance to British repression, and rally colonists in the struggle for freedom. If only on the printed page, Warren's dramatic sketches were effective in all of these ways and a hit, to boot, for their sheer entertainment value.[4]

Notwithstanding her uncommon intellect and political savvy, Warren's venture into public authorship came with misgivings and a sense of transgression. Granted, writing in secrecy spared her the ridicule her brother had endured, retribution from officials and political opponents, and dismissal of her work as the rantings of a woman. But she had been raised to believe that writing and politics—all of public life, in fact—were the natural domain of men and that domestic matters were the proper realm of women. And though she resisted the limitations on her gender and believed that women possessed equal ability if afforded equal education, she treasured her role as a mother and homemaker in its own right, on its own merits. The well-being of her family was her highest priority. That was God's will; writing took second place. "Heaven has so ordained the lot of female life," she once wrote, "that every literary attention, must give place to family vocations."[5]

Mercy's attitude was broadly consistent with an eighteenth-century gender role that some modern historians have termed

* Puritan strictures on the stage dated back to seventeenth-century England. At the start of the Civil War in 1642, Protestant parliamentarians banned dramatic performance and shut down theaters in London. Among them was Shakespeare's Globe, which Puritans proceeded to demolish.

"republican motherhood," with which she is widely associated. According to this view, American women during the revolutionary period had a role to play in politics but understood that their influence should be exercised through their responsibilities as mothers. They should be educated in the ideals of republicanism and civic virtue so that they might pass those values on to their children. Republican mothers would uphold the ideals of patriotism and sacrifice by instilling them in the next generation.[6]

There were few greater champions of democratic republicanism than Mercy Otis Warren. Her Congregationalist upbringing produced a devoted custodian of virtue and righteousness; her entire body of writing—letters, poems, plays, essays, and history—testifies to her bent for moral instruction. At this moment in her life, however, she could not confine her efforts to the domestic realm. Her political convictions, the acts of British tyranny, and the heinous attack on her brother made that no longer enough. Harm to her sons or husband continued to be her greatest fear, but the stakes were too high to hold back. With the respect and support of the two men who mattered to her most, her brother James and her husband James, she entered the public arena.

The first two installments of *The Adulateur* appeared in the *Massachusetts Spy,* a radical patriot weekly, on March 26 and April 23, 1772; the full-length version (with apparently unauthorized cast and plot extensions) was released in pamphlet form the following year.[7] Few readers failed to grasp the satire or recognize the thinly veiled setting and characters.

The play takes place in an oppressed mythical kingdom called Upper Servia, whose hard-earned freedom has fallen victim to "the sullen ghost of bondage." Now, in this once-noble land, "insulting soldiers / Tread down our choicest rights, while hoodwink'd justice / Drops her scales"—the very picture of Massachusetts under British rule.[8]

The greedy, self-serving governor of Upper Servia, an unmistakable caricature of Thomas Hutchinson, is the "shameless tyrant" Rapatio. From the outset, Rapatio swears revenge on the "ten-thousand monsters" who have assaulted his chambers and ransacked his possessions. "If there is any secret sympathy" among the patriots of Upper Servia, he warns, "I'll trample down the choicest of their rights, / And make them curse the hour that gave me birth."[9]

Foremost among Rapatio's minions are his brother-in-law, Limput, and Limput's brother, Lord Chief Justice Hazelrod, brashly lampooning Hutchinson's top allies and henchmen, Lieutenant Governor Andrew Oliver and Superior Court Justice Peter Oliver. The real-life identities of Secretary of State Dupe, Captain Gripeall, Captain Bagshot, Limput, and the rest of Rapatio's cronies may have faded over the centuries, but contemporary readers were sure to recognize them as other members of the Hutchinson-Oliver faction. So popular was Warren's play in patriot circles that some names stuck: "Rapatio is now gone to Middleboro to consult with his Brother Hazelrod," Samuel Adams wrote to a friend about a meeting of Tory leaders.[10] Names began popping up in the press as well.[11]

Opposing Rapatio in heroic defense of Upper Servia and the cause of freedom are the brave and honorable Brutus, "Chief of the Patriots," and his dedicated brothers-in-arms, Cassius, Junius, and Portius. In the starkest black-and-white terms, Brutus and his patriot faction are cast as the moral (not just political) antithesis of the unscrupulous and savage Tory surrogates. Brutus, the paragon of honesty and righteousness, "sprang from men who fought, who bled for freedom."[12]

As a fictional creation, Brutus sprang straight from the heart of Mercy Otis Warren. Here was her brother Jemmy, in all his passion and brilliance, returned to the stage of colonial affairs and the vanguard of the fight for liberty. Like Brutus in Caesar's Rome, whom Mercy remembered as Jemmy's hero, the play's protagonist inspires fellow freedom lovers to defy a ruler's intrigues and save the land from tyranny. In deference to James's sacrifices and Mercy's dramatic license, the true patriot leaders of Massachusetts conceded lieutenant status for the purpose of her sketch: Samuel Adams as Cassius, John Adams as Junius, and John Hancock as Portius.

In *The Adulateur*'s storyline, simple even in the full pamphlet version, the vengeful and bloodthirsty governor, whose ambition from birth has been "to ride triumphant o'er my native land," orders a Boston Massacre–like attack on his countrymen. Brutus, bowed by grief over his fallen compatriots, rises above the gloom and rallies his forces to "rescue freedom . . . and boldly hurl oppression from her basis." Rapatio, meanwhile, schemes against his own people and their "ardent love of liberty," vowing bloodshed, poverty, and bondage as their fate. It is a classic morality play: the highest virtue versus the purest evil. Brutus (James) laments the fate of his people:

> Oh! my poor country! when I see thee wounded,
> And bleeding to death—it pains me to the soul.

He ends the play with a prayer for justice, freedom, and the light of reason:

> And may these monsters find their glories fade,
> Crush'd in the ruins they themselves had made
> While thou my country shall again revive,
> Shake off misfortune, and thro' ages live.
> See thro' the waste a ray of virtue gleam
> Dispell the shades and brighten all the scene.[13]

The combination of biting satire and inspiring rhetoric struck a nerve among New Englanders at a critical juncture. *The Adulateur* was a dire warning and, in no uncertain terms, a call to arms. In the end, after all the name-calling and fun-poking, the author was advocating openly and fearlessly for the armed defense of freedom—the protection of popular rights at any cost.

Only a few close friends and family members knew who that author was. The ones who did know had to have seen the degree of personal satisfaction Mercy derived from publication. Politics and principles aside, it was her first chance to publicly defend the family honor—to avenge the slight against her father and the assault on her brother—by calling out Governor Hutchinson and his Tory sycophants as villains. Her glee in doing so is as evident in the play as her classical education and her enlightened republican values.

Finally, read as psychodrama, *The Adulateur* grants sublimated relief to the author's kindred spirit and her model for the play's protagonist—brother James. No one understood his emotional conflicts and inner turmoil better than Mercy; no one prayed more fervently for their resolution. In elevating Brutus to mythic stature, Mercy brought Jemmy to life as an idealized version of himself, immune to all the confusion and anxiety associated with competing loyalties to King George, his own father, and independence from both.

Mercy Warren, at age forty-four, had found her literary voice and her way into active politics. The patriots had found their secret propaganda weapon. The success of *Adulateur* instilled a new level of confidence in her writing and unleashed a torrent of words in the months and years that followed. With the same "methodological arrangement of time" she had practiced since childhood, Mercy began formulating new blank-verse satires, continued to compose religious lyric poetry, and corresponded extensively with family members, friends, and new acquaintances in the Whig/patriot world.[14] She wrote affectionately to her husband James when he was away on politics. She wrote intimately, sometimes sentimentally, to friends such as Hannah Winthrop and Abigail Adams. And she wrote tenderly, with earnest advice and moral counsel, to her eldest son James at Harvard. (Left unspoken, but most assuredly on her mind, was the object lesson of Uncle James's wayward early days there.) James Warren took to calling his wife "the scribbler"—an endearment she embraced.[15]

Jemmy, in the meantime, was a far cry from the heroic figure of Brutus in Upper Servia. He remained in a fragile state under Captain Souther's watchful eye in Nantasket, with occasional furloughs to visit family members and former colleagues. Raising old ghosts, the critical voice of his father sabotaged whatever calm and stability Jemmy could muster. A letter from the Colonel dated August 1, 1772, let loose a tirade of recrimination on his broken son for his intemperance and general lack of control. "If you continue to go on this way your family will be ruined and you will destroy yourself both soul and body," he fulminated. "You treated your family and me cruelly." Despite all he had done to educate his firstborn and help him realize his "fine prospect," the elder Otis had seen his own "hopes blasted"; he faced "sorrow to the grave." Urging resistance to the "temptations of the Evil one," the Colonel called on his eldest to set aside "unruly passion" (just get over it!) and finally, for everyone's sake, seek salvation in "the worship of God." He signed the letter "your afflicted father."[16]

By the fall of 1772, James Jr. looked as deranged and out of sorts as John Adams ever recalled seeing him. "Mr. Otis came in," Adams wrote in his diary that October, "with his eyes, fishy and fiery, looking and acting as wildly as he ever did."[17] It broke Mercy's heart to observe her brother's declining condition over time—his loss of God-given reason and his removal from the noble task at hand. As she wrote to a friend the following winter,

> It is indeed hard to submit calmly to see those abilities which once equaled and even surpassed many of the first characters, clouded, shattered, and broken: to see the mind of a man so superior, thus darkened, and that man a most affectionate brother, is grief beyond expression.[18]

The frequency and reverence with which Mercy wrote about her brother, in both published works and private correspondence, reflected not only her sadness and sense of loss over his travails but the importance she attached to individual character. Hand in glove with her Puritan morality and Whig ideals, she regarded a principled and upright character as the measure of any person or leader. She saw that quality in her husband, to be sure, but Jemmy set the standard in her mind, no matter his condition. She could not write about him without extolling—as if to safeguard—his dedication and integrity.

Among James Otis's correspondences that Mercy felt most compelled to perpetuate was the one with British Whig historian and activist Catharine Sawbridge Macaulay. Burnishing her brother's stature hardly seemed necessary in this case; Mercy had her own reasons for striking up a relationship. Macaulay's eight-volume *History of England from the Accession of James I to That of the Brunswick Line,* which began appearing in 1763, had established her reputation as England's first female historian. Like Mercy, she had been educated at home and was fascinated with Greek and Roman literature, instilling a love of liberal politics. Macaulay, too, kept close ties with a brother, John Sawbridge, with whom she had grown up on a large country estate and now shared a political ideology. As a member of Parliament and lord mayor of London, Sawbridge was known for his populist, anti-aristocratic views.

Macaulay's mutually admiring relationship with James Otis Jr. had begun with a letter to him in April 1769, as Boston radicals were resisting the Townshend Acts and the entrenchment of British troops. "Sir," she had written,

> Your patriotic conduct and great abilities in defense of the rights of your fellow citizens claim the respect and admiration of every lover of their country and mankind. The principles on which I have written the history of the Stewart monarchs are I flatter myself in some measure correspondent to those of the Guardian of American Liberty.

Including a copy of her book with the letter, Macaulay ended with a request for Otis's view of the situation in America and an expression of her "high admiration."[19]

Mercy, finding a role model in a woman three years her junior, took over James's side of the correspondence in June 1773. Writing to Macaulay from her desk in Plymouth, she invoked shared values and common acquaintances (including John Adams) while conveying regrets on behalf of her incapacitated brother:

> I thank you for the marks of esteem you have heretofore shown to a brother of mine, a Gentleman, eminent for his remarkable exertion of ability in behalf of the expiring liberties of his country. He has not lately been able to make those acknowledgments that are justly in your due; yet I hope he may one day be in a capacity to answer the highest demands that either friendship or society may claim.

Assuming James's function as a commentator on American affairs, Mercy reported that "the rapacious arm of tyranny" had taken hold of the colonies, and that "despotic measures" by the parent state were forcing the people to "vigorous union."[20]

The letter began an exchange and friendship that lasted nearly two decades, until Macaulay's death in 1791. The parallels in the two women's backgrounds, intellectual interests, and political philosophies—both came from locally prominent Whig families that instilled a love of learning and classical republican values—made them transatlantic collaborators in attacking the British government and advancing liberal politics. Macaulay's sprawling *History of England*, a definitive account of the English Civil War, would provide a template and inspiration for Warren's three-volume chronicle of the American Revolution. Not least among the influences of Macaulay's work were its insights into republican principles and the Whig view of history.[21]

Catharine Macaulay was not an outspoken champion of women's rights—none of her writings specifically advocated gender equality—but her stature as a public intellectual permanently altered Mercy's awareness of herself as a woman. It set examples of "worthy character" and independent thinking that bolstered Warren's confidence as she entered the male domain. "The celebrated Mrs. Macaulay" called on Otis and the Warrens during a tour of America in 1784–85, and Mercy was anything but disappointed. "She is a lady whose resources of knowledge seem to be almost inexhaustible," Mercy wrote to her son Winslow.[22]

At the time of her first letter to Macaulay in June 1773, the prospect of armed rebellion—the "calamity of civil war," as Mercy called it—was far from remote in the minds of Massachusetts radicals.[23] The "vigorous union" to which she alluded comprised channels of communication being set up from town to town, colony to colony. The idea of "committees of correspondence," according to Mercy and other historians of the period, originated with her husband James.[24] He "first proposed this institution to a private friend, on a visit at his own house," she later wrote. (Mercy's participation, though highly likely, went unstated.) Samuel Adams, acknowledged as the friend in question, called for the creation of a Boston committee in early November 1772, after the latest British assault on colonial autonomy: a decision to pay superior court judges out of royal customs revenues.[25]

James Otis Jr., "now but a wreck of himself," was listed first among the twenty-one founding members of the Boston committee, in tribute for prior service. Samuel Adams and Dr. Joseph Warren (no relation) were the group's recognized leaders, but Otis, as nominal chairman, managed to deliver the committee's inaugural report to house delegates later in November.[26] While he fell quickly out of the picture yet again, committees of correspondence burgeoned in number and activity. James Warren assembled a group in Plymouth; Elbridge Gerry followed suit up in Marblehead. By January 1773, eighty towns in Massachusetts had created their own committees.[27] (It took the villages of Barnstable nearly two more years.)

"Perhaps no single step contributed so much to cement the union of the colonies and the final acquisition of independence as the establishment of committees of correspondence," Mercy would observe in retrospect.[28] For what started out as loosely connected community groups whose main purpose was to swap information now sprouted up in colony after colony as broad-based shadow governments that superseded provincial legislatures when the British silenced those bodies. At the colonial level and across the network, members rallied opposition to British policies and devised new plans of resistance, from the Boston Tea Party to the First Continental Congress. Thousands of liberty-minded colonists from Massachusetts to South Carolina, among them John Dickinson, Patrick Henry, John Jay, and Thomas Jefferson, ultimately took part in the Warrens' brainchild.

Governor Hutchinson, who at first dismissed the committees and then came to fear them, faced a new challenge to his reputation and authority in the spring of 1773. As had happened before, the scandal revolved around incriminating letters that fell into the wrong hands. In this case, the missives were from Hutchinson and Andrew Oliver to a friend and former treasury minister in England named Thomas Whately. A packet of the correspondence dating back to 1768 and 1769 now came into the possession of Benjamin Franklin, serving in London as an agent of the Massachusetts Assembly. Franklin dispatched the letters to Speaker Thomas Cushing in early 1773 on the condition that he not go public; only members of the committee of correspondence should lay eyes on them.

Cushing immediately showed the letters to Samuel Adams, John Adams, the Warrens, and a handful of other allies—the first reading is said to have taken place at the Warren house—and the contents were damning.[29] Here were the former lieutenant governor and his right-hand man, then the Stamp Act commissioner, criticizing the administration for its inability to control the legislature, urging the installation of crown troops to maintain order, and, most deviously of all, calling for the curtailment of colonial freedoms. For the patriots who read his words, Hutchinson's recommendation came down like a hammer: "There must be an abridgement of what are called English liberties," the governor advised. "A colony distant from the parent state cannot possibly enjoy all the liberty of the parent state."[30]

Samuel Adams and the others stayed quiet for several months, but the evidence of deceit and duplicity in the governor's office was too incriminating not to use. Strategic leaks became part of the ongoing press campaign against the Tall Man, who claimed to have been misrepresented. Finally, in early June, Adams released the letters to the full assembly, which quickly passed two resolutions: one charged subversion of the provincial charter and the rights of colonists; the other called on King George to remove Hutchinson and Oliver from office.[31]

In another propaganda coup for patriot forces, the *Boston Gazette* reported excerpts of the Whately letters, along with editorial and write-in commentary, in mid-June. For subscribers to that publication, the jaw-dropping material came out squarely between two installments of Mercy Warren's latest anti-British satire, *The Defeat,* which appeared in the May 24 and July 19 issues.

The new sketch returned readers to Upper Servia and the hateful rule of Rapatio, hell-bent on enslaving his own people. Brutus, though mentioned twice, is absent from the current scene. Characters from *The Adulateur* who reappear in the sequel include the toady minister Limpet (Andrew Oliver) and the virtuous senator Cassius (Samuel Adams). Among the new characters introduced in *The Defeat* is the "sincere and patriotic" Senator Rusticus, readily identified with James Warren.[32]

Mercy, privy to the Whately letters before they were published, pulls no punches against Governor Hutchinson, already reeling from the scandal. Highlighting the schemes of a shamelessly calculating overlord, act 2 reveals "the covered sting, the half disguised plan" that Rapatio has hatched against Upper Servia. If there was doubt in anyone's mind, Limpet spells out the nature of the plot:

FIGURE 8. A 1773 political cartoon by Paul Revere, titled *The Wicked Statesman; or, The Traitor to His Country at the Hour of Death,* depicts Governor Thomas Hutchinson in the year of the Whately letters affair. The woodcut appeared on the cover of a 1774 almanac called *The Massachusetts Calendar.*
—Courtesy of American Antiquarian Society, Worcester, Massachusetts

> 'Twas deemed impossible [that] Rapatio
> Should plead necessity for an abridgement
> Of native freedom to a British race;
> And urge . . . an armed force to plunder and destroy.[33]

In a triumph of virtue, reason, and the will of the people—not to mention a moment of vicarious revenge for the playwright—Rapatio and his accessories suffer humiliating defeat in a battle reported after act 2. Rapatio dies offstage, but the victory of the people is not final; Warren has one more warning. The tyrant's spirit returns in act 3, introduced by Limpet as the "dangerous foe / of liberty, of truth, and of mankind." The battle between despotism and liberty is eternal, Mercy is saying; the agents of freedom and conscience must be vigilant. In the end, echoing the years of recrimination by her brother and father, she holds an amoral governor and his leading confederate directly responsible for the unhappiness in the land. Limpet concludes with a prophecy to the tyrant's ghost and an implicit challenge to Massachusetts citizens:

> A lifeless effigy won't long suffice,
> But you and I as forfeiture must pay,
> Our hoary heads to this much injured state.[34]

Mercy's political instincts were right on the mark. As the first installment of *The Defeat* riled up readers on both sides of the political divide, news was crossing the Atlantic that would trigger a series of events leading to Hutchinson's downfall and a tipping point in colonial-British relations. On May 10 in London, Parliament passed a measure called the Tea Act, designed to bail out the economically vital but now-floundering British East India Company (EIC). Among other provisions, the law granted the EIC exclusive access to the North American tea market and the right to unload surplus supplies at a steep discount.

Again the British had misread the situation and either misunderstood or ignored colonial sentiment. The decline in price would actually hurt everyday consumers, who had been buying smuggled fare in large quantities since tea was exempt from the repeal of Townshend duties. Now, by allowing the EIC to designate a select group of consignees (receiver-sellers), the Tea Act all at once threatened the colonial market for cheaper contraband, pressured boycotters to end their ban on British supply, and cut out merchants not among the designated few. On the limited list of consignees, moreover, were two sons and a nephew of Thomas Hutchinson himself.

Colonial opposition was slow to build but became widespread and vocal. At best the Tea Act was a reaffirmation of the Townshend tax; at worst it marked the imposition of a new one with tighter restrictions. Handbills screamed that the EIC must not be saved on the backs of colonists. The old precept of James Otis Jr.—no taxation without representation—still applied. While passage of the Tea Act did not ignite the powder keg of colonial anger described in some accounts, it lit a fuse that kept on burning. Colonial dissent grew more heated during the fall of 1773 than at any time since the Stamp Act protests in 1765. Dockworkers in Charleston, Philadelphia, and New York turned away shipments of British tea or unloaded the crates and left the leaves to rot.

In Boston, Governor Hutchinson had his pride to defend and axes to grind. The Whately papers had inflicted new damage on his already battered prestige and London's confidence in him. In response, he hardened his line in support of the crown: its ships would dock and EIC tea would find its way to market, no matter what. In late November and early December, three British cargo vessels—the *Dartmouth, Eleanor,* and *Beaver*—sailed into Boston Harbor, setting up a standoff. Determined patriots stood guard to keep the shipments from reaching the wharf and ordered the captains to return home. Resolute, Hutchinson held the ships at anchor, knowing he could seize the merchandise if it were not unloaded and the duties paid within twenty days of arrival.

But Samuel Adams and the Sons of Liberty had a plan. On the night of December 16, with the deadline for the *Dartmouth* set to expire the next day, a throng of radicals in face-paint and Native costumes gathered at the Old South Meeting House a few blocks from the Town House, then set out for the waterfront. Mercy Warren describes the ensuing events in her history of the Revolution:

> There appeared a great number of persons, clad like the aborigines of the wilderness, with tomahawks in their hands, and clubs on their shoulders, who without the least molestation marched through the streets with silent solemnity, and amidst innumerable spectators, proceeded to the wharves, boarded the ships, demanded the keys, and with much deliberation knocked open the chests, and emptied several thousand weight of the finest teas into the ocean. No opposition was made.[35]

The entire cargo of all three ships—342 opened crates of EIC tea weighing more than 45 tons—sank to the bottom of Boston Harbor.

Massachusetts patriots were jubilant. Hutchinson was stunned and humiliated; the whole incident could have been avoided if he had allowed the ships to leave the harbor. John Adams, recognizing the publicity value of the coup, knew where to turn. Within a matter of days, he addressed a letter to James Warren with a special request to Mrs. Warren, whose first two plays he had adored. "I wish to see a late glorious event celebrated by a certain poetical genius which has no equal that I know of in this country," Adams now wrote. He had a specific approach in mind: to veil the episode in classical allegory: "Tell her that I want a poetical genius to describe a late frolic among the sea nymphs and goddesses."[36]

The scribbler set straight to work and produced what would become her first published poem, "The Squabble of the Sea Nymphs." Adams, marveling at the outcome, made sure it ran on the front page of the *Gazette,* unsigned, on March 21, 1774. In mock-epic style, Warren's new piece spoofed the tea dispute and the events in Boston Harbor with her usual stinging wit. The sea god Neptune, having discovered a shortage of nectar and ambrosia in the land, calls on the goddess Amphytrite and her rival nymph, the fair Salacia, to sample substitutes. Here Warren interjects a bold aside—the closest she ever came in print to advocating a woman's role in politics:

For females have their influence o'er kings,
Nor wives, nor mistresses, were useless things,
Ev'n to the gods of ancient Homer's page;
Then lure, in this polite and polish'd age,
None will neglect the sex's sage advice.

With the two deities locked in debate over the best tea, the "champions of the Tuscararan race" (evoking patriot rowdies dressed as Indians) step in and impose their solution. Siding with the renegade Salacia, they

Pour'd a profusion of delicious teas,
Which, wafted by a soft favonian breeze,
Supply'd the wat'ry deities.

The brazen rebel nymph rejoices in triumph:

The fair Salacia, victory, victory, sings,
In spite of heroes, demi gods, or kings;
She bids defiance to the servile train,
The pimps and sycophants of George's reign.

In the end, "virtuous daughters of the neighboring mead" join in song and dance—the celebration Adams asked for—reverberating over land and sea:

The sea nymphs heard, and all the sportive train,
In shaggy tresses danc'd around the main,
From southern lakes, down to the northern rills.
And spread confusion round Neponsett hills.[37]

"Neponsett hills" alludes to Thomas Hutchinson's home in Milton, on high ground near the mouth of the Neponset River. The wat'ry deities gloat outside his door.

The fuse of independence burned faster during the crisis year of 1774. Misguided policies on the part of the British and imperious governance on the part of provincial administrators, roundly denounced and derided in the popular press, handed patriots one victory after another in the campaign for public opinion. Anti-British sentiment reached into the provinces and took hold in towns and villages. Adamant loyalists dug in harder, however, and the rift between Whigs and Tories grew deeper. Families and friendships strained. "Animosities daily increased," Warren would write, "and the spirits of the people were irritated to a degree of alienation, even from their tenderest connections."[38]

King George and the Tory government, for their part, were vexed beyond a degree. The destruction of British tea was more than an act of vandalism that would have to be repaid. It was a blatant repudiation of English law and imperial rule that could not go unpunished. Parliament responded in the spring of 1774 with a new series of measures aimed at sanctioning the colonists, stifling provincial government, and reasserting crown dominance. The British referred to these laws collectively as the Coercive Acts; Americans dubbed them the Intolerable Acts.

The Boston Port Act, effective June 1, closed the harbor to all traffic, in or out, until the lost tea was paid for. The Massachusetts Government Act revoked the provincial charter, replaced elected colonial officials with appointed ones, and severely restricted town meetings. The Administration of Justice Act stipulated that the trial of royal officials accused of crimes within the colony could be removed to Britain and heard by a British judge. Finally, the Quartering Act allowed authorities to house British soldiers in colonial buildings, including private homes if necessary, at the colonists' expense.

To the citizens of Massachusetts, the overarching purpose of these laws was as plain as the steeple on Old North Church—subjugation. To colonists elsewhere in New England and down the Atlantic seaboard, another message was equally clear: what was happening in Massachusetts could happen anywhere. Parliament had gone too far. Individual rights and colonial charters had been irredeemably violated.

Attachments to the mother country still held strong, but hatred of British rule only grew. The Intolerable Acts were a turning point for many who had wavered, the point of no return for Otises, Warrens, Adamses, and others. In their minds at least, any hope of reconciliation was gone; a sense of dread prevailed. As Mercy observed, "The people trembled for their liberties, the merchant for his interest, the tories for their places, the whigs for their country, and the virtuous for the manners of society."[39] In the other colonies, Parliament's strategy of isolating Massachusetts backfired: the harsh new laws bred solidarity rather than separation, communication rather than isolation. The lines were being drawn.

On June 1, the day the Boston Port Act took effect, a ship carrying Thomas Hutchinson passed quietly through the British blockade and sailed east into Massachusetts Bay, bound for England. Some three weeks before, merchantmen had arrived from the home country carrying a copy of the Coercive (Intolerable) Acts, orders for Hutchinson to report to London, and General Thomas Gage to manage affairs in Hutchinson's absence. Admittedly the patriots had gotten the better of him and had undermined his standing, but the governor left his personal papers and effects at the estate in Milton. He expected to be back.[40]

Thomas Hutchinson never returned to his native Massachusetts and the people he professed to serve. Reviled by his "countrymen" for thirty-five years of condescension and betrayal, old Tommy Skin and Bones stood *against* the Coercive Acts in London.[41] But the crown and Parliament had made up their minds. General Gage was named military governor of Massachusetts and promptly imposed martial law. As for Hutchinson, his fate was much as Mercy Warren had envisioned in *The Defeat*, albeit figuratively: the tyrant's head rolled. Hutchinson stayed on in England, at first to advise the ministry on North American affairs. In the end his fate was the same as that of his dissident ancestor, Anne: permanent exile. Estranged and disillusioned, he spent his final years writing a history of Massachusetts and died in London on June 3, 1780. Warren would look back coldly on his demise:

> Mr. Hutchinson . . . became the object of disgust to all parties. He did not live to see the independence of America established, but he lived long enough to repent in bitterness of soul the part he had acted against a country once disposed to respect his character.[42]

The blockade of Boston Harbor, while it deprived New Englanders of essential supplies, engendered a shared sense of crisis and a new level of cooperation both within Massachusetts and throughout the colonies. All manner of goods and support rolled in from neighboring Connecticut and Rhode Island and as far south as Georgia. Among the faithful, doing without—practicing thrift and self-sacrifice in food, clothing, household supplies, and recreational activities—became an expression of defiance and patriotism. These were precisely the republican values that Mercy Warren held dear, and she lent her voice to the antiblockade movement. In a poem that appeared in the June 1774 issue of *Royal American Magazine,* she directed her plea specifically to the colonial woman of means, urging her to "check her wanton pride / And lay her female ornaments aside."[43]

Outside Boston, meanwhile, resistance mounted. Residents in rural and small-town Massachusetts rose up in alliance with their besieged compatriots during the late spring and early summer of 1774. They took particular umbrage at the Government Act, and they were militant. Salem held a defiant town-hall meeting in late August that the governor's troops failed to disband. In early September, thousands of armed militiamen in Worcester County marched from farm and village into the county seat, where they shut down the court and banished colonial officials. Open insurgencies from Somerville and Danvers to Springfield and Great Barrington sought to throw off British rule for good. General Gage felt hamstrung without more troops.[44]

Change came to Barnstable from the outlying Sandwich area on September 27, 1774. Fed-up citizens, some of them armed, descended on the courthouse where James Otis Sr. was presiding and demanded that he suspend proceedings. Colonel Otis, turning seventy-two and ailing, remained a patriarchal figure in the town and a bigwig in county affairs. He had kept his seat on the Governor's Council, courtesy of Gage, while serving locally as judge of probate and chief justice of common pleas. Concern for his community standing and the well-being of his family made him reluctant to upset the apple cart. He acquiesced to life under the Intolerable Acts, with all their abridgements of colonial liberty—until he couldn't.

FIGURE 9. The Olde Colonial Courthouse, where James Otis Sr. presided during the lead-up to the Revolution, is located at 3046 Main Street in Barnstable. A plaque on the outside wall commemorates the events of September 1774.
—Courtesy of the author

Otis resisted the insurgents at first, arguing the independence of his court. But the patriots refused to back down. Under the new legislation, they insisted, the king's tribunal stood in violation of the provincial charter. That being the case, its judges should refuse all requirements of the Government Act and decline to collect duties. The colonel, seeing the writing on the wall, acceded to their demands and, in due course, the American cause generally.[45] At the same time, ever the shrewd politician, he managed to appease local loyalists and keep his Council seat until full-scale war broke out.

The fuse burned shorter that fall. Resentment of the Intolerable Acts across the colonies gave rise to the First Continental Congress, held in Philadelphia from September 5 to October 26 for the purpose of formulating a collective response. The gathering of fifty-six delegates, with Samuel Adams and John Adams representing Massachusetts, launched a coordinated boycott of British imports and planted the seeds of democratic federalism. James Warren, taking his brother-in-law's place in the patriot leadership at home, was active in the intercolonial correspondence network that organized the Congress. Then in the first week of October, with General Gage dissolving the Massachusetts Assembly under the Government Act, Warren joined other elected representatives as a member of the Provincial Congress, a shadowy, extralegal body that would manage affairs in the colony, except Boston, until the end of the Revolution. Adjourning to Concord, the Provincial Congress elected John Hancock as its first president.

Down in Barnstable, five local villages voted in mid-November 1774 to create a committee of correspondence.[46] Colonel Otis served as the founding moderator; Joseph Otis, who had taken over the family business and hung a large "Liberty" sign at the front of the store, was named clerk.[47] Younger brother Samuel Allyne, in Boston handling financial and trading opportunities for Otis family enterprises, was a moderating force politically and looked after Jemmy during the latter's periodic visits.

Even those grew untenable, however, as James's old patterns—ups and downs amid overall deterioration—persisted. "I know not what to do with him," an exasperated Samuel wrote to Joseph that summer.[48] James's stay at Captain Souther's came to an end in August, leading to another major relapse later that year. Family members and friends reported to the Suffolk judge of probate that his "inconsistent, extravagant and outrageous conduct" was "disturbing the peace of the neighborhood and distressing his family" and asked that he be recommitted.[49]

Once again James's disordered state of mind mirrored the disintegrating state of colonial affairs. The year 1774 was, according to one Barnstable town historian, a "time of difficulty, darkness, and distress."[50] As December drew to a close, Mercy wrote ominously to Catharine Macaulay about what she envisaged for North America and the British Empire:

> I behold the civil sword brandish'd over our heads and an innocent land drenched in blood. I see the inhabitants of our plundered cities quitting the elegancies of life, possessing nothing but their Freedom, taking refuge in the forests. I behold faction and discord tearing up an island we once held dear as our own inheritance, and a mighty empire . . . tottering to the very foundation.[51]

# CHAPTER 10

# "There Is No Receding"

Mercy's involvement in politics reversed the arc of Jemmy's decline: the deeper the crisis grew, the more engaged and emboldened she became. By 1774, she had joined with the Adamses, the Sons of Liberty, and a majority of Massachusetts residents in making the leap her brother had refused: from defiance of the provincial administration to out-and-out rebellion. Her dedication to the republican principles that she and Jemmy had lived by became one with the cause of political independence. Notwithstanding her personal fears and the occasional hesitations of "our weak and timid sex," she would hold fast in her commitment to both popular freedoms and American sovereignty.[1] In a letter that July she referred to her home in Plymouth, still a frequent gathering place and strategic center of the movement, as "Liberty Square."[2]

The admiration and respect of patriot leaders, all of them men, helped Warren to overcome her sense of personal and gender limitation. Their regard for her, she came to understand, was bona fide. They supported her for no other reason than they valued her "sage advice" and the contributions of her pen.[3] Foremost among her champions, on those very grounds, was husband James. "God has given you great abilities," he wrote to her in the spring of 1775. "They are all now to be called into action for the good of mankind, for the good of your friends, for the promotion of virtue and patriotism."[4]

James offered more than praise and encouragement; he played an active role in promoting Mercy's work. When she completed the third of her satiric verse dramas, *The Group,* he proudly sent a copy to John Adams in Philadelphia with a cover letter boasting that she had composed it at "my particular desire."[5] The two-act burlesque, which Adams called a work of genius, debuted in the *Boston Gazette* on January 23 and *Massachusetts Spy* on January 26. Adams arranged the printing of a pamphlet edition, with two additional scenes, that reached audiences in early April. All publications were anonymous.

*The Group* was Warren's most scathing and popular dramatic work to date. The veil of allegory has fallen from the setting of Upper Servia and shifted to Boston itself. Rapatio (Hutchinson) has departed for good—though "his perfidy" lingers—and has given way to a rogue's gallery of Tory councilors and officers: Chief Justice Hazlerod, Judge Meagre, Brigadier Hateall, Secretary Dupe, Simple Sapling, and Crusty Crowbar, attended by "a swarm of court sycophants, hungry harpies, and unprincipled danglers."[6]

The play is a conversation piece among corrupt and villainous leaders who face a dire threat from the people. Although the patriots do not appear and have no voice, they are much on the minds of the Tory cabal. Simple Sapling senses trouble:

> I fear the brave, the injur'd multitude,
> Repeated wrongs, arouse them to resent,
> And every patriot like old Brutus stands,
> The shining steel half drawn—its glitt'ring point

Scarce hid beneath the scabbard's friendly cell,
Resolv'd to die, or see their country free.

"Let them die," replies Brigadier Hateall. "All our hope depends on brutal force / On quick destruction, misery, and death." Hazlerod concurs: "Now let them suffer—I'll no pity feel."[7]

The dark aspect of *The Group* extends to a related theme, equally on the mind of the author: the devastating effects of war, and the debased men who wage it, on wives, mothers, and daughters. Warren's hellish vision comes to life in the words of Brigadier Hateall:

The weeping maid thrown helpless on the world. . . .
The sorrowing mother mourns her starving babes.
Her murdered lord torn guiltless from her side.[8]

The pamphlet version of the play concludes with an epilogue that takes place with the characters leaving the stage at the end of act 2. The curtain parts to reveal a solitary figure, described only as "a Lady." She evokes the specter of battle:

What painful scenes are hovering over the morn,
When spring again invigorates the lawn!
Instead of the gay landscape's beauteous dyes,
Must the stained field salute our weeping eyes.

And she unfolds a grim prophecy:

Till British troops shall to Columbia yield,
And freedom's sons are masters of the field;
Then over the purpled plain the victors tread
Among the slain to seek each patriot dead.[9]

As copies of *The Group* hit the streets, Massachusetts colonists were stockpiling munitions and preparing for war. Two weeks later, on April 19, 1775, patriot blood purpled the fields of Lexington and Concord.

James Warren, in Concord with the itinerant Provincial Congress, left on the eve of the attack and galloped home to Plymouth. From there, with Mercy at his side, he raced Revere-like toward Rhode Island to alert citizens of the British advance.[10] For her part, the reports of bloodshed at Lexington and Concord renewed fears of a life in flight. Plymouth itself was at risk of invasion, and the animosity between patriots and loyalists was as volatile there as it was anywhere. Prominent among local Tories were several of James's relatives on the Winslow side, including a cousin named Ned who rode north to join the British at Lexington.[11] Mercy, upon returning home from Rhode Island, wrote to a friend of her trepidation:

> I am still in a state of suspense—still uncertain whether I shall continue in my own pleasant habitation or whether in a few days, I shall not be obliged to seek a retreat in the wilderness.

The redcoat retreat from Lexington and Concord had confirmed the barbarity of the British as she portrayed them in her sketches. The nightmare envisioned in *The Group* was coming true, she now reported:

> Their brutal fury has . . . led them to perpetuate the most savage acts. I saw yesterday a gentleman who conversed with the brother of a woman cut in pieces in her bed with her new born infant by her side. Are these the deeds of rationals?[12]

Concerned for the Otises in Barnstable, Mercy penned a letter to her father "in this day of general alarm" to offer prayers and to ask his views "on public matters." While referring to Britain as "the Satanic Fiend" and reasserting her faith in providence, Mercy expresses particular dread of the Tory zealots still among them: "I fear more from the wickedness that prevails in this land than from the armed hosts of Britain," she warns.[13]

The Colonel's appeasement of town loyalists had ended with news of the British assault. He immediately ordered the county militia on an eighty-mile march in aid of the patriots. Joseph Otis, unofficially taking command, mustered the men and issued the order, "Forward—Lexington!"* Said to be in the company was James Otis Jr., back in Barnstable and ready to take part in a rebellion he had helped to foment but also resisted. The militia got only as far as Marshfield, a few miles beyond Plymouth, before word arrived to turn back. The skirmish up north had ended.[14]

James Otis Jr. never faced the British in battle. He sat out the early war years at the family estate, now overseen by Joseph and his wife, Maria. It fell on Joseph to restrain his brother during fits of wildness, though physical intervention proved less necessary when Mercy was on hand. With her husband away and her father weakening, she made the trip to Barnstable as often as she could, and the effect on Jemmy was always soothing. Early biographer Elizabeth Ellet reported the memories of Otis family members still living in her time: "Even in the wildest moods of that insanity, with which, late in life the great patriot was afflicted, her voice had power to calm him, when all else was without effect."[15]

Family historians and biographers prone to mythologizing have placed the "great patriot" at the Battle of Bunker Hill on June 17, 1775. He grabbed a musket and sneaked off to fight, the story goes. But the documentary evidence, a letter from James Warren to his wife on the day after the fighting, casts a cloud of doubt on this account. Writing from his rooms at the Edmund Fowle House in Watertown, about ten miles from the scene, Warren assures Mercy of his own well-being and describes the British onslaught: "With a savage barbarity never practiced among civilized nations," he relates, "they have fired and utterly destroyed the town of Charlestown." Then, after reporting the death of patriot leader Dr. Joseph Warren, James adds, "Your

* A roadside tablet in Barnstable today marks "the spot from which the soldiers marched."

brother borrowed a gun, etc., and went among the flying bullets at Charlestown [and] returned last evening at 10 o'clock." Hence the family lore about Jemmy's participation.

But a postscript to Warren's letter raises questions. "Jem," he reports there, "dined with us yesterday . . . and then in the old way got up and went off where I know not."[16] With the fighting at Bunker Hill lasting until evening, could Jemmy have arrived back in Watertown in time for dinner? And if he left the battle scene early, did he just amble off after dinner to carouse around town in his accustomed manner? A more plausible scenario is that the Otis brother who rushed off to Charlestown (and returned to the Fowle House at ten o'clock) was either Joseph or Samuel Allyne; the latter ran a store in Boston at the time.

In the aftermath of Bunker Hill, King George declared the colonies in "open and avowed rebellion."[17] No such proclamation was needed on the American side, as the Second Continental Congress had convened in Philadelphia more than two months earlier to direct the war effort. In Massachusetts, the outbreak of armed conflict brought weighty new responsibilities on James Warren. In late June, the Provincial Congress elected him president, or Speaker, in place of the martyred Dr. Warren. Then came word that the delegates in Philadelphia had appointed him paymaster of the Continental Army. Mercy, who suffered migraines in her husband's absence, was proud and horrified at the level of his involvement.[18]

General George Washington arrived in Cambridge in early July to begin organizing the colonial regiments gathered there. James Warren worked closely with the commander in chief to keep more than twenty thousand troops paid and supplied, no minor task in a time of scarcity. Mercy visited regularly during the summer and fall, usually without her sons. On at least one occasion, the Warrens had a chance to dine with George and Martha Washington, both of whom they admired. Mercy found Martha "amiable in her deportment and sweet in her manners," and the two women corresponded periodically in the ensuing years.[19] On the way to or from Watertown, Mercy would call on her friend Abigail Adams, raising four children and running the family farm in Braintree while John deliberated in Philadelphia.

Mercy's role in the patriot movement enabled her to inform and encourage other republican women from an insider's point of view. Amid full-scale war and a harrowing shortage of food, fuel, clothing, and other necessities, solid information was a treasured commodity among Massachusetts wives and mothers. As a trusted and savvy member of the inner circle, Warren became a fount of war news, political insight, and understanding not otherwise available to the excluded sex. And the benefits of those contacts were mutual. With all of her activities as a propagandist, political adviser, military wife, and mother of five, Mercy's correspondences with female friends—Adams, Hannah Winthrop, Ellen Lothrop, and others—helped on a personal level to endure the stresses of war. The flow of letters brought a reprieve from loneliness, a sisterhood of support, and a chance to vent private concerns.

It was in 1775 as well that Mrs. Warren began taking notes and gathering documents about the events unfolding before her. With British-American hostilities looking more and more like history in the making, she conceived a large-scale political narrative in the style of Catharine Macaulay's. Newspaper articles, pamphlets, handbills, and the accounts of well-placed compatriots were source materials for what she initially called her "annals" and grew into her three-volume history of the American Revolution.[20] Appeals for inside information even went to husband James. In a letter to him late that year, Mercy requested his "best intelligence from the army, from Philadelphia and from every quarter where anything of consequence can be collected."[21]

None of these activities provided a complete diversion from Mercy's anxiety. Fear itself was the response she worked hardest to keep at bay and to hide from outsiders. Only her devotion to freedom superseded it. In an August 2 letter to John Adams, with whom she now corresponded directly, Warren both admitted distress and—with a fierceness belying the "timid sex"—renewed her pledge to the cause:

> I have my fears. Yet, notwithstanding the complicated difficulties that rise before us, there is no receding; and I should blush if in any instance the weak passions of my sex should damp the fortitude, the patriotism, and the manly resolution of yours. May nothing ever check that glorious spirit of freedom which inspires the patriot in the cabinet, and the hero in the field, with courage to maintain their righteous cause.[22]

Even less ladylike was Mercy's exhortation to Adams and his fellow delegates at the Continental Congress in November. She appended her message to a communiqué from her husband during one of her stays in Watertown. American dependency on King George must end, James urged. "You should no longer piddle at the threshold," Mercy added. "It is time to leap into the theatre to unlock the bars, and open every gate that impedes the rise and growth of the American republic."[23]

Conditions in Massachusetts at the start of 1776 were a test of faith for the firmest believers in providence. Twin scourges, both entering their second year, were ravaging the colony: the siege of Boston and an eruption of smallpox. Colonial and British forces were at a standoff: American militia had blocked land access to peninsular Boston and neighboring Charlestown in order to thwart further attack; British regulars captured the high ground of Charlestown in the Battle of Bunker Hill, retaining control of Boston Harbor and creating the deadlock. A deal was worked out that allowed residents to move in and out of town, but dwindling supplies of every conceivable commodity made life difficult for citizens across the colony. The ones who held out in Boston faced the harshest conditions, which only worsened in winter as the harbor froze.

The deadly smallpox virus had visited Massachusetts on multiple occasions in the past but not on this scale since the great epidemic of 1721; few colonists were immune. An effective vaccine lay decades in the future, and inoculation—by a method called "variolation," in which live viral matter was taken from an infected individual and scratched into the skin—carried high risks of death and contagion. The squalor, hunger, and confined population of a city under siege created ideal conditions for the spread of the disease, which followed the same trajectory as revolutionary fervor. And the mortality rate was nearly three in ten.[24]

American troops were more vulnerable than the British, most of whom had been immunized by previous exposure or inoculation. General Washington ordered quarantine or mass inoculation for his regiments; dedicated smallpox hospitals treated soldiers and the public at large. John Adams had had himself variolated in the spring of 1764, during an outbreak of the disease in Boston.[25] Abigail and their four children underwent the procedure in July 1776, with the virus raging again. James and Mercy Warren took their inoculations with the Adams clan in Boston.[26] Mercy waited until November to coax her sons to a hospital in Plymouth, where they stayed several days for aftercare.[27]

Politics afforded little consolation to beleaguered colonials. Independence was a delicate issue at the Continental Congress into the spring of 1776, as Tory sentiment, hopes of reconciliation, and sheer caution all died hard. Loyalists shrank in number and public profile, most dramatically in New England, but family schisms remained common and acrimonious behind closed doors. Ruth Cunningham Otis, for one, never changed her stripes and lived out the war in Boston despite the torrent of abuse directed at Tories. Most who shared her allegiance picked up stakes and fled. The three children of Ruth and James Otis Jr. were divided in partisanship and a source of heartache to both parents.

Out on Cape Cod, James was as volatile as ever but neither rationally disconnected nor emotionally insensitive. News about his eighteen-year-old daughter Elizabeth, or Betsy, came as a devastating blow. She had taken up with a British Army lieutenant named Leonard Brown, who suffered serious injury at Bunker Hill. Brown survived his wounds, and the young couple married on February 25, 1776. James did not attend the wedding, never forgave Betsy, and never saw her again. She relocated with her husband to a small town in Lincolnshire, England—Sleaford, near the port town of Boston—and did not return to America except for a visit long after her father died. Mercy Warren and Abigail Adams found occasion to write to her over the years; James did not.[28]

Betsy's older brother, James III, defied his mother's politics and joined the patriot campaign as an ensign in the new Continental Navy. Providence dealt the family another blow in 1777 as James III fell captive to the British and died aboard the notorious prison ship HMS *Jersey;* he was twenty-two. The youngest of James and Ruth's three children, Mary, was the least worrisome. A young girl at the outbreak of fighting, she later married the son of a Continental Army general and lived into her mid-forties.[29]

The strains and dislocations of the time began to show in the next generation of Warrens as well. James, the eldest of the five sons, came home from Harvard in the spring of 1776, his final year, after a mental breakdown of some sort. It may have been a case, notwithstanding his mother's warnings, of excessive college reveling. In all likelihood it was a depression or worse.[30] Abigail Adams, not one to exaggerate such matters, wrote to her husband that young James was "disordered in his mind."[31] Mercy had to have been panic-stricken at any hint of her brother's affliction, but the younger Warren found his balance several weeks later and returned to Cambridge to complete his degree. Mercy resumed her moralizing: "In greater or lesser disappointments," she wrote to her son back at school, "you must learn equanimity, nor suffer yourself ever to be greatly elated or depressed; in such a world as this, our own actions only are the result of our wills."[32]

Younger brother Winslow, meanwhile, had been old enough to enter Harvard in late 1775 but felt the pull of the military. Whether by free choice or compromise with his parents, he opted instead to stay in Plymouth and help out in his father's absence. That decision was a temporary reprieve for the Warrens' most adventuresome, free-spirited, and often intemperate son. Winslow could hardly have been less like his conscientious, high-minded mother, who fretted endlessly over his comings and goings. Yet she held a special place in her heart for him, "a son who possesses every tender avenue of my soul."[33]

Relief for the city of Boston finally came in March 1776, at the end of a grueling winter. In a stunning feat of engineering and logistics, Continental Army troops under the direction of former bookseller Henry Knox transported sixty tons of heavy artillery from upstate New York and positioned the cannons atop Dorchester Heights, overlooking Boston and the harbor from the south. The British command, caught by surprise, considered a Bunker Hill–style assault but saw the better of it and mobilized for evacuation. Her Majesty's fleet sailed on March 17. All told, twelve thousand redcoats and loyalists—a major portion of Boston's remaining population—fled by boat that day. Colonial militia reclaimed the city, and the theater of war shifted south and west to the Middle Colonies.

The reopening of Boston Harbor revived the hungry and dispirited of New England. Washington and his army dismantled their encampments and marched south. The Provincial Congress went into near-continuous session as the de facto government. Mercy Otis Warren bid good riddance to redcoats, Tory officials, and the loyalists who fled with them with a new pamphlet play, titled *The Blockheads; or, The Affrighted Officers: A Farce.*

Or did she? Glaring differences from preceding works have prompted modern scholars to question Warren's authorship. *The Blockheads* was considerably longer than her three previous plays, written in prose rather than verse, utterly lacking in political idealism or classical allusion, and baldly vernacular—often downright bawdy—in style. The anonymous pamphlet appeared shortly after the staging of an anticolonial satire by British general John Burgoyne called *The Blockade of Boston,* whose live production at Faneuil Hall that January flew in the face of colonial strictures. Warren never claimed *The Blockheads* as her own creation, supporting the case for mistaken attribution. It is entirely plausible, on the other hand, that she composed the original text but that some other writer made additions and alterations prior to publication. That had happened before.

The new work was certainly true to form in its derision of the British and their sympathizers. As the play opens, redcoats and loyalists in Boston face dire circumstances, under siege and hunkered down, "wrangling and starving" among themselves. Fearing capture and cursing their fate, they resolve to drive the rebels from their stronghold but succumb in the end to discord and cowardice. "Loyalty, damn the word," declares loyalist Simple. "I would rather shit my breeches than go without these forts to ease myself," admits an officer named Shallow. The high command sounds retreat, the town is all "uproar and confusion," and "yankee refugees" swarm the departing ships. A haggard redcoat sums up the British adventure: "An everlasting disgrace will attend the distraction in America."[34]

The play's coarse language may seem unlikely for an author of refined manner, but Mercy Otis Warren was no stranger to the talk of stable hands, infantrymen, and a certain patriot firebrand who once assailed British officials as "horse jockeys, gamesters, pimps and whore masters." Could her brother James have had a hand in the play? That is not out of the question, though no one had had to put words in Mercy's mouth when she urged John Adams not to "piddle at the threshold." Finally, the title of the new satire—aside from the pun on "blockade"—suggests a kind of personal signature for the unnamed playwright. Attentive readers recalled the epithet her brother had leveled at British taxmen in the pages of the *Boston Gazette* before his coffeehouse beating in 1769: "superlative blockheads."

The author of the new play, whoever it was, and all Boston patriots could be forgiven their glee at the expulsion of the British. But the city was a shambles. "I can't describe the alteration and the gloomy appearance of this town," James Warren reported to John Adams on July 17. "Ruins of buildings, wharves, etc., etc., wherever you go." The smallpox epidemic was in full rage, and signs of abatement would not appear for at least another month. Boston was one "great hospital for inoculation," according to James. "No business, no busy faces but those of physicians."[35]

The Warrens had come to town for their inoculations the previous weekend, joining Abigail Adams and her children at the home of a relative. James, and presumably Mercy with him, arrived in time for a more celebratory event.[36] On Thursday, July 18, a painter from the North End named Thomas Crafts, an original member of the Loyal Nine and Sons of Liberty, stood on the balcony of the Town House and read the newly minted Declaration of Independence to a jubilant crowd gathered below. To his back and behind the balcony doors lay the Council Chamber where James Otis Jr. had pleaded in the Writs of Assistance Case. The course of events from that moment to this one had been arduous, often precarious, and wholly improbable. The ideological connection—a belief in natural rights and popular sovereignty—was direct. "An act against the constitution is void; an act against natural equity is void," Otis had argued in 1761.[37] "All men . . . are endowed by their Creator with certain unalienable rights," went the Declaration. "Whenever any Form of Government becomes destructive of these ends, it is the Right of the People to alter or to abolish it."

James's contribution was never lost on his sister Mercy, likely on hand for the balcony reading and the removal of lion and unicorn from the front of the building. "Americans could now no more be considered as *rebels,*" she would write in the *History.*

"They were a distinct people, who claimed the rights, the usages, the faith, and the respect of nations, uncontrolled by any foreign power."[38]

Reaction to the Declaration was not all joyous in Barnstable, reflecting old fissures—and inertia—in the community. There was still a sizable contingent of loyalists, but an even larger number of farmers and merchants simply feared British reprisal. So while patriots and Tories argued bitterly, many others stayed quiet. A June vote on legislative instructions regarding independence was telling: thirty electors in favor, thirty-five opposed, and sixty-five abstained. Barnstable thus became the only town in Massachusetts known to vote *against* American independence, though barely a quarter of family heads actually did so.[39]

Colonel Otis summoned everything left of his political skills, commercial contacts, and personal reputation to keep the town on an even keel while marshaling support and resources for war. But his strength was waning. Joseph, who had already taken the helm in family, business, and local political matters, added the titles of brigadier general and court clerk. Primary responsibility for mobilizing men and materiel on the Cape now fell on his shoulders. At General Washington's request, Barnstable County raised a company of 260 men and a massive supply of blankets in 1776; a colony-wide draft later that year tapped another one in every twenty-five men. The Provincial Congress in 1777 lowered the ratio to one in seven and the draft age to sixteen. That yielded eighty-eight more inductees from Barnstable County in June, seventy-two again in April 1778, and seventy-eight in June 1778. Sons of the Cape joined the Continental Navy in inordinate numbers.[40]

The rapid deployment of able-bodied men heightened the strain on community and home life. Fields went unplowed. Fishing boats sat in drydock. Wives and children made do, collected shoes and clothing for the troops, tossed and turned at night.

Brigadier Otis grew concerned that the succession of call-ups had left local villages perilously exposed. "As the enemy are around and threaten danger here," he alerted the assembly in September 1778, "it is like dragging men from home when their houses are on fire."[41]

With crucial campaigns underway in New York, Pennsylvania, and New Jersey, the strategic focus for Cape regiments during the early years of the war was capturing Rhode Island and Narragansett Bay, both critical to home security and the flow of goods. After the British retreat from Boston in 1776, the assembly had appointed James Warren as a major general of the Massachusetts militia, to join two other officers and their brigades in the campaign to secure Rhode Island. With that accomplished, he would march his troops down to New York and join up with Washington's forces.

The news of James's appointment caught Mercy by surprise. For the first and only time, she wrote to her husband in a panic. Her letter of September 15 was no mere "invitation to retirement" like the poem from Clifford Farm a decade since. She would accept whatever James decided, but she pleaded with him to decline the post; surely he could serve his country more ably as a legislator. Mercy was wearing thin:

> How earnestly did I ever entreat my dear Mr. Warren not to accept of an appointment which . . . would involve me in the depths of distress? With my eyes now streaming in tears do I recollect how many honorable, how many profitable, and how many useful employments you have refused, and accepted this one which . . . was as a dagger in my bosom. . . . I feel at present as if I should sink under the weight of my fears.[42]

James accepted the commission but resigned the following August, claiming fatigue.[43] Nor was he happy serving under officers he had outranked as paymaster general.[44] In either case, the decision removed him from the battlefield for the duration of the war. He would make his mark as one of three directors of the Continental Navy Board for the Eastern District, a position he accepted—after more hesitation—in May 1777. The board oversaw shipbuilding, procurement, and general operations of the Atlantic fleet; Warren headed the Boston office. Mercy, having watched their eldest son James ship out to the navy and their middle son Charles leave home for Harvard, found Plymouth "gloomy" in her husband's absence but prayed for the success of his "earnest endeavors."[45]

The surrender of General John Burgoyne, erstwhile playwright, at the Battle of Saratoga in October 1777 marked a critical change in colonial fortunes, as it led directly to France's entry into the war. French support was primarily naval at first, including a joint action with American militia in August 1778 that targeted British garrisons at Newport, Rhode Island. A raging nor'easter wreaked havoc on the French squadron, however, and colonial land forces, numbering more than ten thousand, scrambled in retreat. The British consolidated control of Narragansett Bay, which all but halted the flow of goods to Cape Cod. Allegiance to the colonial cause wavered in some areas. A neutralist party opposed to war formed in Barnstable.

The Otis estate, like other homesteads on Cape Cod, struggled with a depleted male presence for much of the war. The Colonel, beset by infirmities, was "verging fast towards the closing scene," as Mercy put it.[46] Joseph, with his military responsibilities and a seat in the assembly, was rarely at home; his wife, Maria, managed day-to-day domestic affairs. Samuel Allyne, who had served previously on the state Board of War, plugged away in Boston as a collector of clothing for the Continental Army. Jemmy was mostly idle and disengaged, prone to wandering off.

And his mood swings continued. In what would be his last public appearance, during the spring of 1778, James Jr. spoke at the Boston Town Meeting to consider a proposed state constitution that James Warren played a key role in drafting. Calling up old oratorical skills, Otis held forth so persuasively (against the constitution) that the members chose him as moderator for the next session.[47] Soon thereafter he was wandering the streets, drunk and disheveled—"a strolling lunatic," according to one account.[48] "He now appears among the lowest ranks," wrote a Harvard tutor who encountered him on campus. "And though he discovers the ruins of a great mind, yet he is rather a nuisance than a benefit to society."[49]

Mercy despaired of her brother's condition, an ongoing source of sadness amid her worries over the immediate family, the progress of the war, and the cause for which they were fighting. While she was reconciled to Jemmy's incapacity, his suffering and loss of reason pained her no less than ever. Her empathy for his condition—a response demonstrated by Mercy, John Adams, and few others—is palpable in a letter to her husband after one of Jemmy's stopovers in 1778. Between the lines lay her longing for a more rational, tranquil world:

> To see the cold messenger [death] lay his pale hand upon those we love and cover them with the shades of darkness, bears no comparison with the anguish of beholding them deprived of the distinguishing characteristic of men, and that reason, which only sets him above the brute creation and lifts him to the rank of angels, clouded and obscured. You will readily conclude from this reflection that I have felt some pain this evening for an unhappy man—a man once endowed with superior intellect but now miserable in himself and a source of continual anxiety to his friends.[50]

The "cold messenger," meanwhile, drew closer to Barnstable. Mercy stepped up her visits as the Colonel took permanently to bed, sitting beside him and helping Maria direct the staff. Mercy was on her way from Plymouth on November 9 when the "patriarchship" of the Otis family and West Barnstable came to an end. "He breathed his last sigh . . . before I reached his now desolate mansion," she recounted to Abigail Adams.[51]

James Otis Sr. was laid to rest in the West Parish cemetery on King's Highway, a short distance from the family estate and the Great Marsh that had attracted Reverend Lothrop, his Puritan congregation, and John Otis III; the latter's grave lay a few paces away in the same graveyard.

The Colonel's will testified to his thrift as a businessman and severity as a parent, containing meticulous details on past gifts and loans to his children—several of them with interest. Foremost in his reckoning with James Jr. was the "large expense" of his Harvard education and legal training, defrayed more than thirty years earlier. Samuel Allyne incurred a similar charge for his Harvard education. Joseph, conversely, took ownership of the estate house in which he was living and the two acres of land it sat on, "to make him in some measure even with his brothers as to the expense of their education beyond his." James Jr., as the eldest son, inherited a "silver-hilted sword" handed down from his grandfather, along with the Colonel's collection of law books and, "for his comfortable subsistence," an annuity of £90 for the rest of his life.[52]

To his adored Mercy, James Sr. conferred 895 pounds, 6 shillings, 4 pence, in addition to 438 pounds, 4 pence "heretofore given her." She also received a "meadow of sedge ground" on Sandy Neck, half the household linens, and a ten-volume collection of sermons and lectures by Reverend Henry Grove, "which her mother designated for her."[53]

"The tears of affection will long flow over the tomb of an excellent father from the lids of his daughter," Mercy wrote to John Adams.[54]

James Jr., who had a more troubled relationship with the Colonel, was unmoored. It was around this time that he was seen trading law books for alcohol.[55]

## CHAPTER 11

# The Flaming Car

Mercy Warren turned fifty in 1778; James Otis Jr. turned fifty-three. Jemmy had had periods of relative quiescence up to the death of their father, finding comfort in the rhythms of Barnstable life. He walked along the marshes, through the orchards, and up Hinckley Lane to the West Parish Church. He attended town meetings and worship services conducted by Reverend Oakes Shaw, who had succeeded Jonathan Russell as pastor.[1] He sat in on sessions of the Court of Common Pleas and entertained visitors at the Otis estate. But with Jemmy's latest breakdown, the passing of James Sr., and the preoccupations of war, the rest of the family realized it could no longer provide the care or living conditions he needed to hold steady.

Mercy, in particular, was worn and frayed. The eight years since she had taken her brother's place in the patriot campaign had been a whirlwind of clandestine and public resistance for which she was little prepared: writing, advising, and corresponding from the center of a growing storm. Yet in many ways her activity had peaked in the early to mid-1770s, during the lead-up to the war and in its first heady months. Her early propaganda pieces had done their part in stoking rebellion. She had established relationships of trust with the leaders of the movement, lending counsel she knew they valued. Her husband had assumed positions of influence in a cause they shared, and now that cause was *national* in scope.

The fear, anxiety, and loneliness that Mercy experienced throughout those years diminished little after the British left Boston and the major fighting moved south, even as her role and influence began to wane. Her latest plays, if they were her own at all, were less incendiary and more camp, farces rather than satires. No longer was the elm-shaded house in Plymouth a patriot command center; political and military strategies were being hatched on an intercolonial scale in Boston, Philadelphia, and wherever General George Washington set up headquarters. And John Adams, Mercy's most direct conduit of political opinion, left America in February 1778 to serve as an envoy to France.

The political fortunes of her brother Joseph and husband James ran aground at about the same time. On the Cape, popular discontent with war, ongoing shortages, and rampant inflation spurred support for Barnstable's neutralist/opposition party, leading to Joseph's defeat in the May 1778 legislative elections. His reputation for high-handedness and his enmities with rival families, absent his father's political skills, negated any prospect for further elective office. Aside from Samuel Allyne, a delegate to the Second Continental Congress, the Otis political dynasty was in eclipse.[2]

James Warren, who had represented Plymouth in the assembly for twelve years, also lost his seat that May. Lacking the political appetite of his in-laws and frustrated in his navy job by a chronic lack of funding, he was more than ever "wearied by the perplexities and embarrassments of public life . . . and sighing for the felicity of domestic peace."[3] This was Mercy's description of her husband's frame of mind, now fully in sync with her own: ambivalence toward public service and missing a spouse after years of living apart. James would continue on the Navy Board nearly to the end of the war and serve four subsequent terms in the legislature (1779, 1780, 1781, and 1787), but he would never seek national office or accept the kind of remote assignments that Adams and others took on. He had already spurned key positions and would turn down others in the future.

Mercy, for her part, was beyond disappointed with the direction of Massachusetts politics. She was dismayed by the climate of civic life and what she perceived as a decline in public morality. Since the British evacuation, she believed, the republican virtues of thrift, frugality, and self-sacrifice had given way to personal indulgence and wanton materialism. With the harbor open and a populace fed up with deprivation, the moderate politics of John Hancock, his merchant class, and currency depreciation prevailed over the austere radicalism espoused by Samuel Adams and the Warrens. Her husband's election defeat told Mercy plainly enough that character and love of country did not carry the weight they once did. In a poem titled "The Genius of America," published in the *Boston Gazette* on October 5, 1778, she bemoaned the loss of patriotism, the new culture of greed, and the "remarkable depravity of manners" that characterized the times:

> Behold the schedule that unfolds the crimes
> And marks the manners of these modern times. . . .
> The selfish passions, and the mad'ning rage
> For pleasure's soft debilitating charms,
> Running full riot in cold avarice' arms. . . .
> Our country bleeds and bleeds at every pore,
> Yet gold's the deity whom all adore.[4]

Hancock, the first signer of the Declaration of Independence and two-time president of the Continental Congress, was the unlikely new villain in Mercy Warren's good-or-evil universe—or not unlikely at all. He was Boston's wealthiest merchant and lived as lavishly as the despised Governor Thomas Hutchinson, whose favor he curried into the 1770s. To Mercy, who preferred homespun wool over silk, the gilt carriage in which Hancock went about town symbolized the corruption of democratic ideals and Puritan simplicity by which she lived. "His obstinacy, vanity, levity, and ostentation," she once wrote of him, "have created disgust and rendered him contemptible in the eyes of the soberer part of the community."[5]

The sea-change that Hancock stood for, moreover, struck close to home for the Warrens. Typifying the new culture of material indulgence and moral compromise—or a victim of it, in Mercy's eyes—was fair-haired son Winslow. In 1778, at age nineteen, he left home for Boston to seek his fortune among the traders, brokers, and commercial investors whom his Uncle Jemmy once represented and John Hancock now championed. The fortune Winslow sought was strictly financial, but trade was slow and the terms risky in wartime. With no honest prospects, he hung around taverns, mixed with shady characters—those "whose principles (if they have any) are a burlesque on reason," his mother cautioned—and took to gambling.[6] For Mercy, the specter of Jemmy's influence on the next generation had already appeared with the breakdown of eldest son James at college. Fresh parallels in the life of her second and favorite son compounded that concern, along with her general disillusionment.

She was at a low ebb, downcast and disaffected. Her health began to suffer. She had always been wiry-strong, animated, a woman in motion. But her headaches intensified, and she wrote to her husband of "wounded optics."[7] Vision problems, which would come and go for the rest of Mercy's life, were associated with migraines, but they were also after-effects of variolation; Abigail Adams had reported eye troubles months after her inoculation.[8] In addition, Mercy confided to James of "the vapours," a catch-all term for the moodiness, depression, and related symptoms commonly ascribed to women at the time.[9] Her energy began to flag in the period after her father's death and Winslow's move to Boston. The absence of husband James and all but two sons, Henry and George, at Christmas 1778 left her further dispirited.

On the war front, the British tightened their grip on New York City, its strategic harbor, and surrounding areas. General Washington's surprising successes at Trenton and Princeton held New Jersey in early 1777 and boosted American morale, but the British took Philadelphia—the new nation's capital—late that September. France's entry into the war forced a more defensive posture on the part of the British, who withdrew from Philadelphia in the summer of 1778 to fortify their main base in New York City. That July, six thousand French troops under General Jean-Baptiste de Rochambeau occupied the undefended town of Newport, Rhode Island, and established a base of operations in support of the Americans. France's alliance with Spain in 1779 and the outbreak of hostilities between Britain and the Netherlands in 1780 made America's War of Independence just one theater in a wider conflict for King George.

As redcoats and rebels fought to a stalemate in the northern states, the British shifted their focus south to limit the scale of fighting and to enlist loyalist support, believed to be widespread. (They also hoped for armed support on the part of runaway slaves, whom they promised freedom in exchange for joining crown forces.) The capture of Savannah and Charleston, followed by a sweeping victory in the Battle of Camden in August 1780, solidified British control of Georgia and South Carolina, but the mass loyalist turnout never materialized. General Charles Cornwallis's advance north through the Carolinas and into Virginia faltered with the depletion of his troops, dwindling supplies, and a failed rearguard. Washington and Rochambeau gathered their forces and debated next steps.

As the young men of Massachusetts stood and fell in each succeeding battle—no state was more heavily represented in the Continental Army—Mercy Warren sank deeper into depression over public life in Boston and her solitude in Plymouth.[10] Hancock and everything he stood for were in ascendancy. He would soon become the first governor of the state, and, according to Warren, "the spirit of accumulation [was] rampant."[11] Down on the South Shore, meanwhile, she felt "too much secluded from society" and despondent over her wayward son, who rarely visited.[12]

Even her writing stalled. She could not "awake the sleeping muses," as she put it in a letter to Abigail Adams. "Clio is deaf . . . and Melpomene is starved," implying that both her history of the revolution and her playwriting had foundered. She felt disconnected creatively and alienated from the community at large. All nine muses, she remarked, were "sickned by the unpromising aspect of the decayed village of Plimoth."[13]

By mid-1779, Mercy hit bottom. Her emotional state expressed itself in a host of physical ailments, a tendency that her brother, in all his instability, never exhibited. She held back nothing in a June 1 letter to husband James:

> I have suffered such an uncommon faintness, languor, and some pain for three days, that I could scarcely move about. I got into the chaise on Saturday to see if the air of Eel River would not be a little more salutary. Returned exceedingly fatigued.[14]

James, recently reelected to the Massachusetts Assembly and named to the Continental Congress, declined the latter appointment over concern for Mercy's "trembling nerves and palpitating heart." His response to her on June 6, concealing his worry but announcing that decision, exudes the kind of tenderness and encouragement that always lifted his wife's spirits. "What next can I do better than write a saint," he begins. "She has good sense. She has exalted virtue and refined piety." He challenges her to buck up and resume writing: "Why . . . should I attempt to explore the reasons . . . that a mind, possessed of a masculine genius well stocked with learning, fortified by philosophy and religion, should be so easily impressed by the adverse circumstances or inconveniences of this world."[15]

Her next play, *The Motley Assembly: A Farce,* came out later in 1779, unattributed and in pamphlet form. Tradition ascribes the work to Mercy Warren, though again she took no credit and contemporary scholars dispute her authorship. The best argument on her behalf lies in the subject matter of the play and its consonance with her thinking at the time rather than the literary form or style.* The targets are no longer British oppressors and their Tory sympathizers but fickle and greedy Americans—aristocratic men (Turncoat, Esquire Runt, et al.) and high-society women (Mrs. Flourish, Mrs. Taxall, Mrs. Bubble, and their daughters)—who sip tea in parlors and surrender their patriotism, honor, and republican virtue for "taste and fashion." The final scene takes place in a Boston coffeehouse, the domain of tea boycotters and the working class, where a soothsaying sea captain named Careless decries "the conduct of some of this town who profess themselves Whigs . . . [but are] the most treacherous characters among you." The play ends with a grim evocation of lost patriotism and compromised principles, a tongue-lashing in rhymed couplets:

> Blush Boston! Blush! Thy honest sons bewail,
> That dance and song over patriot zeal prevail,
> That Whigs and Tories (joined by wayward chance)
> Should hand in hand lead on the sprightly dance. . . .
> Here lured by fashion, opposite interests join,
> And lull their cares and rage, in cards and wine.[16]

At the confluence of her politics, republican values, and Puritan sensibility lay a set of democratic principles that connected

---

* The text, however, bears some striking similarities to Warren's letters of roughly the same period: The assembly, exclaims Mrs. Flourish in the play, "is a *burlesque* upon the name." Mercy, in a letter to son Winslow in December 1779, warns of men "whose principles . . . are a *burlesque* on reason." The character of Careless in the play declares that "it is the duty of every Whig to discountenance such indecent *raillery* and abuse" toward women; likewise, Mercy admonishes Winslow in another letter against "a peculiar asperity, disgust, or *raillery* at the [female] sex in general." *The Motley Assembly,* scenes 1, 4, in *The Plays and Poems of Mercy Otis Warren,* ed. Benjamin Franklin (Delmar, NY: Scholars' Facsimiles and Reprints, 1980), emphasis added; MOW to Winslow Warren, December 4, 1779, *MOWSL,* 119, emphasis added.

Mercy's public and private lives. Her brother James had lived by the same egalitarian precepts. They were children of privilege but opposed slavery, lived modestly, and stressed character and thrift to their children. "I am no courtier," James wrote in the *Boston Gazette* during the hard-currency debate of the early 1760s. "I desire neither poverty nor riches and thank God heartily that I have neither."[17] Mercy conveyed a similar outlook, politically and personally: "I believe the grandeur, magnificence and wealth of states seldom promotes either the virtue or happiness of individuals; where there is the most simplicity of life and manners there is most felicity," she wrote to friend Hannah Winthrop.[18]

The ethic of thrift and simplicity appeared to be lost on twenty-year-old Winslow, who let it be known in March 1780 that he would be leaving shortly for the Netherlands to make his mark as a commission agent. Mercy, who had not seen him in more than three months, took the news hard. It had been another long, dark winter in gloomy Plymouth. There had been little to ease her feelings of isolation, and she felt ineffectual as a mother and wife. She poured her heart out in a letter to husband James:

> My children leave me early, and I seem to grow useless to them, and I am sometimes ready to think you could serve the public as well and perhaps better unembarrassed by anxieties for me. I am not hypocrite enough to conceal the regrets that prey upon my mind and interrupt my peace though I have a thousand times resolved it for your sake.... As no mortal voice breaks in upon the silent contemplation, I sometimes recover myself by a shower of tears.[19]

Winslow finally visited in early April, spent two or three days, then left. Prior to his departure for Europe in mid-May, his mother wrote to John Adams in France to ask his help in making introductions and pointing her acquisitive son in the right direction. "The views of this young gentleman are chiefly of a commercial nature," she admitted.[20]

It would be another a year before Winslow reached the Continent. A squadron of the Royal Navy captured his frigate a few days out of Boston Harbor and escorted it to St. John's, Newfoundland, where he and the other passengers spent the summer as prisoners. By sheer good fortune, older brother James was serving on the American warship *Alliance* as it passed through Newfoundland; he got word to the family that Winslow was safe.[21] Transported to London in October, Winslow was free to roam the city—except for a brief period while under suspicion of espionage—and granted passage to Holland the next May.

The year 1781 was decisive in the fight for independence and turbulent in the lives of the Warrens and Otises. The war staggered toward resolution, as Continental Army troops under Major General Nathanael Greene regained control of the southern interior during the first half of the year. In the late summer, Washington and Rochambeau marched a combined army of seven thousand men from New York to the Virginia peninsula, where they joined forces with the Marquis de Lafayette and the French fleet in laying siege on Cornwallis at Yorktown.

The thirteen colonies, meanwhile, came together under a loose governing document called the Articles of Confederation, which took effect on March 1. Massachusetts had ratified the agreement as early as March 1778; Barnstable voted against it on the grounds that it yielded too much power to the central government.[22] The Warrens were satisfied that the articles preserved the sovereignty of the separate states well enough, though Mercy wished for a stronger endorsement of religious freedom and Christian values.[23]

Samuel Allyne Otis had assumed legal custody of his brother James upon the death of James Sr., but his wartime duties and participation in the state constitutional convention precluded close supervision. Mercy commiserated with Jemmy over the loss of his son and abandonment by his daughter, closely followed by the death of their father, but neither she nor Joseph was in a position to look after him. And so, sometime in the late 1770s or early 1780s, the family arranged for Jemmy to board at the home of a well-to-do farmer and old friend in Andover named Jacob Osgood.[24] Otis would spend his remaining years at the Osgood home, enjoying interludes of tranquility between the kinds of overexcited or depressive episodes that had plagued him since the night at the British Coffee-House.*

Notwithstanding their republican values and the vice of easy money, the Warrens in January 1781 indulged in the purchase of a sprawling estate—elegant mansion, expansive fields, stables, and outbuildings—overlooking the Neponset River in Milton. For James, who craved a return to gentleman farming after the war, the property was instantly alluring. For Mercy, almost any change from Plymouth center—"the early asylum of our ancestors," she quipped—would have been welcome.[25] The Milton house was just ten miles from Boston, six miles from the Adams's farm in Braintree, and thirty miles (barely three hours by carriage) from Jemmy in Andover. The price was daunting, but the high ground and open spaces were irresistible to both of them. "What sort of mistress I shall make at the head of a family of husbandmen and dairymaids I know not," she teased James. "I think there cannot be a pleasanter spot."[26]

Beyond the gracious interiors and grand vistas, the Milton property came with an added attraction for the Warrens—one that made it uniquely appealing. It was the very estate that Thomas Hutchinson had made home after the ransacking of his Boston mansion in the Stamp Act riots of 1765. Mercy, James, and their youngest son, George, left Plymouth for Milton on June 1, 1781, seven years to the day after the despised governor and archenemy of the Otises had departed the colony for good. Sea nymphs danced on Milton Hill once again.

* The two-story farmhouse, featuring an asymmetrical four-bay facade, pedimented center doorway, and rear el, still stands at 116 Osgood Street in Andover. See "116 Osgood Street," Andover Historic Preservation, https://preservation.mhl.org.

After all their time apart, Mercy and James were reunited under one roof. She had been "recovering fast" at the mere prospect of change, then in her new surroundings, but the respite was short-lived.[27] On June 6, the thirty-six-gun frigate *Alliance* limped into Boston Harbor after a fierce encounter with the Royal sloops *Atalanta* and *Trespassy* off the Grand Banks of Newfoundland. The *Alliance* prevailed but at great structural and human cost. Six men died, and twenty-six were injured. Among the latter were the ship's captain, James Barry, whose wounds to the left shoulder forced him below decks at the height of battle, and Lieutenant James Warren, who took a cannon ball to the right knee.[28] Warren arrived by stretcher at his parents' doorstep a few days later, his life in the balance. He would survive the injury but lose the leg to amputation.

Here was Mercy's worst fear, or terrifyingly close to it, come true. Her "anxiety, agitation and fatigue" returned with a vengeance, triggering a recurrence of her vision problems and depression.[29] And the bad news continued. Sons Charles and Henry, both at Harvard, had developed chest congestion and nagging coughs during the winter and spring of 1781. Henry, whom she described as an "amiable, active, obliging youth" of seventeen, recuperated in due course. Charles, nineteen, "pursue[d] his studies with industry and sobriety" despite worsening symptoms of consumption, or "white plague"—tuberculosis.[30]

In the same September letter in which she told Winslow of these developments, Mercy acknowledged her own "decayed health and weakened eyes." She concluded the correspondence with a gentle plea for his return to America, "if peace should be restored to the contending nations."[31] Yorktown was just coming under siege at the time, and the fighting ended three weeks later. Winslow remained in Europe.

Generals Washington and Cornwallis negotiated the terms of surrender, but the British commander failed to appear for the official ceremony on October 19; he claimed to have taken ill. French and American troops faced each other in two lines on the battlefield; the British marched somberly between them in full dress uniform, flags furled. General Charles O'Hara, standing in for Cornwallis, extended the sword of surrender to Rochambeau, who declined in favor of Washington. The American leader in turn deferred to his second-in-command, Major General Benjamin Lincoln.

When her vision improved, Mercy Warren included the following account in her history of the revolution:

> As general Lincoln had recently felt the mortification of yielding himself and his troops into the hands of the royal army, he was selected to conduct the military parade and receive the submission of the British veterans. This might be thought by some to wear rather too much the air of triumph; but it was judged a kind of compensation for his own military misfortune, while it might call into exercise the feelings of benevolence. These ever operate more strongly on the human character from the experience of sufferings, except in such ferocious minds as are actuated only by the principles of revenge.[32]

The "mortification" Major General Lincoln had suffered was surrendering to British forces after the Battle of Charleston the previous year. Beyond the lesson in humanity, Mercy had a personal interest in this particular detail of the Yorktown proceedings. Lincoln, a native of Hingham, Massachusetts, was the brother-in-law of her friend Hannah Quincy, also a cousin of Abigail Adams. More importantly, he was the father-in-law of Mercy's niece Mary Otis Lincoln—Jemmy's younger daughter. Family, friends, and politics all were connected.

"Mr. Otis lived to see the independence of America," Warren wrote in her *History,* "though in a state of mind incapable of enjoying fully the glorious event which his own exertions had precipitated."[33] Jemmy lived simply and without turmoil at the Osgood farm, his own calm retreat. According to early biographers, he stayed close to the house and spent much of his time indoors, reading or lying in bed. He grew heavy and lackadaisical, usually in good humor, on a diet consisting mainly of bread and milk. His relationship with the Osgood family was warm and amiable. Several visitors and James himself came to believe, yet again, that he had returned to sanity. "I have this day attended divine service and heard a sensible discourse," reads a fragment of his journal, "and thanks be to God I now enjoy the greatest of all blessings, *mens sana in corpore sano.*"[34]

Samuel Allyne thought James was well enough to come to Boston and arranged in 1782 for his son, Harrison Gray Otis, to transport him by gig (a light, two-wheeled carriage) from Andover. Along the way, the two discussed Harrison's legal education and James's prospective patronage; no support was ever forthcoming. James stayed with Samuel Allyne in Boston for a few weeks, during which he argued a case in the Court of Common Pleas. He was successful in his pleadings but displayed little of his old flair—"he appeared a sun shorn of beams," Harrison reported—and left for Andover when the excitement got to be too much.[35]

James Otis Jr. made his last visit to Boston in April 1783, at the invitation of Governor Hancock. According to several accounts, the two men met alone in the Council Chamber and chatted privately.[36] According to other accounts, Otis was a special guest at Hancock's formal dinner to celebrate Congress's ratification of a preliminary peace agreement with Britain.[37] In either case, the heady atmosphere and flood of memories—the chaos and ordeal of trying times, the enemies and allies come and gone, the successes and recriminations of a fragile soul in the eye of a storm—all washed down in toasts of wine, were James's undoing.

Samuel Allyne, on hand in case of distress, recognized the signs and hurried his brother home.

According to James himself, who remained agitated for weeks thereafter, the evening culminated somewhat differently. In his version, two sheriff's deputies arrived at his room after dinner to take him back to Andover. "Those villains seized me in my [nightshirt]," he scrawled in a note to Hancock. "They were for dragging me through the streets and mob which had assembled. . . . Hurried me through the town in a damned savage, barbarous manner—over the ferry and to Andover (though very lame and unwell)."[38]

It was shortly after his return to the Osgood house that Otis is said to have gathered his books, correspondence, legal documents, and other papers in a giant pile and burned them over a period of two days. Yet a letter many years later from John Adams to William Tudor, Otis's biographer, suggests a slightly different timeframe. Adams told of an inquiry he had made to James's expatriate daughter Elizabeth as to whether she had a copy of Otis's book on Greek prosody, which Adams had read as a young man. Elizabeth wrote back from England that she "had not had a line from her father's pen in some time"; she knew, however, that "he had spent much time, and taken great pains, to collect together all his letters and other papers, and, in one of his unhappy moments, committed them all to flames." Adams noted in his letter to Tudor that he sent the inquiry to Elizabeth "since my return from Europe"—which put the exchange back in mid- to late 1779.[39] So perhaps Otis burned his possessions on more than one occasion.

There is less uncertainty about James's death, eerily fitting in its suddenness and drama. On Friday afternoon, May 23, 1783, five weeks after the dinner with Governor Hancock, a thunderstorm came up in Andover that sent residents of the Osgood house scurrying inside. James was standing in one of the interior doorways, leaning on the frame and commenting to the assembled group, when a lightning bolt struck the chimney. The current flashed from chimney to roof rafters to doorpost, through Otis, and to the floor. He fell dead instantly, Jacob Osgood catching him before he hit the ground. He was fifty-eight. Not a single mark was found on his body save the scar on his forehead.

Otis was "as extraordinary in death as in life," Adams wrote upon hearing the news.[40] James had always expected to die abruptly; in times of despair he yearned for God to strike him down. But a notion crept into the family lore that James had confided to Mercy on multiple occasions that he hoped, even expected, to die by lightning specifically. That narrative entered the written record in *The Life of James Otis, of Massachusetts,* in which William Tudor quotes Jemmy (or a family member quoting him) verbatim: "My dear sister, I hope when God Almighty in his righteous providence shall take me out of time into eternity, that it will be by a flash of lightning."[41] In more fanciful later accounts, James's purported hope came to be characterized as a "foregleam" and a "presentiment."[42]

In any event, Jemmy's words are apocryphal, nowhere to be found in surviving correspondence. What the archives do contain is a letter from Mercy to niece Elizabeth (still Betsy to her), dated June 15, 1783, that informs her of her father's passing. In it Mercy tells of James's sadness and frustration during the many years since his injury, faculties diminished, useless to society. In short, death by lightning may well have been Jemmy's final wish; at the very least it was an apt metaphor for his quick, painless demise. The reality, as far as Mercy was concerned, was the redemption he deserved. As she wrote to Betsy,

> he often invok'd the messenger of death to give him a sudden release from a life become burdensome in every sense, but then the calm interval of a moment permitted him the recollection of his integrity. Thus have we beheld the divine commission—the flaming car—which

> has wafted from the world one of the greatest yet most unhappy of men.[43]

For all his misgivings and shortcomings, Mercy viewed her brother as the first martyr to the American Revolution. She concluded the letter to Betsy with a moving defense of his character and achievements, as flawed as they seemed to his estranged daughter:

> While the pen of a sister, agitated by the tenderest feelings, can scarcely touch the outlines, history will doubtless do justice to a character to whom America is more indebted for the investigation of her rights and the defense of her liberties than perhaps any other individual. It was the masterly precision of his pen, and the early and vigilant exertion of his abilities that laid the foundation of a glorious Revolution.[44]

The Brotherhood of Masons arranged a lavish public funeral in Boston, attended by old colleagues in law, government, and the patriot movement.[45] Otis took his place in the Cunningham family plot at the Granary Burying Ground, a short walk from the Town House, now called the Old State House. His wife, Ruth, whom he forgave in his will for all their differences, was buried alongside him at her death on November 6, 1789. Otis never forgave Elizabeth for her betrayal; he bequeathed her five shillings.[46]

# CHAPTER 12

# Wresting a Female Pen

Exactly where James Otis Jr. would have stood in post-revolutionary politics and the debate over a federal constitution is open to conjecture. His crusade against British despotism in the 1760s fell short of an outright call for independence; his respect for the sovereignty of king and Parliament left him suspect among radical patriots. And yet, whatever his equivocations, Otis's fiery arguments against imperial taxation and violations of individual freedom suggest that he would have subscribed to his sister's pure form of republicanism.

Second only to God and family, these were the truths that Mercy Warren valued most and that governed the rest of her life in politics: limited government, popular sovereignty, and the interests of the many over the few. She and her brother were old-school liberals, tried and true believers in John Locke and the doctrine of natural rights.

The signing of the Treaty of Paris on September 3, 1783, officially ending the War of Independence, brought a measure of peace and tranquility not seen in nearly a generation. "The discordant sounds of war that had long grated the ears of the children of America, were now suspended," Mercy would write. "The benign and heavenly voice of harmony soothed their wounded feelings."[1] The reality of independence eased the pain of everything the Warrens had endured—the impairment of a brother and a son, fractures in the family, years of living apart—but the couple was to find little peace or solace amid the family tragedies and political disappointments still to come.

In the battle over the U.S. Constitution and the ideological direction of the country, Mercy defended her republican principles with all the passion and intellect of her fight for independence. At the same time, with the fledgling nation facing crises of identity and economic stability during the 1780s and early 1790s, crises in the Warren family tested Mercy and James in ways that paled in comparison with their wartime challenges. In both realms, politics and family life, there were constant reminders of her brother Jemmy, the ideals he stood for, and the demons he fought.

James Warren, finally retired from the Navy Board, hoed turnips on Neponset Hill and assisted James Jr. in his recuperation. Mercy, who had always hoped that the house and grounds might lure her sons to the nest, saw her wish come true in the fall of 1783. All five boys were on hand together: James Jr. was making progress despite occasional tremors; Charles was breathing more easily; Henry and George were studying hard; and Winslow, back from Europe and Philadelphia, awaited a diplomatic assignment he had been soliciting through his father's contacts in Congress.

But the domestic bliss proved fleeting. By February 1784, James Jr. had fallen into a prolonged depression, and Charles's condition had taken a turn for the worse. Winslow, meanwhile, losing patience in his wait for a consulship, left for Boston and arranged for a return to Europe with no position in hand. Henry went back to Harvard, and George rode off to study in Rhode Island, leaving the Warrens alone in caring for their two ailing sons.[2]

Mercy's sadness over the departure of George, the last of her brood, was exceeded only by her despair over Charles's relapse;

the chances of a full recovery were looking remote. Winslow sailed for Lisbon in the spring, stopping on the way to cavort in London. Charles, seeking a healthier climate, left for the Caribbean island of Hispaniola in August. Contributing even further to Mercy's sense of loss was the departure that same summer of Abigail Adams, who joined her husband in France.

For relief and escape, Mercy turned to writing as her eyesight permitted. In the same way that Jemmy, John Adams, and husband James had motivated her in the past, now it was Winslow who provided the spark. During his stay in Milton, he urged her to attempt a classical drama that set the pursuit of liberty in a foreign context. The result, penned in a second-floor study during the winter of 1783–84, was a five-act tragedy titled *The Ladies of Castile.* It began with Mercy's dedication and open letter "To a Young Gentleman in Europe, at whose Request a regular Dramatick Work was first attempted."[3]

Featuring dramatic plot lines and fully drawn characters, the play takes place in sixteenth-century Spain during the reign of Holy Roman Emperor Charles V. The central characters are two women, Doña Maria and Doña Louisa, whose husbands die in rebellion against the crown and in defense of it, respectively. Maria is a woman of action and high principle with whom the author plainly identified. (Mercy often used the pseudonym "Marcia" in signing letters to husband James and the Adamses.) She is the wife of one martyred freedom fighter, Don Juan de Padilla, and the sister of another, Don Francis. Like Mercy taking up the cause of her fallen brother, Maria vows revenge for Juan's death; she concocts a plan to rob the church and bankroll the rebel cause. "I will avenge my lord," she declares. "I will never despair, till my soul flies / and mixes with the bold exalted shades [spirits of the deceased]."[4] Jemmy, dead less than a year when Mercy wrote those lines, clearly was on her mind.

Doña Louisa, in counterpoint to Maria, is a daughter of the villainous regent Don Velasco but (like Mercy's niece Elizabeth) loves an adversary of her father, in this case Maria's brother

Francis. Whereas Maria refuses to "wail . . . in vulgar grief" over Don Juan's fate and fights bravely on his behalf, Louisa responds to Francis's death by taking her own life. True to history as well as tragedy, the rebellion fails and the heroes die. (Charles V put down an uprising in Castile, called the Revolt of the Comuneros, in 1520–21.) Maria, in the meantime, has evoked the spirit of James Otis Jr., John Locke, and Brutus of Upper Servia in declaring the creed of popular sovereignty and natural rights:

> Yet justice's sword can never be resheath'd,
> 'Till Charles is taught to know we will be free;
> And learns the duty a monarch owes,
> To heaven—the people—and the rights of man.[5]

Mercy was not just rehashing old themes or writing in a vacuum. She intended the play as a warning to fellow citizens about the corruption of principles that threatened the budding republic. "The design of the writer," she acknowledged in a prefatory note, was "to cultivate the sentiments of public and private virtue in whatsoever falls from her pen."[6]

The same message and motif animate her next work, written in the winter of 1784–85.[7] *The Sack of Rome* is another five-act tragedy in blank verse, this time classical in setting as well as form. The drama takes place in fourth-century Rome during the reign of Emperor Valentinian, another in Mercy Warren's succession of ruthless tyrants. Barbarian hordes threaten the empire from without; despotism, corruption, and vice threaten from within. Like *The Ladies of Castile,* the play revolves around two women at the center of political turmoil: Empress Edoxia (Valentinian's wife) and their daughter, Eudocia. Love, filial duty, and political allegiance are complicating factors once again, with operatically tragic results.

Eudocia's fiancé, a nobleman named Gaudentius, is the son of a slain Roman general who seeks revenge against his father's murderer, Emperor Valentinian. Eudocia persuades Gaudentius to elope instead, but the approach of invading Vandals scuttles their plan. Valentinian meets his fate at the hands of another vengeful noble, Petronius Maximus, who seeks marriage with the widowed Edoxia. She, desperate to save Rome and herself, allows marauding Vandals into the city—which dooms her, Gaudentius, Eudocia, and the republic.

Theatrical performance was still rare in New England, but *The Sack of Rome* carried a lesson that Warren wanted delivered live. The epilogue includes her plea:

> Pray let it pass at least a night or two;
> And if the moral in this pious age
> Should let it have a week upon the stage;
> Some gambling fools by Maximus's fate
> Might learn their follies ere it was too late.[8]

With no prospects for staging the play stateside, Mercy sent a copy to John Adams in London with an appeal for help. Adams replied several months later with admiration for the work but discouraging news about the British theater scene. "Nothing American sells here," he reported. "There is a universal desire and endeavor to forget America." Instead, Adams suggested, she should focus on her history of the Revolution.[9]

Mercy found solidarity and inspiration during the Milton years in her associations with like-minded republicans. Thomas Jefferson spent several weeks in Boston during the summer of 1784 en route to his ministerial posting in France. The Warrens came to know him at the Winter Street home of Samuel and Betsey Adams, staunch allies in the crusade for civic virtue.[10] Catharine Macaulay Graham, an object of scandal in England for her marriage to a much younger man, was a long-awaited and revered visitor to the Warren estate that November. "I think her not only a learned but a virtuous, worthy character, with much sensibility of heart and dignity of manner," Mercy gushed.[11] Elbridge Gerry, James's friend and former assembly colleague from the

North Shore, was among the Massachusetts Whigs who shared the Warrens' enmity for the kind of freewheeling, improvident government personified by Governor John Hancock. State politics had become a "burlesque," Mercy concurred. "Nothing less than an American monarchy is in contemplation."[12]

Popular discontent across Massachusetts, as in other states, was more economic than political. The war effort had saddled Congress with debts totaling $40 million by 1784; the individual states shouldered another $21 million.[13] Paper currency, printed to excess, lost purchasing power. Lending rates climbed higher. Basic commodities grew scarcer even as luxury imports poured in. The Warrens, covering Winslow's losses to boot, had difficulty making payments on the Milton mansion. Joseph Otis protected the Barnstable estate, the warehouse, and all family possessions by transferring them to heirs. And Samuel Allyne, ending two years as speaker of the state assembly, declared bankruptcy in 1785.[14]

Amid the tensions over money and class, the Warrens began taking heat for their outspoken views. James was reelected to the Continental Congress but declined to serve "with men unacquainted with or indifferent to the principles of the Revolution."[15] Political adversaries skewered him for turning down public service yet again. Mercy, for her part, submitted signed articles to the press that criticized institutions she deemed uncivil, from the Hancock administration to a high-society social club called the Sans Souci. In response, the *Boston Gazette* published an anonymous letter that gave Mercy a taste of the personal abuse heaped on Jemmy in the 1760s. Warren's "literary accomplishments are known," the letter began, but "she prostitutes her time and talents . . . to blast the character of some of the most worthy of our citizens."[16]

For the Warrens, however, the financial squeeze and political attacks were trivial compared to the miseries suffered at home. Charles returned from Hispaniola somewhat improved in spring 1785, but his chest pain and fever reappeared within a few months. Mercy and James, acceding to his wish to spend time with Winslow, put Charles and a servant on a ship to Portugal in the fall. But on a cold morning in early December, as Mercy was "contemplating the situations of my sons at the distance of a thousand leagues," she was astonished to hear the front door open and Winslow call from downstairs.[17] He had heard from Congress that the treaty of friendship with Portugal had not materialized and that there would be no position for him in Lisbon. Winslow claimed not to have received his mother's letter about Charles's visit; or else, in his disappointment, anger, and mounting debt, he simply disregarded it. In any case, Winslow and Charles had crossed paths in the middle of the Atlantic Ocean.

"My next thought," Mercy wrote to Charles when the shock wore off, "was the disappointment you must suffer by the absence of [your] brother."[18] What the Warrens in Milton did not know was that Charles had not survived the voyage. They received a letter in early 1786 with the news of his death in Sanlúcar, Spain, on November 30, 1785. He was twenty-four.

Winslow, hopelessly self-centered and endlessly forgiven, had more surprises in store. He returned to America heavily in debt to Dutch bankers, among others, and expected his father to bail him out. But James Warren, with steep obligations of his own, had no more help to give. Winslow was in trouble. In March 1786, an agent for the Dutch creditors named John Codman served Winslow with court papers as he passed through Connecticut. Later that month, in a stunning evocation of his Uncle Jemmy, Winslow confronted Codman on the floor of the Boston Stock Exchange. Retired general Henry Jackson, on hand for the events of the day, reported a "caning match" in which Winslow beat the defenseless agent with a heavy walking stick, leaving him badly bruised.[19]

The downward spiral of the Warren family mirrored the economic difficulties and deepening malaise of many Americans during the Confederation period. Federal and state debts were ruinous. Congress had no authority to tax directly, and state governments were loath to do so while citizens faced crippling shortages, soaring inflation, and a squeeze on credit. Mercy Warren took a mother's perspective in characterizing the situation:

> Americans felts themselves in such a state of infancy, that as a child just learning to walk, they were afraid of their own movements. Their debts were unpaid, their governments unsettled, and the people out of breath by their long struggle.[20]

In Massachusetts, where James Otis Jr. and Samuel Adams had made tax resistance a matter of popular pride, incoming governor James Bowdoin sought to ease the debt burden and bolster a depleted treasury by raising property taxes and collecting unpaid levies. The effects were harshest in the rural, western part of the state, where farmers strapped by the failing economy went bankrupt in waves—but not without a fight. Direct action against the administration began in August 1786 with the forced shutdown of several state courts to block foreclosure proceedings. Under the leadership of a bankrupt farmer and former Continental Army officer named Daniel Shays, the protest movement grew rapidly into armed rebellion.

In January 1787, reviving the fervor and rhetoric of freedom-loving, antitax patriots, a 1,500-man insurgent force marched on the town of Springfield with plans to seize a federal armory and use the weapons to overthrow the state government. A volunteer Massachusetts militia, funded by wealthy eastern merchants because the treasury was broke, succeeded in halting the advance and quelling the rebellion over the next month. Two agitators were hanged; Shays was pardoned. The three thousand state recruits, under the command of General Benjamin Lincoln (five years removed from Yorktown), included Mercy and James's son Henry as well as their nephew Harrison Gray Otis.[21] Both were cousins of General Lincoln's daughter-in-law Mary Otis Lincoln—thereby connecting James Otis Jr. with that side of the conflict as well.

James Warren, as a citizen-farmer, sympathized with the Shays rebels, their limited representation in government, and the oppressive measures of state authorities. Mercy held both sides accountable. While blaming the administration for "drawing the reins of power much too tight," she condemned the uprising in no uncertain terms and dismissed any comparison to the patriot cause.[22] The difference, as she saw it, was that the Shaysites had taken arms against a duly constituted popular government rather than a tyrannical monarchy. "They were too ignorant," she grumbled, "to distinguish between an opposition to regal despotism and a resistance to a government recently established by themselves."[23]

In the end, what the episode demonstrated most clearly to political leaders was the weakness of America's governing document. Under the Articles of Confederation, the nation was unable to pay its bills or maintain civil order. The federal union needed to be strengthened.

The year 1787 marked the return of James and Mercy Warren to the "warring passions" of politics. It had been six years since their move to Milton, and the gild was off the lily. They were alone in the grand estate and missed their sons. It had been more than a year since Charles's death. James Jr. had moved to Hingham and was teaching school. Winslow, ordered to a Connecticut debtors' prison the previous November, had managed to escape custody and was back in Boston. George studied law in Northampton, opened a practice that floundered, and resettled on land his father owned near Kennebunk, Maine. Henry eventually joined him there.

For sixty-year-old James Warren, the exertions of farming had grown arduous, and Shays's Rebellion created a viable opening into politics. The country party had nominated him for governor in 1785 and lieutenant governor in 1786, but the prospects of success were slim to none. Then, in late May 1787, in a wave of anti-Bowdoin liberalism following the Shays trouble, John Hancock won back the governorship and Warren regained his seat in the assembly; colleagues old and new elected him speaker.

Less than a week before the Massachusetts balloting, meanwhile, delegates to the Constitutional Convention had gathered in Philadelphia to begin revising the Articles of Confederation. No one attached greater importance to the deliberations than Mercy Otis Warren. Writing to John Adams in London during the lead-up to the convention, she hatched a new childrearing metaphor to express her concern over the state of the republic. Left implicit but readily understood by a family friend was her allusion to son Winslow:

> Perhaps America is in the predicament of an adventurous youth, who has disengaged himself from parental authority, before the maturity that might have taught him to make a proper use of his freedom.[24]

Mercy and James could hardly have been more chagrined at the outcome of the convention. Fortunately, the proposed Constitution, signed by the delegates on September 17, 1787, would not become binding until nine of the thirteen states voted for ratification. The result was nearly a year of fierce debate in newspapers, pamphlets, taverns and coffeehouses, and the halls of government from state to state. Tiny Rhode Island, which resisted any federal interference in its affairs, refused to participate in the Philadelphia Convention from the beginning. Several delegates from other states walked out of the gathering in protest; three, including Elbridge Gerry, declined to sign the final draft.

The loose coalition of Americans who rejected the stronger national government envisioned in the Constitution came to be called, pejoratively at first, Anti-Federalists. Prominent voices in the movement included Patrick Henry, George Mason, and Edmund Randolph of Virginia; Luther Martin of Maryland; George Clinton and Robert Yates of New York; and Samuel Adams, John Hancock, and Mercy and James Warren of Massachusetts.

What, exactly, was the new "liberty" they had fought for? How much of it should they embrace? Mercy framed the core issue as objectively as she could in a letter to Catherine Macaulay Graham, but she left little doubt as to which side she was on:

> Our situation is truly delicate and critical. On the one hand, we stand in need of a strong federal government, founded on principles that will support the prosperity and union of the colonies. On the other we have struggled for liberty and made costly sacrifices at her shrine, and there are still many among us who revere her name too much to relinquish, beyond a certain modicum, the right of man for the dignity of government.[25]

Anti-Federalists rejected the Constitution on any of several related grounds. Most of them feared that the new federal government would be too powerful and devolve into the very kind of despotism the colonists had just overturned. The office of the presidency, in particular, threatened monarchy. Other opponents, not only in Rhode Island, were most concerned that the sovereignty of individual states would be compromised; the federal government would be too far away and too amorphous to serve the needs of individual states and communities. Still others worried that personal rights and liberties—such as free speech, freedom of religion, and fair trial—were at risk; the draft Constitution contained no guarantees.

These and other arguments against the new blueprint reached citizens at large through a slew of newspaper articles, broadsides, and pamphlets that began appearing within days of the draft. The burst of public criticism elicited a prompt and sustained response from Alexander Hamilton, James Madison, and John Jay in a series of eighty-five influential articles—initially called *The Federalist,* later *The Federalist Papers*—that explained the Constitution and promoted ratification. Whereas the *Federalist* authors would famously publish their essays under the pseudonym "Publius," the Anti-Federalists submitted their articles under such pen names as "Cato" (believed to be George Clinton), "Brutus" (likely Robert

Yates), "Federal Farmer" (Richard Henry Lee or Melancton Smith), and "Helvidius Priscus" (James Warren).

Prominent among the Anti-Federalist papers for its erudition and florid style was a twenty-three-page pamphlet that appeared in late February 1788 under the title *Observations on the New Constitution, and on the Federal and State Conventions.* The first edition, signed "A Columbia Patriot," carried a printer's note that credited the work to the Warrens' old friend and confederate Elbridge Gerry.[26] It was not until the 1930s that the Harvard legal scholar and historian Charles Warren, Mercy and James's great-great grandson, discovered her reference to the "Columbian Patriot" tract—with a copy enclosed—in a December 1787 letter to Catharine Macaulay Graham in England.[27] That discovery corroborated textual evidence of Mercy's own authorship.*

While it may have lacked the philosophical rigor of brother James's anti-British pamphlets from the 1760s, Mercy's *Observations* drew on her lifetime in letters—classical history, Enlightenment thought, and the literary canon—in assailing the proposed Constitution. And it was as emphatic as anything her brother ever wrote. Her objections to the document ran the gamut from government structure and underlying principles to the process of ratification.

The three-branch system of checks and balances, Warren declares, would be a "many headed monster, of such motley mixture, that its enemies cannot trace a feature of Democratic or Republican extract." The new system would afford no protection of "rights of conscience" or freedom of the press, no limit on judiciary power, no guarantee of trial by jury, inadequate legislative representation, attenuated state sovereignty, and "no provision by a bill of rights to guard against . . . dangerous encroachments

* One clue in the text is an allusion to the settings of Warren's two most recent plays, imperial Rome and sixteenth-century Spain: "The virtues of Cato could not save Rome, nor the abilities of a Padilla defend the citizens of Castile from falling under the yoke of Charles." MOW, *Observations on the New Constitution, and on the Federal and State Conventions* (Brooklyn, NY: N.p., 1788), 21.

of power." On the last point, Mercy pauses to remember brother James's case against unreasonable search and seizure:

> I cannot pass over in silence the insecurity in which we are left with regard to warrants unsupported by evidence—the daring experiment of granting writs of assistance in a former arbitrary administration is not yet forgotten in the Massachusetts; nor can we be so ungrateful to the memory of the patriots who counteracted their operation.[28]

Underpinning the eighteen points of disagreement enumerated in Warren's essay are what she refers to as "first principles": human freedom, natural rights, and government by popular sovereignty. Invoking both John Locke and the Declaration of Independence, she posits that "man is born free and possessed of certain unalienable rights. . . . The origin of all power is in the people." At the same time, though she warns from the beginning of the "wretched effects of slavery," she invokes the concept of bondage time and again as an analogue of despotism or the antithesis of liberty, rather than the economic system and social order oppressing hundreds of thousands of living Americans. The three-fifths clause of article 1 goes unmentioned.[29]

While mounting a wide-ranging case against Federalism and the new order, *Observations* would have been less than vintage Mercy Warren had it not cast the entire debate in Manichaean terms—a struggle between liberty and tyranny, principle and avarice, common people and the "aristocratical" class. Should darker impulses prevail, she concludes, reason and virtue would be the last refuge of the faithful:

> While the statesman is plodding for power, and the courtier practicing the arts of dissimulation without check—while the rapacious are growing rich by oppression, and fortune throwing her gifts into the lap of fools, let the sublimer characters, the philosophic lovers of freedom who have wept over her exit, retire to the calm shades of contemplation, there they may look down with pity

> on the inconsistency of human nature, the revolutions of states, the rise of kingdoms, and the fall of empires.[30]

Husband James may have recalled the words of a much younger wife and emerging poet. In the heady months after the Stamp Act, during his first term in the General Court, Mercy had implored him to retire from politics—to quit the smoky town and all its folly for the "calm retreat" of Clifford Farm. Now, with the Revolution won but the larger cause in jeopardy, retiring to "calm shades of contemplation" appeared to be their lot after all. For true lovers of freedom, solace would lay in the Whig view of history: kingdoms and empires passing, a true democratic republic yet to come.

The saving grace was compromise. At the heart of it was a demand on the part of Anti-Federalists like Samuel Adams, Elbridge Gerry, and the Warrens for a set of amendments that would ensure the rights of citizens. At the Massachusetts Ratifying Convention in early 1788, by which time five other states had voted in favor of the Constitution, Anti-Federalist leaders struck a deal with their Federalist counterparts: the Anti-Federalists would vote in favor of the Constitution, and the Federalists would support their amendments. Based on that compromise, the full state convention voted to ratify on February 6.

Warren's *Observations,* released later that month, helped solidify the case for a bill of rights in the uncommitted states.* Several of them agreed to the overall Constitution under the same conditions as Massachusetts, ensuring ratification by the end of June 1788.[31] Incorporating a bill of rights became one of the first orders of business for the new federal government, with formal adoption coming in December 1791. By the time she wrote about it in her *History,* Mercy acknowledged that "the

* The pamphlet's influence was likely strongest in New York, where 1,630 copies were distributed among Anti-Federalist county committees and the text appeared in the *New York Journal* on April 2, 1788. In the five months following publication, New York, Maryland, New Hampshire, and South Carolina voted for ratification based on the Massachusetts compromise. All states would vote later on the adoption of amendments in what became the Bill of Rights.

government of the United States stood on a basis which rendered the people respectable abroad and safe at home."[32]

She and her late brother had done more than their part in making it so. The first ten amendments addressed many of the rights, privileges, and limitations on federal authority that Mercy had demanded in her pamphlet. The Fourth Amendment protection against "unreasonable searches and seizures" was directly attributable to James's assertion in the Writs of Assistance Case that "a man's house is his castle."

In June 1788, with the Constitution on the brink of ratification, the Warrens sold the Milton estate and returned to Plymouth. It was time for a change. Neponset Hill was never the haven they had hoped for; they may have even concluded it was jinxed. While Thomas Hutchinson dreamed of his "humble cottage" for the rest of his days in exile, the Warrens' seven years there had been a litany of mishaps and disappointments.[33] James was glad to be relieved of the financial burden; Mercy, with the war over, was ready to resume life in Plymouth. She settled contentedly in the Main Street house, he traveled to Boston for legislative sessions, and together they escaped to Clifford Farm as time allowed. "We are again happily fixed I believe for the remainder of life," Mercy wrote to Catharine Macaulay Graham.[34]

The Adamses sailed home from England during that same month, June 1788, and purchased an estate in Braintree they called Peacefield, not far from their old farm. But the years, the distance, and politics had strained relations between the two couples. Mercy, who cleaved to her morals and never set foot outside New England, suspected that the grandeur and luxury of European courts had corrupted her old republican friends. Rumors of James Warren's complicity in Shays's Rebellion compounded any hard feelings John may have harbored over his friend's repeated refusals of service. And Adams, despite extended stints in the Old World, was an active and engaged Federalist. He insisted to Mercy that life in Europe had not changed him, but his politics *had* shifted from the ardent republicanism of the Revolution. Anti-Federalists denounced his ideas for a new American system, laid out in a three-volume screed titled *Defence of the Constitutions of Government of the United States* (1787–88), as monarchical and aristocratic.

Ratification of the Constitution had not put an end to political arm wrestling, as competing interests vied for influence in the first federal government. There were no formal parties in the elections of 1788–89, and George Washington, everyone's choice for president, stood above the fray. Down the line, however, there was still a deep divide between Federalists and Anti-Federalists. The former prevailed in the executive branch, with Adams winning the vice presidency (to the personal pride and political distress of the Warrens) and with Washington naming Alexander Hamilton and John Jay to high-level cabinet posts. Hamilton's centralizing economic policies set the overall direction of the administration.

The divisions were more pronounced in congressional elections. Federalist and proadministration candidates won a decisive majority in both the House and Senate, but Anti-Federalist and anti-administration forces martialed a viable opposition. In Massachusetts, two of eight seats went to Anti-Federalist candidates, Elbridge Gerry and Jonathan Grout; Samuel Adams in the 1st district and James Warren in the 5th both lost badly.

The Otis family, in a partisan twist, did find a place in the national government. Samuel Allyne, a committed Federalist and Hamiltonian who had opposed his sister and brother-in-law in the ratification debate, was rewarded for his service to Washington's army and the Continental Congress by being named (with Adams's backing) secretary of the Senate, a high-level administrative position. In that capacity, he held the Bible on which George Washington placed his hand to take the oath of office on April 30, 1789.

The Warrens, meantime, hunkered down in Plymouth. With the Federalists firmly in control, they kept a low profile and held their tongues (for the most part) about politics. Mercy, unable "to write with that energy and pathos that such a subject requires," tabled her history of the Revolution.[35] There would be little interest in an exhaustive account of the nation's founding, or its emergence as a commercial republic, from the perspective of an old-fashioned liberal and Anti-Federalist. Besides, she had another project in mind.

A younger generation of female writers—including slave poet Phillis Wheatley, essayist Judith Sargent Murray, and poet and novelist Susanna Haswell Rowson (Jemmy's former student from Nantasket)—had had successful books published under their own names. Why couldn't Warren? Anonymity was no longer necessary for political cover or physical safety. And she had reams of manuscript, old and new, ready to share.

Finding a publisher was no problem. Isaiah Thomas, who had carried Mercy's early verse dramas in the *Massachusetts Spy,* printed and released her 252-page collection from his Boston printing office in September 1790. *Poems, Dramatic and Miscellaneous,* by "Mrs. M. Warren," gathered her two recent tragedies, *The Sack of Rome* and *The Ladies of Castile,* and eighteen poems dating from the prerevolutionary period to that summer. The volume opens with a laudatory dedication to George Washington, begging indulgence from "a lady of his acquaintance."[36]

The selection of verse offered a telling portrait of the author at age sixty-two. Leaving out her early satires and farces, she chose to include her most ambitious and representative works of political drama, spiritual faith, and personal devotion. *The Sack of Rome* and *Ladies of Castile,* with their underlying themes of filial duty and fraternal love, were pleas from the political sidelines to combat vice and rescue the revolutionary ideal. A trio of poems originally published in 1774—"A Political Reverie," "Squabble of the Sea Nymphs," and "To the Hon. J. Winthrop, Esq."—recalled the patriotic zeal she had helped stoke in her brother's name. "Lines, Written after a Very Severe Tempest," date unknown, suggested the act of God that took Jemmy's life ("lightnings fly from pole to pole . . . those flying shafts of death") but was, in the end, an affirmation of faith.[37] Also included in the volume were poems dedicated to husband James, sons Winslow and Charles, and recently deceased friend Hannah Winthrop. The book contained everything that mattered most to her: political and moral principles, religious beliefs, and the people she loved.

The lead-off piece in the poetry section and the newest item in the collection, "To Mrs. Montague, Author of 'Observations on the Genius and Writing of Shakespeare,'" has garnered particular interest among modern Warren biographers. Composed in July 1790, the poem is an encomium to British literary critic and arts patron Elizabeth Montagu and a declaration of solidarity with all female writers. If the sons of Britain failed to live up to Shakespeare's lofty standards, Warren hazards, women should take up the challenge:

> A sister's hand may wrest a female pen,
> From the bold outrage of imperious men.[38]

The poem deserves its place of prominence in the first book to carry Mercy Warren's name. It is the most unflinching statement of literary aspiration and feminine pride in all of her published work.

# CHAPTER 13

# The Last Frail Reed

In the spring of 1791, the newly constituted Federal District Court of Massachusetts heard the case of the two Dutch bankers, Nicholaas and Jacob Van Staphorst, against Winslow Warren. Complicating matters for Mercy and James was the fact that the Van Staphorsts had granted loans to the United States which John Adams had arranged as minister to the Netherlands. In mid-May, the district court ruled in favor of the Dutchmen and sentenced Warren to one month in debtors' prison. "Humanity has wept that the first victim of experiment in the United States was the son of General Warren and the nephew of the celebrated Mr. Otis," his aggrieved mother commented to Secretary of War Henry Knox, organizer of the cannon expedition back in 1775–76 and another family friend.[1] "A corrupt influence is apparent," she wrote to Winslow, seemingly blameless again.[2]

Upon completion of his jail term, Winslow joined the Second Infantry Regiment of the U.S. Army, with a rank of second lieutenant, thanks to Secretary Knox. Serving in the military would erase his debts. Under the command of General Arthur St. Clair, a friend of President George Washington with a tarnished war record, the regiment set out in June 1791 for tribal territory beyond the Ohio River. Winslow left without saying goodbye to his parents.

Camped on Miami and Shawnee land near the headwaters of the Wabash on the night of November 3–4, the ill-prepared federal troops were awakened by the war cries of a thousand Native warriors emerging from nearby woods. In the worst defeat of U.S. forces ever suffered at the hands of American Indians—an event referred to in history texts as the Battle of the Wabash, or St. Clair's Defeat—more than nine hundred white soldiers and settlers lost their lives. Among the dead was Second Lieutenant Winslow Warren; General St. Clair found his way to safety.

Word reached Plymouth in early December. Mercy Warren was beside herself with grief and anger. She had opposed a federal standing army to begin with. Now she decried St. Clair's failure of leadership and the administration's "wanton attempt . . . to exterminate the simple tribes or drive them from their native inheritance."[3] For the young United States, the Wabash massacre was the deadliest tragedy since the battles for independence. For Mercy, the death of her beloved Winslow was the deepest shock and greatest test of faith since the beating of brother James. She hardly spoke and did not pick up a quill for weeks.

Opening up to friend Janet Livingston Montgomery four months later, she finally penned, "I am seized with emotion too violent and painful to be endured."[4] Notwithstanding previous hardships and a lifelong trust in God's providence, Mercy's faith was shaken to the core. She began an elegiac poem for Winslow, "Written in Deep Affliction," with these plaintive lines:

> My God! relieve my wounded heart,
> Thou know'st the conflicts of my breast,
> The source of pain—the recent smart,
> The sorrows that my heart invest. . . .
> In woes 'lorn garb I silent mourn
> My filial son—my faithful *friend.*[5]

Mercy lost another faithful friend in the year of Winslow's passing. That May she had written to Catharine Macaulay Graham to congratulate the Whig historian on her pamphlet praising the French Revolution and criticizing a treatise by the Irish statesman Edmund Burke that repudiated the uprising.[6] Such were American politics at this juncture that Burke's essay found an enthusiastic audience among Federalists despite the common values of the French and American Revolutions, the vital U.S. alliance with France, and fresh memories of British despotism. "Some . . . professed republicans," Mercy complained to Catharine, "are now become the advocates for monarchy and all the trappings of royalty."[7]

Warren arranged an American edition of Macaulay's pamphlet, including her own introductory note, to promote its antimonarchical values at a critical moment: the last several states were about to vote on the Bill of Rights. The author, however, did not live to see the volume or perhaps even the letter from Plymouth. She died on June 22, 1791.

Toward the end of a dismal year, relief to Mercy's "wounded heart" came in two forms, one personal and one political. On November 1, three days before the debacle that took Winslow's life, the Warrens' fourth son, Henry, was married. The bride was Mary (Polly) Winslow, another descendant of Plymouth settler Edward Winslow and General John Winslow, who had built the house on Main Street. Henry would be the only Warren son to take a wife and have children. The couple moved onto the farm at Eel River, just as Mercy and James had as newlyweds, and Polly gave birth to the first of their nine surviving children the following September 25. It was a baby girl, in the pink of health, whom they named after her grandmother. They called her Marcia.

The political relief was final ratification of the ten amendments making up the Bill of Rights on December 15, 1791.

Partisan disagreement continued to simmer in the Washington administration, heating to a low boil after Thomas Jefferson took over as secretary of state from John Jay in 1790. Disputes over national policy had as much to do with economic interests and foreign ties as they did with the scope of government. Federalists such as Alexander Hamilton and John Adams, seeking to expand American commerce, advocated protective tariffs, investment in infrastructure (such as roads, bridges, and ports), and an active relationship with the nation's largest trading partner—Great Britain. Jefferson and fellow Republicans (opponents of the Federalists, sometimes called Democratic-Republicans), favoring independent-minded yeoman farmers and their bucolic vision of America, called for low taxes and tariffs, small government, and close ties with America's wartime ally—France.

President Washington struggled to keep the rivalry in check, but the rift grew wider and the dialogue harsher as the idealism of the French Revolution gave way to the Reign of Terror in 1793. Federalists questioned how far liberty could extend before devolving into populist tyranny. Republicans viewed any desire for a well-organized central authority as a dangerous embrace of absolutism. At the heart of the matter was the question of human nature: Were people fundamentally good and just? Left to their freedom, would they act in the common interest, to preserve the rights and well-being of all? Or could society at large not be trusted to maintain order and serve justice? Was a strong government necessary to keep the people in check?

Jefferson, most notably, subscribed to the Lockean view that people are born with a blank slate and not naturally inclined toward selfish interests or dominance over others. Those are learned behaviors, resulting from defects in the social environment, including institutions of civic authority. Improving the quality of life thus means liberating people as much as possible from government. The goal of the American experiment, wrote Jefferson, was to "show by example the sufficiency of human reason for the care of human affairs."[8] The Federalists viewed humanity in grimmer terms. All men should be equal before the law, they believed, but not all men are born with equal means. People scramble and compete viciously for wealth, power, and material well-being; *that* is the law of nature. A robust, centralized system of government is therefore necessary to protect the rights and interests of ordinary working people from privileged elites and to promote growth and opportunity broadly.

Mercy Warren, shocked by the greed and selfishness of fellow citizens since the Revolution, had less faith in people than Jefferson did. "Passion, prejudice, and error are characteristics of human nature," she had stated in her pamphlet on the Constitution.[9] And while no one advocated more strenuously for social and economic equality or against a new American aristocracy, her resistance to strong central government rested instead on an abiding fear of state authority and the willingness of ordinary people to submit to it. "Mankind," she cautioned newly installed Vice President John Adams, "are much more prone to servile compliance to the will of power than to a sober and rational attention to that freedom and independence which is the just claim of nature."[10]

Adams had startled her with a comment made in the weeks before his swearing in. "The people of our united America find it much easier to institute authority than to yield obedience," he wrote to her. What *he* feared was that "there is not enough spirit of union to insure obedience to the laws."[11] It was a telling statement from a figure in the innermost circle of power, with a blunt rebuttal from an old friend and confederate far removed from it. The disparity in their views of humanity lay at the heart of their political estrangement and, inevitably for two priggish characters, their growing personal tensions.

The Warrens and Adamses had not seen each other since before Abigail departed for London in 1784. Incipient political differences, largely unspoken at first, and John's rise in federal government kept them apart even after the Adamses returned stateside in 1788. Mercy, never shy about seeking patronage from friends in high places, wrote her old mentor to congratulate him on becoming vice president and to curry favor for husband James and son Winslow (before his trial and enlistment).[12] Adams's delayed response and refusal to find them jobs—special assistance of this kind would "belie the whole course of my public and private conduct and all the maxims of my life," he finally replied—struck Mercy as a betrayal of their friendship and "the purest principles" on which it was founded.[13] A series of miscommunications, real or perceived slights, and open or veiled accusations magnified their differences in the period that followed. Mercy lay low in Plymouth and James held a seat on the Governor's Council (1792–94) while Adams served the Federalist agenda in Philadelphia.

Abigail, who had taken her husband's side in the spat with Mercy over patronage, made a surprise visit to Plymouth in August 1796; Mary Otis, the wife of Samuel Allyne, came along for moral support.[14] Once bosom friends and wartime helpmeets, Mercy and Abigail had not been together for more than twelve years. The two republican mothers, both grandmothers now, spent several pleasant days in the house on "Liberty Square" and strolling along Plymouth Harbor; they had much to talk about. Subsequent correspondence suggests that they reached at least a tacit understanding that politics should not stand in the way of friendship—a proposition that would be sorely tested in the decade ahead.

In mid-September 1796, President Washington announced in a published letter—his historic Farewell Address—that he would not be seeking a third term. Because he had run unopposed in 1789 and 1792, the election of 1796 would be America's first contested presidential race. It was also the first U.S. election to involve formal parties, despite Washington's warning that loyalty to party over country was the "worst enemy" of popular government. The Federalists put up John Adams as their candidate;

the opposition Democratic-Republicans backed their party's cofounder and ideological father, Thomas Jefferson. In the Electoral College balloting that fall, Adams edged out his southern rival, seventy-one to sixty-eight. Under the rules then in place, this meant that Adams would become president and Jefferson vice president.[15] The two men took the oath of office on March 4, 1797, at Congress Hall in Philadelphia.

The Federalist victory kept Mercy Warren in the political wilderness. Plymouth, a Tory stronghold during the war, was a firm Federalist town now, which limited her social interactions and forced an unnatural reticence. In her early seventies, she was gray and frail. Eyeglasses were common in late eighteenth-century America but inadequate to her crippled vision. Her intellect and judgment, on the other hand, were as sharp as ever. James had suffered recurring bouts of gout and other creeping illnesses, but he stayed active with son Henry as a local leader of the minority party. The Warrens' marriage, ever loving, was a boon to both of them, while they reveled in a growing brood of grandchildren. Marcia got three younger brothers before the end of the decade—Winslow, Pelham, and Charles—promising future generations of Warrens. Mercy made cursory inquiries with publishers about her history of the Revolution, but the unfinished manuscript collected dust for most of the 1790s.

The Adams administration, meanwhile, was floundering. It remained neutral in the war between Britain and the French Republic, but a diplomatic incident in 1797–98 referred to as the XYZ Affair triggered a succession of naval encounters with France that historians dubbed the Quasi-War. Purportedly to strengthen national security, Federalists in Congress passed a legislative package—the Alien and Sedition Acts—which President Adams signed into law in the summer of 1798. The four bills, portents of xenophobic nationalism, made it harder for immigrants to become citizens, allowed the president to imprison or deport noncitizens from a hostile country or any others he deemed "dangerous," and imposed criminal penalties for publishing false and damaging statements against the government.

The real motives were blatantly political. Publishers of Democratic-Republican newspapers were convicted, jailed, and forced to cease publication. The curtailments of individual liberty and violations of constitutional principle confirmed everything Mercy Warren had warned about unchecked federal power. And the main perpetrator was, of all people, her former revolutionary compatriot and literary adviser, the admirer of her brother James, and an early member of the Sons of Liberty. Anger over the Alien and Sedition Acts would be the undoing of the Adams presidency and Federalist ascendancy.

Already dubious about the nation's future, Mercy felt even more alienated from affairs of state. For the nation as a whole, the death of George Washington on December 14, 1799, came as a sad and unifying respite from all the wrangling. For the Warrens, a further shock likewise kept politics in perspective. Youngest son George, who had followed in the family footsteps as a legislative representative from Maine, came down sick in late 1799. He wrote in January that the unknown illness had worsened to the point that he canceled a trip to Boston. Weeks passed with no further updates. Finally, in March 1800, Henry rode north to check on his brother's condition. He arrived too late. George had passed away on February 5; he was thirty-three.

Physically diminished and emotionally racked, Mercy faced this latest test with a proud and stubborn fortitude. "The waves have rolled in upon me—the billows have repeatedly broken over me," she wrote to Samuel Allyne, "yet I am not sunk down."[16]

Pluck and resilience did little to improve Mercy's eyesight, which worsened to the point that she gave up writing almost entirely. Sometime after George's death in 1800, eldest son James Jr. left his teaching job in Hingham and returned to Plymouth to open a school and assist his mother as a secretary and amanuensis (scribe). Having a second pair of eyes revived her spirits as well as her correspondence. By February 1802, it had been a full year since she was able to read a page or take up her pen, but, she reported to friend Sarah Gray Cary, "I tread down the remnant of life with a tolerable degree of cheerfulness—my days are tranquil, my nights not wearisome."[17]

Contributing to her good spirits, for sure, was a promising transformation in national politics. In the election of 1800, opposition to high taxes and the Alien and Sedition Acts sent Adams and the Federalists to a stinging defeat at the hands of Jefferson and the Democratic-Republicans. It was the first and only presidential election to pit an incumbent against his vice president. More importantly, it marked the first time in world history that power transferred peacefully from one political party to another. For Mercy, the major cause for optimism was the rescue of the fledgling republic from what she perceived as the aristocratic Federalists and their dangerous ideas of government. Looking on from lofty "shades of contemplation," she saw a triumph of reason and a reaffirmation of revolutionary ideals—the natural and inevitable path to freedom laid out before her. Jefferson later referred to the election as "the revolution of 1800." It was, he said, "as real a revolution in the principles of our government as that of 1776 was in its form."[18]

President Adams, in the end, had few scruples about assigning government jobs to Federalist friends and relatives; Jefferson proved equally generous to his allies. Rewards for loyalty and service devolved to the Warren family in the form of prized patronage positions: son Henry was named customs collector for the port of Plymouth, and James Jr. became the town's postmaster. James Sr. won an honorary appointment in 1804 as one of the state's presidential electors and had the satisfaction of voting for Jefferson's reelection.

For Mercy, the revival of republicanism made her history of the Revolution ripe for completion, which she accomplished with James Jr.'s help in the first years of the new century. In her buoyancy over the Bill of Rights and the Jeffersonian revolution, she could end the saga on a hopeful note:

> The wisdom and justice of the American governments, and the virtue of its inhabitants, may, if they are not deficient in the improvement of their own advantages, render the United States of America an enviable example to all the world, of peace, liberty, righteousness, and truth.[19]

The final three-volume work, totaling more than 1,300 pages, carried a formidable title: *History of the Rise, Progress and Termination of the American Revolution. Interspersed with Biographical, Political and Moral Observations.* The publisher, Ebenezer Larkin of Boston, launched subscription sales in early 1805 and distributed 1,500 leather-bound copies, volume by volume, through the following year. Among the first to subscribe was Jefferson, who ordered sets for himself and his entire cabinet.[20]

There had been other in-depth chronicles of the American Revolution, but none brought to bear the access to leadership, the female perspective, and the intellectual and literary brilliance of Warren's *History.* She had little interest in battles scenes or military strategy; she left those to the men. As promised in the subtitle, her primary concerns were the competing politics, philosophical principles, and central characters of the revolutionary movement. And while she declared a commitment to "the most exact impartiality," her purpose was patently ideological.[21] She regarded her task as one of establishing and passing on a particular set of values, ideals, and understandings—teaching philosophy by example.[22]

The text begins with a definition of history and a statement of purpose that reflected the dualities so prevalent in Warren's writings: good versus evil, right versus wrong, and the conflicting impulses in human nature:

> History, the deposit of crimes and the record of everything disgraceful or honorary to mankind, requires a

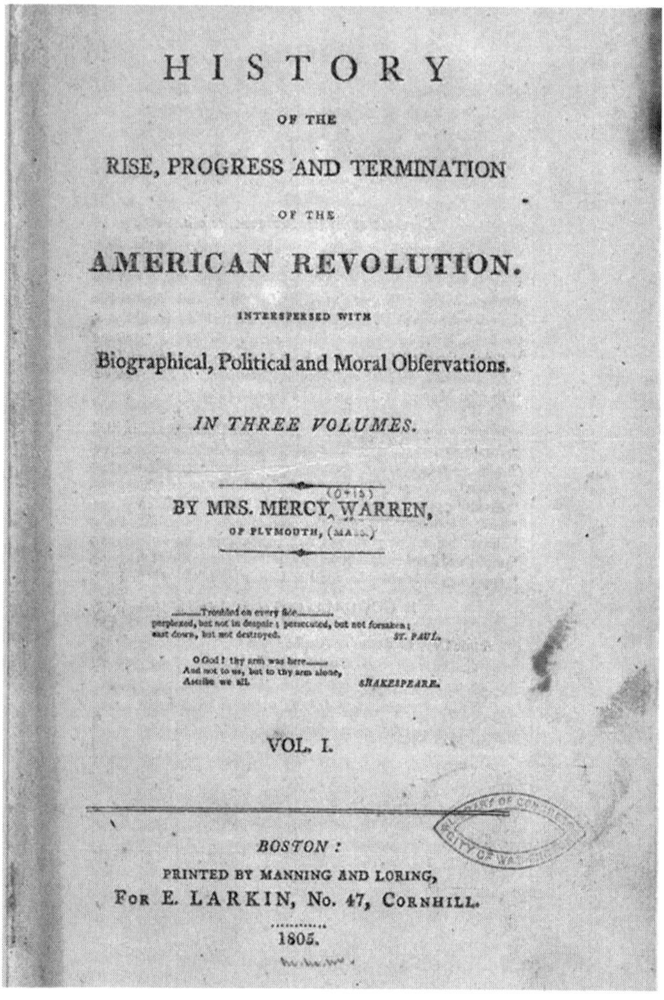

HISTORY

OF THE

RISE, PROGRESS AND TERMINATION

OF THE

AMERICAN REVOLUTION.

INTERSPERSED WITH

Biographical, Political and Moral Obſervations.

*IN THREE VOLUMES.*

BY MRS. MERCY WARREN,

OF PLYMOUTH,

——Troubled on every ſide,——
perplexed, but not in deſpair; perſecuted, but not forſaken;
caſt down, but not deſtroyed. *ST. PAUL.*

O God! thy arm was here,——
And not to us, but to thy arm alone,
Aſcribe we all. *SHAKESPEARE.*

VOL. I.

*BOSTON :*

PRINTED BY MANNING AND LORING,
FOR E. LARKIN, No. 47, CORNHILL.

1805.

FIGURE 10. Mercy Otis Warren did not complete her three-volume history of the American Revolution until a favorable turn in national politics—the election of Democratic-Republican Thomas Jefferson in 1801. Warren's partisan account began appearing four years later; Jefferson ordered copies for his entire cabinet. —Courtesy of American Treasures of the Library of Congress, Washington, DC

> just knowledge of character, to investigate the sources of action; a clear comprehension, to review the combination of causes; and precision of language, to detail the events that have produced the most remarkable revolutions. . . . The study of the human character opens at once a beautiful and a deformed picture of the soul.[23]

The account proceeds from there, laying out epic battles between liberty and tyranny, reason and passion, self-sacrifice and greed from the first rumblings of disaffection in the 1760s to the contentious politics of the 1800s.

Character sketches based on personal acquaintance, with no shortage of critical judgment, gave readers candid introductions to many of the era's most prominent figures. In the parade of heroes and villains, those who led the Revolution and respected its republican values (Samuel Adams, Joseph Warren, James Warren et al.) were uniformly men of integrity, honor, devotion, and sobriety; anyone who opposed or compromised the pursuit of liberty (Francis Bernard, Thomas Hutchinson, John Hancock et al.) were men of intrigue, dark design, self-aggrandizement, and, more often than not, privilege.

First and foremost among the champions of liberty was Mercy's brother James, to whom she devoted more space by far than any individual of the era:

> The celebrated Mr. Otis [is] justly deemed the first martyr to American freedom; and truth will enroll his name among the most distinguished patriots who have expired on the "blood-stained theatre of human action."
>
> This gentleman, whose birth and education was equal to any in the province, possessed an easy fortune, independent principles, a comprehensive genius, strong mind, retentive memory, and great penetration. To these endowments may be added that extensive professional knowledge which at once forms the character of the complete civilian and the able statesman.[24]

The adulation went on from there. The Enlightenment philosophy that had bound Mercy and James together as teenagers and defined their life's work still burned inside her. Recording the history of the Revolution was her chance not only to reinforce those ideals but to ensure due recognition for the first colonist to stand up for them. The next part of her tribute recalls Hamlet's famous soliloquy on human perfection,* naming attributes that her brother and the prince had in common: wit, charm, a silver tongue, and a hot temper:

> In his public speeches, the sire of eloquence, the acumen of argument, and the lively sallies of wit, at once warmed the bosom of the stoic and commanded the admiration of his enemies. To his probity and generosity in the public walks were added the charms of affability and improving converse in private life. His humanity was conspicuous, his sincerity acknowledged, his integrity unimpeached, his honor unblemished, and his patriotism marked with the disinterestedness of the Spartan. Yet he was susceptible of quick feelings and warm passions, which in the ebullitions of zeal for the interest of his country sometimes betrayed him into unguarded epithets that gave his foes an advantage, without benefit to the cause that lay nearest his heart.[25]

Warren's *History* was the culmination of all her efforts to promote freedom, to burnish the family name, and to exert influence in the public arena as a woman. Given its strong political bias and her gender, however, she expected the reception to be tepid. It was. Sales were modest, reviews mixed. One suggested that a woman had no business writing about such matters, faulting Warren for not accepting that "all political attentions lay out of the road of female life."[26] Her most important work was all but forgotten until the twentieth century.

---

* Act II, scene ii: "What a piece of work is man! How noble in reason, how infinite in faculties, in form and moving how express and admirable, in action how like an angel, in apprehension how like a god; the beauty of the world; the paragon of animals."

Among the last of Mercy's acquaintances to read and comment on the *History* was John Adams. Since leaving the presidency, he had retired to Peacefield to lick his political wounds and begin his autobiography. Still, it was telling that almost two years had passed since the publication of Warren's work and that he, who had encouraged the project from the start, had not read it. Their relationship stood at arm's length; Mercy and John had never come to the understanding about friendship and politics that she and Abigail had.

He finally waded into the tomes in 1807, sailing along until reaching the passages about himself in volume 3. "Mr. Adams was undoubtedly a statesman of penetration and ability," the assessment begins, "but his prejudices and his passions were sometimes too strong for his sagacity and judgment." And there was more. Upon his return from Europe, Mercy wrote, citizens perceived that Adams had "relinquished the republican system and forgotten the principles of the American revolution." Then came the zinger, which he had heard before but never from Mercy: "Mr. Adams's former opinions were beclouded by a partiality for monarchy."[27]

Warren thought she was telling it like it was. Adams felt personally attacked. He protested in a long, overheated letter on July 11, pointing out "in the spirit of friendship" a litany of errors that she might correct in a future edition. Never in his life, he insisted, had he "taken one public step or performed one public act from passion or prejudice." He was even more vehement in answering the charge of monarchism: "This fact I deny, and entreat you to mention to me the evidence."[28]

There was little "spirit of friendship" in Adams's rebuttal. Defensiveness gave way to open resentment against the Warrens and their political allies. "If I were to measure out to others the treatment that has been meted to me," he ended, "I could make wild work with some of your party. Shall I indulge in retaliation or not?"[29]

Adams's July 11 missive touched off a two-month war of words, and it was no quasi-war. The salvos shot back and forth between Quincy and Plymouth—ten letters from him and five from her—through the end of August. Mercy, immediately upon receiving his first complaint, responded with cool surprise and veiled hostility. "It was very unexpected to me this day to receive a letter from Mr. Adams," she opened, "nor can I conceive of anything that should occasion a resentment in his bosom." Then came her first jab—an oblique reference to the shift in political climate: "Had not the irritation of the times or some cause unknown have agitated his mind too much, I should not have received a letter couched in such terms as his." Finally, without apology or regret, Mercy defended her observations of Adams. She meant everything she wrote, including allusions to his "natural irritability of temper."[30]

Adams fired back page after page, letter after letter, with a vehemence of someone who felt his reputation at stake. Mercy maintained her composure for most of the exchange and stood by her account of history. Even nearing eighty, however, she was still sensitive to male rebuke. He finally drove her to exasperation:

> ADAMS, JULY 30, 1807: It seems as if your pen could not possibly approach my name without issuing some insinuation of meanness and awkwardness, or, in other plainer words, without venting some spiteful hint.[31]
>
> WARREN, AUGUST 1: If one or the other is done in this instance, it is by your own pen—a pen from which I have lately received so much abuse, unfriendly, ungenerous, and ungentlemanly treatment that my indignation is too much raised to reply to every particular of your dark, unfounded suspicions.[32]
>
> ADAMS, AUGUST 15: Mrs. Warren, it is my opinion and that of all others of any long experience that I have conversed with, that your History has been written to the taste of the nineteenth century, and accommodated to gratify the passions, prejudices, and feelings of the party

> who are now predominated. The characters are not such as you esteemed them in the times when they acted, but such as will please the present fashion.[33]
>
> WARREN, AUGUST 27: I now forbear further remarks. The lines with which you concluded your late correspondence cap the climax of rancor, indecency, and vulgarism. Yet, as an old friend, I pity you; as a Christian, I forgive you; but there must be some acknowledgment of your injurious treatment or some advances to conciliation, to which my mind is ever open, before I can again feel that respect and affection towards Mr. Adams which once existed in the bosom of MERCY WARREN.[34]

There was no conciliation on either side. A lifelong friendship all but ended. Some four years later, at the urging of mutual friend Elbridge Gerry, then the governor, Mercy Warren and John Adams exchanged notes. Abigail Adams traveled alone to Plymouth in late summer 1812, already sixteen years since the last visit, and the two women swapped locks of hair. As a token of friendship, Abigail sent Mercy a custom-made ring that contained intertwined wisps of her own hair and John's. She also had a brooch made in which Mercy's locks had been set; Abigail kept that piece for herself. "I shall hold it precious," Abigail wrote.[35]

Mercy had occasion to contact John in July 1814, this time to ask a favor. She had learned that a Mr. Samuel Barrett was claiming authorship of her 1775 satiric play *The Group.* Did Adams remember it (he had arranged its original publication) and would he vouch for her as the author?[36] Certainly, Adams replied, only one person could have written such a piece. In mid-August 1814, he took a coach to the Boston Athenæum and inscribed a copy with a testimonial of Warren's authorship to his "certain knowledge."[37]

Yet old grudges, political and personal, died hard. Unbeknownst to Mercy, Adams had disparaged her account of the revolution in an April 1813 letter on military policy to Vice

President Elbridge Gerry. "History is not the province of the ladies," he blurted.[38]

In February 1811, fifty years after James Otis Jr. challenged British authority in the Writs of Assistance Case, the mental illness that had debilitated King George III for decades forced him into permanent seclusion and led Parliament to designate his eldest son (later George IV) as prince regent. Britain, locked in commercial warfare with Napoleonic France, had forbidden the United States from trading with the French and impressed thousands of American merchant sailors into the Royal Navy. U.S. patience with the Tory ministry, now in full charge of government affairs, was running thin.

Most of the older-generation American revolutionaries by this time had died or retired from public life. John Hancock passed way in October 1793 after years of failing health. Patrick Henry died in June 1799. Samuel Adams left politics in 1797 after one term as Massachusetts governor and died of his tremor condition in October 1803. Alexander Hamilton succumbed to wounds suffered in his pistol duel with Jefferson's vice president, Aaron Burr, in July 1804.

The fact of James Warren's extended illness and advanced years—he turned eighty-two in 1808—little diminished Mercy's grief at his passing on November 28. He was her husband of fifty-four years and still "the star of her attention." Warren took his place in the family plot on Burial Hill in Plymouth, the gravesite of *Mayflower* passengers and their descendants since the seventeenth century. Mercy chose a line from Psalm 37 for his epitaph: "Mark the perfect man, and behold the upright: for the end of that man is peace." The cemetery was a short walk from the elm-shaded house on Main Street, so Mercy could visit often.

The slightly younger cohort of patriots now at the helm of the federal government—Thomas Jefferson, James Madison, Elbridge

Gerry, and George Clinton—were all Democratic-Republicans and all incensed at Britain's assaults on U.S. nationhood. Merchants and Federalists across Massachusetts opposed armed conflict, but British naval attacks pushed President Madison and public sentiment toward a "second war of American independence." Congress issued its formal declaration on June 18, 1812.

Mercy once again found herself at odds with her neighbors. The town of Plymouth joined other maritime villages in notifying the president that it favored peace.[39] The declaration was purely rhetorical and far from unanimous, but limited militia and financial support from New England crippled the U.S. war effort. British naval forces occupied Maine and used it as a launching point for a naval blockade of Massachusetts in 1814. Towns on the South Shore and Cape Cod faced a constant threat, as British warships hovered off the coast. Small private vessels carrying smuggled goods were captured and destroyed. British fleet commanders were known to extort local communities in exchange for holding their fire.[40]

Mercy Warren remained active in politics and vigilant to her dying day against threats to American freedom. In one of her last letters, dated June 30, 1814, she conveyed the same fortitude she had felt in the early days of the Revolution:

> We are hourly expecting the depredations of the British. I would not have you think me alarmed by womanish fears or the weakness of old age. I am not. I sit very tranquilly in my elbow-chair—patiently awaiting the destination of providence with regard to myself, my family, my friends, and my country.[41]

After the death of brother Joseph Otis in September 1810, Mercy and Samuel Allyne were the last surviving members of their birth family. Samuel Allyne stopped in Plymouth on his way to Washington in the spring of 1814 and, upon leaving, lingered on the path for a last look back. Mercy could tell that he "never expected to behold her faded countenance again in this world."[42] He did not. Samuel Allyne Otis died shortly after arriving home, on April 22.

Mercy looked to providence to spare her the kind of prolonged demise her father and husband had suffered.[43] Her eyesight was completely gone, but her mental faculties were undiminished. She came down violently sick on the night of October 13 and died in the early morning of Wednesday, October 19—the thirty-third anniversary of the British surrender at Yorktown. Her two surviving sons were at her bedside when she passed. "She expired with great calmness and perfect recollection of her mind," Henry wrote later that morning to his Aunt Maria, Joseph's widow in Barnstable. "And thus the *last* frail reed is broken."[44]

Mercy was laid beside husband James on Burial Hill, overlooking Main Street in Plymouth. Nearby in the same cemetery lay the graves of Edward Doty, Richard Warren, Governor William Bradford, and other founders of the 1620 settlement.

# Epilogue

> Those we call the Founders were living men. None was perfect. Each had his human flaws and failings, his weaknesses. They made mistakes, let others down, let themselves down. . . . They were imperfect mortals, human beings.
>
> —DAVID MCCULLOUGH,
> "The Course of Human Events," 2003

Massachusetts, like much of the young republic, burgeoned economically in the period following the War of 1812; social change, however, came more slowly. Whaling and shipbuilding flourished; automated textile mills processed tens of thousands of bales of cotton each year, sustaining the staple crop of the South and the tragedy of human slavery. America's first public high school, the English Classical School in Boston, opened in 1821; it was for boys only. Massachusetts became the first state to impose compulsory smallpox vaccination in 1809, but other states banned the practice and outbreaks of the disease returned; Native American peoples were hit the hardest. The Asylum for the Insane in Charlestown, one of the earliest institutions of its kind in North America, admitted its first patient in October 1818; humane treatment of the mentally ill was a reform movement still decades away.

The maritime villages of Barnstable, which suffered inordinate wartime privation once again, entered their heyday when the British blockade lifted. Salt production brought heightened prosperity. Cod and mackerel fishing thrived. New shipyards served a booming demand. When Barnstable celebrated its two hundredth anniversary in the fall of 1839, according to one local history, "the town was at its acme of strength and beauty; its harbor was busy with shipping and its shores were white with salt works." What never changed was the town's piety and provincialism: "Its many spires of church and school edifices point to God and knowledge," the narrative continued. "The statistics indicate no beggars in the town, no idlers or sots, and only three in jail—and they foreigners."[1]

In Plymouth, the economic mainstays of fishing and shipping likewise revived after the war. The number of locally owned ships devoted to overseas and coastal shipping went from virtually none during the blockade to more than a hundred by 1820; foreign trade skyrocketed. Light manufacturing came to the town as well, with a cotton factory and a rolling mill on the Eel River and the Plymouth Cordage Company (producer of rope and rigging) in a new factory on the waterfront. A high school for girls opened in 1836, with classes held in the lower level of Pilgrim Hall (1824).[2] Mercy Warren would have been delighted even though her two granddaughters were too old to attend. James Warren Jr. served as the town postmaster until his death on August 5, 1821, at age sixty-three. Henry Warren kept busy as customs collector until 1820; he died on July 6, 1828, at age sixty-four.

With one exception, the Warren grandchildren lived well into adulthood. The fifth-born, James, died at age twelve just months prior to his grandmother. The eldest, Marcia Warren (1792–1858), married a lawyer named John Torrey and donated the manuscript of her grandmother's *History* to Harvard. The second-born, Winslow Warren (1795–1870), practiced medicine in Plymouth. Pelham Winslow Warren (1797–1848) was clerk of the Massachusetts House in the 1820s and followed in his father's footsteps as customs collector for the port of Plymouth. Charles

Henry Warren (1798–1874) served as a district attorney, judge, member of the Massachusetts senate, and president of the Boston and Providence Railroad, one of the first in the country.[3]

Notable in later generations of the Warren family were attorney Winslow Warren (1838–1930), a U.S. commissioner and customs collector for the port of Boston, and his son Charles Warren (1868–1954), the Harvard legal scholar and Pulitzer Prize–winning historian who established Mercy's authorship of *Observations on the New Constitution.*

On the Otis side, James the Patriot did not live to meet either of his two grandsons from daughter Mary Otis Lincoln—physician Benjamin Lincoln (1786–1813) or attorney James Otis Lincoln (1787–1818). Neither of them had children.[4] According to records in Lincolnshire, England, daughter Elizabeth Otis Brown lived until April 1839 and bore a son named Leonard (ca. 1777–1848). He married but had no children either, thereby ending James Otis Jr.'s branch of the family.[5]

Among James and Mercy's nieces and nephews, Samuel Allyne's son Harrison Gray Otis (1765–1848)—who had driven his uncle by gig from Andover to Boston in 1782—rose to prominence as a leader of the Federalist Party, U.S. attorney, president of the state legislature, U.S. representative and senator, and third mayor of Boston. Amassing a fortune in Beacon Hill real estate, he became the scion of one of Boston's elite Brahmin clans. One of Harrison's grandsons, James Otis (1836–1898), was active in New York Republican politics and the Gilded Age elite of Manhattan and Newport, Rhode Island. Other names on the family tree include Elisha Otis, founder of the Otis Elevator Company; historian Samuel Eliot Morison; and one more James Otis, a mayor of San Francisco in the 1870s.

Genealogical history and probate records in Massachusetts show that at least three members of the Otis family in the nineteenth century had property placed in custody because of insanity and two more because of debt.[6]

James Otis Jr. and Mercy Otis Warren came from affluence but only in provincial terms. To the wealthy and powerful of Boston, they were outsiders. Their father rose to a modest level of influence and then was shut out. James Jr. pleaded in court on behalf of the merchant class but was never truly *of* it. Mercy came to despise it. Their activities in the 1760s and early 1770s placed them at the center of the rebel movement, but they fired no shots, signed neither the Declaration of Independence nor the U.S. Constitution, and were outsiders to the new federal government.

Despite active roles in the crisis of America's birth, James and Mercy, each in their own way, hesitated, held back, withdrew. They were ordinary people of uncommon family pride, Congregational faith, and a predisposition to mental illness. They were proud, resentful, and dedicated to the cause but skittish. They harbored fears, at times crippling.

James was a living, breathing contradiction: a firebrand lawyer and politician who craved a life of scholarship; a man driven by family pride who loathed his father; a lawyer to the elites who detested slavery and the aristocracy; a rebel agitator who valued social order, the rule of law, and respect for authority. He was the Hamlet of revolutionary America, brilliant and articulate but torn by ambivalence. Swept from the scene in a perfect storm of internal conflict, political circumstance, and physical trauma, he was the patriot the nation forgot.

Mercy was the model of poise and refinement compared with her brother but no less spirited—all qualities reflected in her writing. Yet in many ways she, too, felt pulled in opposite directions. Popular sovereignty and republicanism were like religion to her, while the well-being of her family was her deepest concern. She was moved to action but called her husband and sons home repeatedly. She was harshly critical of political opponents and anyone who crossed her family (Thomas Hutchinson, John Hancock, even John Adams), but she excused and forgave the Otis men (her father, her brother James, her son Winslow) for

FIGURES 11 and 12. Seven-foot bronze statues of James Otis Jr. and Mercy Otis Warren, by the Cape Cod sculptor David Lewis, were erected outside the *Barnstable* County Courthouse on July 4, 1991—proper reminders of the siblings' contributions to America's founding and the relationship that inspired them.
—Courtesy of the author

any failure or shortcoming.[7] She cherished her traditional role as wife and mother but elevated her voice and exerted her influence as a republican woman.

With all their doubts and hesitations, what motivated James and Mercy—and what set them apart from their peers—was their fierce devotion to principle and each other. The ideas they discovered in youth became the guiding lights of an independent United States. James was the first to assert the rights of colonists in the public square; Mercy was one of the purest and most eloquent champions of those freedoms. Without writing or signing any of the founding documents, they played key roles in bringing Enlightenment theories of government to the American experiment.

If John Adams was right that the real Revolution was the "change in principles, opinions, sentiments, and affections of the people," then James Otis Jr. and Mercy Otis Warren must be counted among the nation's true founders.[8] They established ideals and swayed opinion at crucial moments throughout the period; their flaws and failings were no more “human” than those of the giants. Their love and respect for each other, born of childhood companionship and a shared passion for learning, sustained them in ideological battles that helped define and establish the American system of government. They had the courage of their convictions and paid dearly for them—James in physical and mental well-being, Mercy in domestic tranquility, friendships, and place in history.

Their greatest legacies lie, in the end, in the same realm of principles, opinions, and sentiments in which they traded as patriots. The Otises were founders of an ideological tradition whose central tenets galvanize adherents to the present day. In the ongoing national dialogue over the meaning of “liberty”—the ever-evolving *idea* of America—their political descendants have perpetuated a set of precepts that have animated conservative and libertarian thought through changing times: limited government, resistance to taxes, the inviolability of private property, states’ rights over federal authority, and the sanctity of personal freedoms. By the same token, the Otises’ belief in social equality, the common good over personal interest, and ordinary people over the business elite helped lay the groundwork for a political tradition we now identify as liberal or progressive. Their footprints, side by side, are discernible in all of it.

# Acknowledgments

I am grateful to the many individuals and institutions that provided research guidance, access to resources, historical and literary insights, manuscript review, publishing support, and personal encouragement at every stage of this undertaking. The author takes full responsibility for any inaccuracies, misinterpretations, or oversights that future writers on this subject may find cause to rectify.

Materials made available at or through the Massachusetts Historical Society in Boston form the true spine of this book: Mercy Otis Warren Papers, 1709–1841; Otis Family Papers, 1701–1800; Warren-Adams Letters; Adams Papers; period newspapers; and other sources identified in my endnotes. I am thankful to that great institution and its staff for their help in accessing the collections.

Research librarians at the Rare Book and Manuscript Library, Columbia University, were generous with their time and assistance in exploring the original Otis Family Papers, 1687–1868, and the Gay-Otis Family Papers, 1740–1900.

The Pilgrim Hall Museum in Plymouth, Massachusetts, furnished highly welcome transcripts of Mercy's correspondence and pointed me to archival materials at multiple locations.

Directors and staff at the Barnstable Historical Society (BHS) and neighboring Sturgis Library offered firsthand guidance on local resources and history. Special appreciation is reserved for

Nancy Viall Shoemaker, a village historian affiliated with BHS, for sharing her extensive knowledge of the Otis family and area landmarks.

The Perkins and Bostock Libraries at Duke University, treasure troves of secondary source materials, made their stacks, service-center holdings, and study areas available for virtually unlimited use. Among secondary sources, the works of Rosemarie Zagarri, Jeffrey Richards, and Nancy Rubin Stuart were most instrumental in piecing together the Otises' lives and writings. Stuart offered useful tips on navigating Mercy's correspondence.

This work would not see the light of day but for the perseverance and good counsel of my agent, Barbara Collins Rosenberg, and the dedicated efforts of staff at the University of Massachusetts Press: Editor in Chief Matt Becker, EDP Manager Sally Nichols, Production Editor Rachael DeShano, and Copy Editor (extraordinaire) Margaret A. Hogan. I wish to thank as well the two anonymous readers who peer-reviewed a late draft of this book; their recommendations were invaluable.

Manuscript revisions along the way benefited from the comments of gentle readers whom I am pleased to be able to thank in print: Richard Hacker, Jim Wright, Beth Navon, Jonathan Markow, Jane Benbow, Bill Davis, Mary Davis, and Nancy Viall Shoemaker. My appreciation goes out to Michael Hacker for his research assistance, Renee Sall and Linda Solomon for their guidance on publicity and social media, Susan Greendyke of the Massachusetts State House Art Commission, former editorial colleagues at M. E. Sharpe and Grolier/Scholastic, and all the friends and family members whose warm encouragement sustained this undertaking more than they know.

This book is dedicated to my wife, Julie, for everything she has brought to the process—joy, devotion, an open ear, a keen eye, and tolerance for all my time with another family—and to my stepchildren, Liz and Luke, for sharing their lives, their familial bond, and, on occasion during the course of this project, their living space.

# *Notes*

## ABBREVIATIONS

| | |
|---|---|
| *DAJA* | *Diary and Autobiography of John Adams,* 4 vols., ed. L. H. Butterfield (Cambridge, MA: Belknap Press of Harvard University Press, 1961). |
| GOFP | Gay-Otis Family Papers, ca. 1740–1900, University Archives, Rare Book and Manuscript Library, Columbia University, New York. |
| *HRPT* | Mercy Otis Warren, *History of the Rise, Progress, and Termination of the American Revolution,* 3 vols. (Boston: Larkin, 1805). |
| JOJ | James Otis Jr. |
| *JOJW* | *The Collected Political Writings of James Otis,* ed. Richard Samuelson (Indianapolis, IN: Liberty Fund, 2015). Also available online at Library of Liberty, https://oll.libertyfund.org/titles/collected-political-writings. |
| *LPJA* | *Legal Papers of John Adams,* 3 vols., ed. L. Kinvin Wroth and Hiller B. Zobel (Cambridge, MA: Belknap Press of Harvard University Press, 1965). |
| MHS | Massachusetts Historical Society, Boston. |
| MOW | Mercy Otis Warren. |
| MOWP | Mercy Otis Warren Papers, 1709–1841, Massachusetts Historical Society, Boston. |
| *MOWSL* | *Mercy Otis Warren: Selected Letters,* ed. Jeffrey H. Richards and Sharon M. Harris (Athens: University of Georgia Press, 2009). |
| OFP | Otis Family Papers, 1687–1868, University Archives, Rare Book and Manuscript Library, Columbia University, New York. |
| PAP | "The Plays and Poetry of Mercy Otis Warren," handwritten manuscript, MS Am 1354.1, Houghton Library, Harvard University, Cambridge, MA. |
| *PDM* | Mercy Otis Warren, *Poems, Dramatic and Miscellaneous* (Boston: Thomas and Andrews, 1790). |
| *PJA* | *Papers of John Adams,* 18 vols. to date, ed. Robert J. Taylor et al. (Cambridge, MA: Belknap Press of Harvard University Press, 1977–). |

*WAL* *Warren–Adams Letters, Being Chiefly a Correspondence among John Adams, Samuel Adams, and James Warren,* 2 vols. (1743–1777 and 1778–1814), Massachusetts Historical Society *Collections,* vols. 72–73 (1917, 1925).

*WJA* *The Works of John Adams,* 10 vols., ed. Charles Francis Adams (Boston: Little, Brown, 1850–1856).

## INTRODUCTION

1. John Adams to William Tudor, June 1, 1818, *WJA,* 10:317.
2. John Adams to William Tudor, February 25, 1818, *WJA,* 10:291.
3. For an account of efforts in the early nineteenth century to recreate national heroes and the regional rivalries in doing so, see Daniel Boorstin, *The Americans: The National Experience* (New York: Random House, 1965), 2:357–62.
4. There is no documentary evidence that Otis ever used the phrase "Taxation without representation is tyranny."
5. John Adams to James Warren, April 9, 1774, *PJA,* 2:82, emphasis added; Adams to Warren, March 18, 1780, *PJA,* 9:64.
6. Alexander Hamilton to MOW, July 1, 1791, *WAL,* 2:326, emphasis added.
7. Thomas Jefferson to James Warren, March 21, 1801, *The Writings of Thomas Jefferson,* ed. H. A. Washington (New York: J. C. Riker, 1853–1855), 4:376, emphasis added.
8. John Adams to William Tudor, June 1, 1818, *WJA,* 10:317.
9. William Tudor, *The Life of James Otis, of Massachusetts* (Boston: Wells and Lilly, 1823), 488, xviii.
10. Notable essays include Bernard Bailyn's introduction to Otis's political pamphlets in *Pamphlets of the American Revolution, 1750–1776,* ed. Bernard Bailyn (Cambridge, MA: Belknap Press of Harvard University Press, 1965); Ellen Elizabeth Brennan, "James Otis: Recreant and Patriot," *New England Quarterly* 12, no. 4 (December 1939): 691–725; Richard A. Samuelson, "The Constitutional Sanity of James Otis: Resistance Leader and Loyal Subject," *Review of Politics* 61, no. 3 (Summer 1999): 493–523; and James R. Ferguson, "Reason in Madness: The Political Thought of James Otis," *William and Mary Quarterly,* 3rd ser., 36, no. 2 (April 1979): 194–214.

## CHAPTER 1: FLAME OF FIRE, CALM RETREAT

1. For accounts of the Boston fire of 1760, see *Boston Evening-Post,* March 24, 1760, and Brian Deming, *Boston and the Dawn of American Independence* (Yardley, PA: Westholme, 2013), 1–2.
2. For details on the Council Chamber and court proceedings that day, see John Adams to William Tudor, March 29, 1817, *WJA,* 10:245–48.

3. John J. Waters, *The Otis Family in Provincial and Revolutionary Massachusetts* (New York: Norton, 1975), 117.
4. Thomas Weston, *Peter Oliver, the Last Chief Justice of the Superior Court of Judicature of the Province of Massachusetts Bay* (Boston: Cupples, Upham, 1886), 17.
5. Waters, *The Otis Family,* 119.
6. According to Hutchinson, as reported by ally Peter Oliver, JOJ "swore that he would set the province in a flame." Douglas Adair and John A. Schutz, ed., *Peter Oliver's Origin and Progress of the American Rebellion: A Tory View* (San Marino, CA: Huntington Library, 1961), 163. JOJ denied he ever made that statement. JOJ to *Boston Gazette,* April 11, 1763, *JOJW.*
7. Thomas Hutchinson, *History of the Colony and Province of Massachusetts-Bay* (Cambridge, MA: Harvard University Press, 1936), 1:88.
8. Maurice Henry Smith, *The Writs of Assistance Case* (Berkeley: University of California Press, 1978), 264.
9. John Adams, Diary, January 1, 1759, *DAJA,* 3:275.
10. The painting now belongs to a private collection.
11. For Adams's abstract of the arguments at court, ca. April 1761, see *LPJA,* 3:135–44, 139–40 (quotation).
12. Ibid., 3:141.
13. Ibid., 3:142.
14. Ibid., 3:144.
15. Quoted in John Adams to William Tudor, August 16, 1818, *WJA,* 10:349.
16. John Adams to William Tudor, June 1, 1818, *WJA,* 10:314–15.
17. John Adams to William Tudor, March 29, 1817, *WJA,* 10:247–48.
18. Ibid., 10:247.
19. The description of Clifford Farm comes in part from Annie Russell Marble, "Mistress Mercy Warren: Real Daughter of the American Revolution," *New England Magazine* 28 (1903): 166–67.
20. MOW to Hannah Winthrop, February 1773, quoted in Nancy Rubin Stuart, *The Muse of the Revolution: The Secret Pen of Mercy Otis Warren and the Founding of a Nation* (Boston: Beacon, 2008), 26.
21. For dates and details on notable life events for the Warrens, here and elsewhere, see especially Stuart, *Muse;* Rosemarie Zagarri, *Woman's Dilemma: Mercy Otis Warren and the American Revolution,* 2nd ed. (1995; Hoboken, NJ: Wiley, 2015); and Jeffrey H. Richards, *Mercy Otis Warren* (New York: Twayne, 1995).
22. "The sublime": that which is terrifying in art and nature, as articulated in Edmund Burke's treatise *A Philosophical Inquiry into the Origin of Our Ideas of the Sublime and Beautiful* (London: R. and J. Dodsley, 1757). The contradistinction of "beauteous and sublime" in the final paragraph of MOW's poem suggests that she was familiar with Burke's recent essay.

23. MOW, "On Winter," Edmund M. Hayes, "The Private Poems of Mercy Otis Warren," *New England Quarterly* 54, no. 2 (June 1981): 204–5.
24. Ibid., 199–224. For the poems not published in Hayes, see PAP.
25. Stuart, *Muse,* 26.
26. *James Warren,* oil on canvas, ca. 1763, by John Singleton Copley, Museum of Fine Arts, Boston.
27. *Mrs. James Warren (Mercy Otis),* oil on canvas, ca. 1763, by John Singleton Copley, Museum of Fine Arts, Boston.
28. *HRPT,* 1:27.
29. MOW, "To J Warren Esqr," Hayes, "The Private Poems," 206–7.
30. JOJ to MOW, April 11, 1766, *WAL,* 1:2.
31. Ibid.

## CHAPTER 2: ROOT AND FIBER

1. Henry David Thoreau, *Cape Cod* (Boston: Ticknor and Fields, 1865), 252.
2. On the natural landscape and early settlement of Barnstable, see Simeon Deyo, *History of Barnstable County, Massachusetts* (New York: H. W. Blake, 1890), chap. 19, and Donald Grant Trayser, *Barnstable: Three Centuries of a Cape Cod Town* (Hyannis, MA: Goss, 1939).
3. On transportation and mail service in early Barnstable, see Deyo, *History of Barnstable County,* 110, 122–23.
4. John J. Waters, *The Otis Family in Provincial and Revolutionary Massachusetts* (New York: Norton, 1975), 73.
5. Rosemarie Zagarri, *A Woman's Dilemma: Mercy Otis Warren and the American Revolution,* 2nd ed. (1995; Hoboken, NJ: Wiley, 2015), 7.
6. Alice Brown, *Mercy Otis Warren* (New York: Charles Scribner's Sons, 1896), 11.
7. Deyo, *History of Barnstable County,* 11.
8. On the early economy of Barnstable, see Deyo, *History of Barnstable County,* and Trayser, *Barnstable.*
9. On John Otis II and John Otis III, see Waters, *The Otis Family,* chaps. 2–3; William Augustus Otis, *A Genealogical and Historical Memoir of the Otis Family in America* (Chicago: W. A. Otis, 1924), 55–56, 70–71; and John A. Schutz, *Legislators of the Massachusetts General Court, 1691–1780: A Biographical Dictionary* (Boston: Northeastern University Press, 1997), 300.
10. Otis, *Genealogical and Historical Memoir,* 70.
11. For more on the West Parish of Barnstable Congregational Church and 1717 meetinghouse, see "West Parish Congregational Church, Barnstable Massachusetts," Historic Structures, http://www.historic-structures.com, and "Historical Highlights of the 1717 Meetinghouse," 1717 Meetinghouse Foundation, http://www.1717meetinghouse.org.

12. On Reverend Russell, the West Parish, and the Great Awakening, see Waters, *The Otis Family,* 73; "History Happens Here," West Parish of Barnstable, https://westparish.org; and Walter R. Goehring, *The West Parish Church of Barnstable: An Historical Sketch* (West Barnstable, MA: West Parish Memorial Foundation, 1959).
13. Waters, *The Otis Family,* 58–60.
14. On the domination of a few local families, see ibid., 61; Deyo, *History of Barnstable County,* 400; and Amos Otis, *Genealogical Notes of Barnstable Families* (Barnstable, MA: Goss, 1890).
15. Harriet Beecher Stowe, *Oldtown Folks,* in *The Writings of Harriet Beecher Stowe,* Riverside ed. (Boston: Houghton Mifflin, 1896), 9:261.
16. On James Sr.'s youth and early adult life, see Waters, *The Otis Family,* chap. 4.
17. On Mary Allyne and her family, see ibid., 63, and Katharine Susan Anthony, *First Lady of the Revolution: The Life of Mercy Otis Warren* (Garden City, NY: Doubleday, 1958), 22–23.
18. On the Otis family lifestyle, see Waters, *The Otis Family,* 65, and Nancy Rubin Stuart, *The Muse of the Revolution: The Secret Pen of Mercy Otis Warren and the Founding of a Nation* (Boston: Beacon, 2008), 11.
19. On the family estate and furnishings, see Trayser, *Barnstable,* 445; Waters, *The Otis Family,* 64 (quotations); Stuart, *Muse,* 11; and Zagarri, *Woman's Dilemma,* 8.
20. Waters, *The Otis Family,* 98–99; Anthony, *First Lady,* 26.
21. Henry C. Kittredge, *Cape Cod: Its People and Their History* (Boston: Houghton Mifflin, 1930), 64.
22. Leonard H. Smith and Norma H. Smith, *Vital Records of the Town of Barnstable and Sandwich: An Authorized Facsimile Reproduction of Records Published Serially, 1901–1935* (Baltimore: Clearfield, 1976), 81. On the question of whether JOJ owned slaves as an adult, see J. L. Bell, "James Otis, Jr., and Slavery Revisited," Boston 1775, June 8, 2017, http://boston1775.blogspot.com. Bell concludes that there is no reliable evidence.
23. On Otis Sr.'s rise in local politics, see Waters, *The Otis Family,* chap. 4, and Zagarri, *Woman's Dilemma,* 29.
24. Waters, *The Otis Family,* 75.
25. On profiteering by Otis Sr. in the Seven Years' War, see Waters, *The Otis Family,* 101–2.
26. Otis, *Genealogical and Historical Memoir,* 83.
27. John Adams, *DAJA,* June 8, 1762, 1:227.

## CHAPTER 3: CHILDHOOD BONDS

1. For more on the "borning room" and birthing practices in colonial New England, see Richard W. Wertz and Dorothy C. Wertz, *Lying-In: A History*

of *Childbirth in America* (New Haven, CT: Yale University Press, 1989), 13, and Katharine Susan Anthony, *First Lady of the Revolution: The Life of Mercy Otis Warren* (Garden City, NY: Doubleday, 1958), 25.

2. C. Dallett Hemphill, *Siblings: Brothers and Sisters in American History* (New York: Oxford University Press, 2011), 2; Wertz and Wertz, *Lying-In*, 2–3.
3. Wertz and Wertz, *Lying-In*, 19; Rosemarie Zagarri, *Woman's Dilemma: Mercy Otis Warren and the American Revolution*, 2nd ed. (1995; Hoboken, NJ: Wiley, 2015), 8.
4. Wertz and Wertz, *Lying-In*, 2.
5. Anthony, *First Lady*, 33.
6. The surviving samples include an elaborately embroidered card-table cover on display at Pilgrim Hall in Plymouth and a finely stitched silk pincushion archived at the MHS.
7. *Mrs. James Otis (Mary Allyne Otis)*, oil on canvas, 1760, by John Singleton Copley, Roland P. Murdock Collection, Wichita Art Museum, Wichita, Kansas.
8. MOW to Janet Livingston Montgomery, March 18, 1779, *MOWSL*, 110.
9. For relevant background on the colonial family, see Stephanie Coontz, *The Social Origins of Private Life: A History of American Families, 1600–1900* (New York: Verso, 1988), 78, 82; James Ciment, ed., *Colonial America: An Encyclopedia of Social, Political, Cultural, and Economic History* (Armonk, NY: M. E. Sharpe, 2006), 2:330; and Zagarri, *Woman's Dilemma*, 8–9.
10. MOW to James Warren, February 1775, MOWP.
11. Quoted in Zagarri, *Woman's Dilemma*, 11.
12. John J. Waters, *The Otis Family in Provincial and Revolutionary Massachusetts* (New York: Norton, 1975), 90.
13. On the separation of brothers and sisters in colonial families, see Hemphill, *Siblings*, 26–27.
14. For more on reading and literacy in colonial New England, see Ciment, *Colonial America*, 3:724; Zagarri, *Woman's Dilemma*, 10–11; and Jeffrey H. Hacker, ed., *Colonial Roots: Settlement to 1783* (Armonk, NY: M. E. Sharpe, 2014), 145.
15. On schools and schooling in Barnstable, see Frederick Freeman, *The History of Cape Cod: The Annals of Barnstable County and of Its Several Towns* (Boston: Rand and Avery, 1860–62), 2:291–97, and Simeon Deyo, *History of Barnstable County, Massachusetts* (New York: H. W. Blake, 1890), 376.
16. John Clark Ridpath, *James Otis, The Pre-Revolutionist* (Milwaukee, WI: Campbell, 1898), 16.
17. Alice Brown, *Mercy Otis Warren* (New York: Charles Scribner's Sons, 1896), 25.

18. No known manuscripts or transcripts of Reverend Russell's sermons survive to the present day, but for their influence on MOW, see Anthony, *First Lady*, 32.
19. Ray Raphael, "The Righteous Revolution of Mercy Otis Warren," Gilder Lehrman Institute of American History, AP U.S. History Guide, www.gilderlehman.org.
20. On Whig foundations of the American revolutionary movement and Declaration of Independence, see Lee Ward, "Revolutionary Constitutionalism: Laboratories of Radical Whiggism," in *The Politics of Liberty in England and Revolutionary America* (New York: Cambridge University Press, 2004), 396–425; G. H. Guttridge, *English Whiggism and the American Revolution* (Berkeley: University of California Press, 1942); and Linda C. Raeder, "Edmund Burke: Old Whig," *Political Science Reviewer* 35, no. 1 (Fall 2006): 115–31.
21. Brown, *Mercy Otis Warren*, 19–20.
22. Ibid., 20, 25.
23. Ibid., 19.

## CHAPTER 4: PROSPECTS, POSSIBILITIES, AND CONTAGIOUS ENTHUSIASMS

1. Andrew Schlesinger, *Veritas: Harvard College and the American Experience* (Chicago: Ivan R. Dee, 2005), 28.
2. Harvard University, *Harvard University Handbook: An Official Guide to the Grounds, Buildings, Libraries, Museums, and Laboratories* (Cambridge, MA: Harvard University Press, 1936), 15–26; *Harvard College in 1740*, engraving by William Burgis, Library of Congress (LC-USZ62-2105).
3. Harvard University Research Guides, 17th/18th Centuries Curriculum Overview, https://guides.library.harvard.edu.
4. John J. Waters, *The Otis Family in Provincial and Revolutionary Massachusetts* (New York: Norton, 1975), 11; Clifford K. Shipton, "James Otis," in *Sibley's Harvard Graduates*, vol. 11, *1741–1745* (Boston: Massachusetts Historical Society, 1960), 584.
5. Waters, *The Otis Family*, 111n3.
6. James Otis Sr. to JOJ, August 1, 1772, GOFP.
7. Will of James Otis Sr. (attested copy), April 21, 1774, GOFP.
8. Shipton, "James Otis," 247.
9. Waters, *The Otis Family*, 112.
10. Harvard University Research Guides, 17th/18th Centuries Curriculum Overview; Waters, *The Otis Family*, 111.
11. Shipton, "James Otis," 247.
12. The oft-repeated anecdote of the fiddle first appeared in William Tudor, *The Life of James Otis, of Massachusetts* (Boston: Wells and Lilly, 1823),

8–9, possibly on the basis of a firsthand account; the addition that James never played again comes from John Clark Ridpath, *James Otis: The Pre-Revolutionist* (Milwaukee, WI: Campbell, 1898), 17.

13. Estimates of the crowd size range from fifteen to thirty thousand in various sources.
14. "This Month in Harvard History," *Harvard Gazette,* October 14, 2004; Samuel Atkins Eliot, *Sketch of the History of Harvard College* (Boston: Little and Brown, 1848), 65.
15. Schlesinger, *Veritas,* 30.
16. Shipton, "James Otis," 247.
17. Waters, *The Otis Family*, 136.
18. JOJ to James Otis Sr., 1760, quoted in Tudor, *Life*, 12; JOJ to *Boston Gazette,* January 11, 1762, *JOJW.*
19. John Locke, *Two Treatises of Government* (London: Awnsham Churchill, 1690), 2nd treatise, chap. 2, sec. 4; chap. 7, sec. 87.
20. On the Nathan Prince incident, see "Papers of Nathan Prince, 1714–1747," Biographical Note, Harvard University Archives, https://hollisarchives.lib.harvard.edu.
21. JOJ to James Otis Sr., April 4, 1743, OFP.
22. On Harvard commencement, see Schlesinger, *Veritas,* 25–26; Katharine Susan Anthony, *First Lady of the Revolution: The Life of Mercy Otis Warren* (Garden City, NY: Doubleday, 1958), 36–37; and Alice Brown, *Mercy Otis Warren* (New York: Charles Scribner's Sons, 1896), 28–29.
23. MOW to James Warren, April 4, 1778, MOWP.
24. The entirely plausible view of Waters, *The Otis Family*, 113.
25. JOJ to James Otis Sr., 1760, quoted in Tudor, *Life,* 12.
26. Shipton, "James Otis," 302; Waters, *The Otis Family*, 113.
27. JOJ to James Otis Sr., 1760, quoted in Tudor, *Life,* 10.
28. Quoted in John Adams to William Tudor, June 5, 1817, *WJA,* 10:264–65.
29. Waters, *The Otis Family*, 114.
30. Joseph Otis to James Otis Sr., January 8, 1749, OFP.
31. Anthony, *First Lady,* 40.
32. See Waters, *The Otis Family*, chap. 5.
33. On the delegation to Maine, see Andrew Stephen Walmsley, *Thomas Hutchinson and the Origins of the American Revolution* (New York: New York University Press, 1999), 27.
34. Ridpath, *James Otis,* 22.
35. Waters, *The Otis Family*, 115; John R. Galvin, *Three Men of Boston* (New York: Crowell, 1976), 15; Rosemarie Zagarri, *Woman's Dilemma: Mercy Otis Warren and the American Revolution,* 2nd ed. (1995; Hoboken, NJ: Wiley, 2015), 14.

36. On the Halifax case, see Galvin, *Three Men,* 15, and Shipton, "James Otis," 249.
37. Quoted in John Adams, Autobiography, *WJA,* 2:124.
38. Quoted in Tudor, *Life,* 36; Shipton, "James Otis," 249. (Hutchinson often referred to himself in the third person.)
39. JOJ to *Boston Gazette,* May 13, 1765, *JOJW.*
40. Shipton, "James Otis," 248.
41. Waters, *The Otis Family,* 116.
42. Galvin, *Three Men,* 15; Waters, *The Otis Family,* 115–16.
43. Shipton, "James Otis," 249.
44. Tudor, *Life,* 10.
45. On the courtship and wedding, see Zagarri, *Woman's Dilemma,* 16–17.
46. The insight of ibid., 18.
47. Tudor, *Life,* 20; Shipton, "James Otis," 248.
48. Waters, *The Otis Family,* 116.
49. Shipton, "James Otis," 248; Anthony, *First Lady,* 46.
50. *An Historical Catalog of the Old South Church* (Boston: N.p., 1883), membership and covenant lists; Shipton, "James Otis," 248.
51. Anthony, *First Lady,* 47.
52. On *The Rudiments of Latin Prosody* and its Greek sequel, see Tudor, *Life,* 15–16; Anthony, *First Lady,* 47; Galvin, *Three Men,* 14; and Shipton, "James Otis," 249.
53. Anthony, *First Lady,* 47.
54. Shipton, "James Otis," 248.
55. Thomas Hutchinson, *The History of the Colony and Province of Massachusetts-Bay* (Cambridge, MA: Harvard University Press, 1936), 1:iii, ii; 2:342.
56. Quoted in "Liberty! The American Revolution," PBS, www.pbs.org.
57. *HRPT,* 1:79.
58. JOJ, *Boston Gazette,* January 31, 1763, *JOJW.*
59. Bernard Bailyn, *The Ordeal of Thomas Hutchinson* (Cambridge, MA: Belknap Press of Harvard University Press, 1974), 16n, 129, 244.
60. On the land bank issue, see Galvin, *Three Men,* 40–42.
61. *Diary and Letters of His Excellency Thomas Hutchinson, Esq.,* ed. Peter Orlando Hutchinson (Boston: Houghton Mifflin, 1884–86), 1:53.
62. Galvin, *Three Men,* 18, 17.
63. Walmsley, *Thomas Hutchinson,* 12.
64. James Otis Sr., memorandum, April 15, 1757, OFP, quoted in Waters, *The Otis Family,* 105.
65. On JOJ's growing involvement in politics, see Galvin, *Three Men,* 16, and Waters, *The Otis Family,* 116.

66. Waters, *The Otis Family*, 105–6. On the sale of whaleboats specifically, see Thomas Pownall to James Otis Sr., August 25, 1757, OFP.
67. Galvin, *Three Men*, 17.
68. Hutchinson, ed., *Diary and Letters*, 1:65.
69. Galvin, *Three Men*, 20, citing *Boston Gazette*, April 11, 1763.
70. According to Hutchinson, JOJ threatened to "set the province in a flame" (see chap. 1, note 6).
71. JOJ to *Boston Gazette*, April 4, 11, 1763, *JOJW*.

## CHAPTER 5: LOCKE STEP

1. On John Winslow's ancestry and his relation to James Warren, see Maria White Bryant, *Genealogy of Edward Winslow of the Mayflower and His Descendants* (New Bedford, MA: E. Anthony, 1915).
2. MOW, "A Sigh," Edmund M. Hayes, "The Private Poems of Mercy Otis Warren," *New England Quarterly* 54, no. 2 (June 1981): 210.
3. MOW to Winslow Warren, March 25, 1780, *MOWSL*, 131.
4. John Locke, *An Essay Concerning Human Understanding* (London: Awnsham Churchill, 1690), book 4, chap. 19 ("Of Enthusiasm"), para. 4.
5. MOW, "A Thought on the Inestimable Blessing of Reason," Hayes, "The Private Poems," 213–14.
6. MOW, "An Address to the Supreme Being," ibid., 223–24.
7. Locke, *An Essay Concerning Human Understanding*, book 2, chap. 1: "Let us then suppose the mind to be, as we say, white paper, void of all characters"; Locke, *Some Thoughts Concerning Education* (London: A. and J. Churchill, 1693), paras. 41–43, 64–66, 139, 200, 147.
8. See especially MOW to James Warren, February 11, 1772, *MOWSL*, 67.
9. Juliana Seymour, *On Management and Education of Children: A Series of Letters Written to a Niece* (London: J. Roberts, 1754).
10. MOW to Abigail Adams, July 25, 1773, MOWP.
11. MOW to Winslow Warren, December 4, 1779, *MOWSL*, 118.
12. On sibling relationships in the colonial period, see C. Dallett Hemphill, *Siblings: Brothers and Sisters in American History* (New York: Oxford University Press, 2011), 32–41.
13. Thomas Hutchinson, *History of the Colony and Province of Massachusetts-Bay* (Cambridge, MA: Harvard University Press, 1936), 3:166.
14. Good summaries of the political issues and maneuverings can be found in John J. Waters, *The Otis Family in Provincial and Revolutionary Massachusetts* (New York: Norton, 1975), 138–43, and John R. Galvin, *Three Men of Boston* (New York: Crowell, 1976), chap. 3.
15. JOJ to *Boston Gazette*, December 21, 1761.

16. Thomas Hutchinson to William Bollan, April 23, 1762, *The Correspondence of Thomas Hutchinson*, ed. John W. Tyler and Elizabeth Dubrulle (Boston: Colonial Society of Massachusetts, 2014–), 1:162.
17. JOJ, *A Vindication of the Conduct of the House*, in *JOJW*, 84, 86.
18. On the role of pamphlets in the revolutionary movement, see Bernard Bailyn, *Pamphlets of the American Revolution, 1750–1776* (Cambridge, MA: Belknap Press of Harvard University Press, 1965), and Gordon Wood, ed., *The American Revolution: Writings from the Pamphlet Debate, 1764–1772* (New York: Library of America, 2015).
19. John Adams to William Tudor, April 5, 1818, *WJA*, 10:310.
20. Typically in pseudonymous letters, e.g., *Boston Evening-Post*, March 28, 1763.
21. Samuel Allyne Otis to Joseph Otis, February 14, 1763, OFP. Samuel was not joining in the derision. In this and another letter on March 18, he assured Joseph and the rest of the family that JOJ's allies would stand by him despite such ridicule.
22. For especially compelling arguments to this effect, see Andrew Stephen Walmsley, *Thomas Hutchinson and the Origins of the American Revolution* (New York: New York University Press, 1999), 40–41, and Waters, *The Otis Family*, chaps. 6–7.
23. Waters, *The Otis Family*, 131.
24. Walmsley, *Thomas Hutchinson*, 41.
25. *Boston Evening-Post*, March 21, July 11, 1763.
26. Samuel Adams, "Instructions of the Town of Boston to its Representatives in the General Court," May 1763, *The Writings of Samuel Adams*, ed. Harry Alonzo Cushing (New York: G. P. Putnam's Sons, 1904), 1:5.
27. Bailyn, *Pamphlets*, 414.
28. JOJ, *The Rights of the British Colonies Asserted and Proved*, in *JOJW*, 158, 140.
29. Ibid., 149.
30. For an insightful analysis of the conflict in JOJ's thinking, see James R. Ferguson, "Reason in Madness: The Political Thought of James Otis," *William and Mary Quarterly*, 3rd series, 36, no. 2 (April 1979): 194–214.
31. JOJ, *Rights of the British Colonies Asserted and Proved*, 140.
32. George Henry Moore, *Notes on the History of Slavery in Massachusetts* (New York: Appleton, 1866), 51.
33. JOJ, *Rights of the British Colonies Asserted and Proved*, 120.
34. *HRPT*, 1:27.
35. JOJ, *A Vindication of the British Colonies*, in *JOJW*, 186.
36. Richard A. Samuelson's explanation for much of the contradiction in JOJ's writings, as argued in "The Constitutional Sanity of James Otis: Resistance Leader and Loyal Subject," *Review of Politics* 61, no. 3 (Summer 1999): 493–523.

37. *Boston Evening-Post,* May 13, 1765. See also J. L. Bell, "Jemmy's in the Caucus, and Jemmy's with the Reps," Boston 1775, January 12, 2008, http://boston1775.blogspot.com.
38. John Adams to William Tudor, March 11, 1818, *WJA,* 10:296.
39. William Gordon, *The History of the Rise, Progress, and Establishment of the Independence of the United States of America* (New York: Samuel Campbell, 1801), 1:119–20.
40. *HRPT,* 1:31.
41. The events of August 14 are well described in Robert Middlekauff, *The Glorious Cause: The American Revolution, 1763–1789,* rev. ed. (New York: Oxford University Press, 2005), 93–94, and Galvin, *Three Men,* 96–98.
42. Thomas Hutchinson to Richard Jackson, August 30, 1765, Tyler and Dubrulle, eds., *Correspondence,* 1:291.
43. Ibid.
44. *WJA,* 1:71.
45. Galvin, *Three Men,* 135.
46. Josiah Quincy, *Reports of Cases Argued and Adjudged in the Superior Court of Judicature of the Province of Massachusetts Bay between 1761 and 1772* (Boston: Little, Brown, 1865), 172.
47. *Peter Oliver's Origin and Progress of the American Rebellion: A Tory View,* ed. Douglas Adair and John A. Schutz (Stanford, CA: Stanford University Press, 1962), 52.
48. John C. Miller, *Origins of the American Revolution* (Boston: Little, Brown, 1943), 145; Galvin, *Three Men,* 105.
49. Thomas Hutchinson to Richard Jackson, April 21, November 16, 1766, Tyler and Dubrulle, eds., *Correspondence,* 1:427, 470.
50. JOJ, *Considerations on Behalf of the Colonists,* in *JOJW,* 242, 243, 254.
51. Francis Bernard to Thomas Pownall, October 19, 1765, quoted in Galvin, *Three Men,* 112.

## CHAPTER 6: ANXIOUS WEARISOME DAYS AND NIGHTS

1. JOJ to James Otis Sr., January 8, 1766, OFP.
2. Ibid.
3. James Otis Sr. to Joseph Otis, February 4, 1766, OFP.
4. In the earliest known correspondence between them, dated April 11, 1766, Jemmy included the following in his discussion of events in Boston: "I have written diverse letters within the period you mention and will write you many more." JOJ to MOW, *WAL,* 1:1–2.
5. William H. Davis, *History of the Town of Plymouth, with a Sketch of the Origin and Growth of Separatism* (Philadelphia: J. W. Lewis, 1885), 82–83.
6. MOW, "To J Warren Esqr," Edmund M. Hayes, "The Private Poems of Mercy Otis Warren," *New England Quarterly* 54, no. 2 (June 1981): 206–7.
7. MOW to John Adams, December 16, 1778, *MOWSL,* 105.

8. John Adams, *DAJA*, January 16, 1770, 1:349.
9. MOW to James Warren, January 10, 1776, *MOWSL*, 62. The full comment reads, "a weak infatuated woman who has heretofore brought innumerable difficulties upon her own family." In this case, "infatuated" means fatuous or foolish. The comment, according to volume editor Jeffrey H. Richards, "probably means Ruth Cunningham Otis, . . . [was] a person much disliked by MOW and the other Otises" (62).
10. "John Hampden to William Pym: Essays from the *Boston Gazette*," January 27, 1766, *JOJW*, part 3, sec. 7. See also John R. Galvin, *Three Men of Boston* (New York: Crowell, 1976), 118–20.
11. *HRPT*, 1:34.
12. Declaratory Act, para. 1., "Great Britain: Parliament—The Declaratory Act; March 18, 1766," The Avalon Project, Lillian Goldman Law Library, Yale Law School, https://avalon.law.yale.edu.
13. *Boston Evening-Post*, June 9, 1766 (supplement), quoted in Ellen Elizabeth Brennan, "James Otis: Recreant and Patriot," *New England Quarterly* 12, no. 4 (December 1939): 722.
14. Thomas Hutchinson to William Bollan, June 11, 1766, *The Correspondence of Thomas Hutchinson*, ed. John W. Tyler and Elizabeth Dubrulle (Boston: Colonial Society of Massachusetts, 2014–), 1:439.
15. JOJ to MOW, April 11, 1766, *WAL*, 1:1–2.
16. On sisters Eliza and Abigail and their death dates, see Hayes, "The Private Poems of Mercy Otis Warren," 215n.
17. JOJ to MOW, April 11, 1766, *WAL*, 1:1–2.
18. Clifford K. Shipton, "James Otis," in *Sibley's Harvard Graduates*, vol. 11, *1741–1745* (Boston: Massachusetts Historical Society, 1960), 269.
19. On assembly elections and colonial politics in 1766, see Galvin, *Three Men*, 129–37, and John J. Waters, *The Otis Family in Provincial and Revolutionary Massachusetts* (New York: Norton, 1975), 158–63.
20. Waters, *The Otis Family*, 161, citing JOJ to Robert Treat Paine, August 14, 1766.
21. Galvin, *Three Men*, 137.
22. Thomas Hutchinson to Thomas Pownall, December 8, 1766, Tyler and Dubrulle, eds., *Correspondence*, 1:487.
23. Francis Bernard to the Earl of Shelburne, December 22, 1766, *The Papers of Francis Bernard*, ed. Colin Nicolson (Boston: Colonial Society of Massachusetts, 2007–15), 3:276.
24. *HRPT*, 1:45.
25. John Dickinson to JOJ, December 5, 1767, *HRPT*, 1:412–13.
26. Ibid., 1:414.
27. A photograph of the front page, *Boston Chronicle*, December 21, 1767, can be viewed at "The Boston Chronicle," MHS Collections Online, http://www.masshist.org.

28. *HRPT,* 1:54.
29. A transcription of the original text and image of the letter as it appeared in the *Journals of the House of Representatives of Massachusetts* (Boston: Green and Russell, [1767–68]), can be found in the MHS Collections Online.
30. Quoted in William Tudor, *The Life of James Otis, of Massachusetts* (Boston: Wells and Lilly, 1823), 317.
31. This account of the *Liberty* incident relies heavily on Galvin, *Three Men,* chap. 14.
32. Quoted in Ellen Chase, *The Beginnings of the American Revolution: Based on Contemporary Letters, Diaries, and Other Documents* (New York: Baker and Taylor, 1910), 97.
33. On JOJ's speech, the reaction to it, and the delivery of documents to Governor Bernard, see Galvin, *Three Men,* 158–59, and Shipton, "James Otis," 274.
34. JOJ's rant is recounted in Francis Bernard to the Earl of Hillsborough, September 9, 1768, *Papers of Francis Bernard,* 4:299.
35. Ibid., 297.
36. Lord Hillsborough, secret letter to General Thomas Gage, commander of British forces in North America, June 8, 1768, *Papers of Francis Bernard,* 4:373.
37. *HRPT,* 1:65.
38. Elizabeth Mayhew to Thomas Hollis, July 27, 1766, William H. Bond, "Letters from Thomas Hollis of Lincoln's Inn to Andrew Eliot," *Proceedings of the Massachusetts Historical Society* 99 (1987): 88.
39. Benjamin Rush, *A Memorial Containing Travels through Life or Sundry Incidents in the Life Dr. Benjamin Rush* (Philadelphia: Louis Alexander Riddle, 1905), 102.
40. Galvin, *Three Men,* 205, 218.
41. JOJ to MOW, April 11, 1766, *WAL,* 1:1–2.
42. Waters, *The Otis Family,* 181.
43. Simeon Deyo, *History of Barnstable County, Massachusetts* (New York: H. W. Blake, 1890), 11.

## CHAPTER 7: A COMET PASSES

1. For more on taverns, coffeehouses, and pubs in colonial Massachusetts, see David W. Conroy, *In Public Houses: Drink and the Revolution of Authority in Colonial Massachusetts* (Chapel Hill: University of North Carolina Press, 1995), and Sharon V. Salinger, *Taverns and Drinking in Early America* (Baltimore: Johns Hopkins University Press, 2002).
2. John Adams to Benjamin Rush, August 28, 1811, *WJA,* 9:637.
3. On the Crocker Tavern, see "History," Crocker Tavern House, https://crockertavern.com.

4. The St. John's Lodge, "the oldest duly constituted and chartered Masonic lodge in the Americas," was founded at the Bunch-of-Grapes on July 30, 1733. Jeremiah Gridley was master of the lodge at the time he sponsored JOJ in the early 1750s. See "Our History," St. John's Lodge, https://www.saintjohnsboston1733.com.
5. Samuel Adams Drake, *Our Colonial Homes* (Boston: Lee and Shepard, 1894), 155.
6. *Boston Chronicle,* August 17, 1769.
7. *Boston Gazette,* April 17, 1769 (supplement).
8. Quoted in John Clark Ridpath, *James Otis, The Pre-Revolutionist* (Milwaukee, WI: Campbell, 1898), 73–74; Ellen Chase, *The Beginnings of the American Revolution: Based on Contemporary Letters, Diaries, and Other Documents* (New York: Baker and Taylor, 1910), 129.
9. The event is recounted in Clifford K. Shipton, "James Otis," in *Sibley's Harvard Graduates,* vol. 11, *1741–1745* (Boston: Massachusetts Historical Society, 1960), 277, and John R. Galvin, *Three Men of Boston* (New York: Crowell, 1976), 179.
10. *Boston Gazette,* August 21, 1769.
11. On the events of August 14, 1769, see "The True Sons of Liberty of Massachusetts Gather to Celebrate the Fourth Anniversary of the Stamp Act Riots, 14 August 1769," MHS Object of the Month, August 2015, http://www.masshist.org.
12. "New England Weather, Summer 1769," Colonial Sense: The Web Site for All Things Colonial, http://www.colonialsense.com.
13. *Boston Gazette,* September 4, 1769, signed advertisement.
14. Ibid.
15. On the two meetings, see John Adams, *DAJA,* September 2, 1769, 1:342.
16. John Adams, *DAJA,* September 3, 1769, 1:343.
17. JOJ to the *Boston Gazette,* September 4, 1769.
18. John Adams, *DAJA,* September 4, 1769, 1:343.
19. Galvin, *Three Men,* 185; Ray Raphael, *Founders: The People Who Brought You a Nation* (New York: New Press, 2009), 77.
20. Galvin, *Three Men,* 185, citing *Letters and Diary of John Rowe: Boston Merchant, 1759–1762, 1764–1779* (Boston: W. B. Clark, 1903), 191; Edward L. Pierce, "Diary of John Rowe," *Proceedings of the Massachusetts Historical Society,* 2nd series, 10 (1895–96): 59.
21. For accounts of the coffeehouse altercation, see *Boston Gazette,* September 11, 18, 1769 (John Gridley's affidavit of testimony); *Boston Evening-Post,* September 11, 1769; Robert Middlekauff, *The Glorious Cause: The American Revolution, 1763–1789,* rev. ed. (New York: Oxford University Press, 2005), 205–6; Raphael, *Founders,* 77–78; Shipton, "James Otis," 278; and Galvin, *Three Men,* 185–87.

22. *London Chronicle,* November 4, 1769.
23. Samuel Adams, "Article Signed 'An Impartialist,' *Boston Gazette,* September 25, 1779," *The Writings of Samuel Adams,* ed. Harry Alonzo Cushing (New York: G. P. Putnam's Sons, 1904), 1:383–85.
24. Widely attributed to John Adams but uncorroborated; the earliest identifiable source is Katharine Susan Anthony, *First Lady of the Revolution: The Life of Mercy Otis Warren* (Garden City, NY: Doubleday, 1958), 70.
25. "An Impartialist," *Boston Gazette,* September 11, 1769.
26. MOW to JOJ, September 10, 1769, *MOWSL,* 3–5. The copy of this letter in MOW's letterbook, part of the MOWP, was written out by her son James as her amanuensis and carries the incorrect date of September 10, 1770.

## CHAPTER 8: PRIVATION TO A FRIEND

1. John Adams, *DAJA,* October 19, 1769, 1:344. JOJ was "conversible enough, but not extravagant," Adams continued, "not rough, nor sour."
2. Meeting of November 13, 1769, *Report of the Record Commissioners of the City of Boston, 1758 to 1769* (Boston: Rockwell and Churchill, 1886), 301.
3. Quoted in Thomas Hutchinson to Francis Bernard, November 27, 1769, *The Correspondence of Thomas Hutchinson,* ed. John W. Tyler and Elizabeth Dubrulle (Boston: Colonial Society of Massachusetts, 2014–), 2:421.
4. John Adams, *DAJA,* January 16, 1770, 1:348.
5. Some "opposition to reason," John Locke wrote, "is found in most men." The root cause, except for persons "under the power of an unruly passion" and "fit for Bedlam," is what he called "a wrong connection of ideas." Locke, *An Essay Concerning Human Understanding* (London: Awnsham Churchill, 1690), book 2, chap. 23.
6. On attitudes toward and treatment of the mentally ill in colonial America, see Mary Ann Jimenez, *Changing Faces of Madness: Early American Attitudes and Treatment of the Insane* (Hanover, NH: University Press of New England, 1987).
7. John Adams, *DAJA,* February 26, 1770, 1:350.
8. *Boston Gazette,* March 12, 1770.
9. John Rowe, Diary, March 16, 1770, *Proceedings of the Massachusetts Historical Society,* 2nd series, 10 (1896): 74. A Boston merchant and selectman, Rowe is perhaps best known as the owner of the *Eleanor,* one of the ships later involved in the Boston Tea Party.
10. Joseph Otis to James Otis Sr., March 19, 1770, OFP.
11. *HRPT,* 1:87.
12. MOW, "A Thought on the Inestimable Blessing of Reason," Edmund M. Hayes, "The Private Poems of Mercy Otis Warren," *New England Quarterly* 54, no. 2 (June 1981): 213–14.

13. On Otis's political about-face in 1771, see John R. Galvin, *Three Men of Boston* (New York: Crowell, 1976), 219–20; John J. Waters, *The Otis Family in Provincial and Revolutionary Massachusetts* (New York: Norton, 1975), 178–80; and Clifford K. Shipton, "James Otis," in *Sibley's Harvard Graduates*, vol. 11, *1741–1745* (Boston: Massachusetts Historical Society, 1960), 282.
14. John Adams, *DAJA*, May 15, 1771, 2:14.
15. On the lawsuit against John Robinson, see Shipton, "James Otis," 279; Galvin, *Three Men*, 224, 232; and Katharine Susan Anthony, *First Lady of the Revolution: The Life of Mercy Otis Warren* (Garden City, NY: Doubleday, 1958), 72.
16. In one incident reported by John Adams, he berated a server at the British Coffee-House for failing to place four candles on the table. Adams, *DAJA*, August 8, 1771, 2:49.
17. On the finding of insanity and assignment of a custodian, see Shipton, "James Otis," 282–83, and Galvin, *Three Men*, 22.
18. Quote variously attributed to Thomas Hutchinson, December 1771: Anthony, *First Lady*, 72; Shipton, "James Otis," 283; and James H. Stark, *The Loyalists of Massachusetts and the Other Side of the Revolution* (Boston: W. B. Clarke, 1907), 35. A post-chaise was a horse-drawn carriage built for long-distance post travel (via relay stations). Hutchinson implied that JOJ was being removed to custody far from Boston society.
19. "Letter from Hannah Winthrop to Mercy Otis Warren, 1 January 1772," MHS Collections Online, http://www.masshist.org.
20. Jimenez, *Changing Faces of Madness*, 50.
21. MOW to JOJ, December 28, 1771, MOWP.
22. On JOJ's life and activities around Hull, see "Notes: Reminiscences of James Otis," *Historical Magazine* 10 (1866): 13–14, and Shipton, "James Otis," 283.
23. Marion Rust, *Prodigal Daughters: Susanna Rowson's Early American Women* (Chapel Hill: University of North Carolina Press, 2008), 6.
24. On Susanna Rowson, see ibid., and Patricia L. Parker, *Susanna Rowson* (Boston: Twayne, 1986).

## CHAPTER 9: THE SCRIBBLER

1. John Adams to Hezekiah Niles, February 13, 1818, *WJA*, 10:283.
2. An idea advanced by Harvard professor David Armitage. See Armitage, "Every Great Revolution Is a Civil War," in *Scripting Revolution: A Historical Approach to the Comparative Study of Revolutions*, ed. Keith Michael Baker and Dan Edelstein (Stanford, CA: Stanford University Press, 2015), 57–68, 269–71.
3. *HRPT*, 1:100.
4. For further background on Puritan strictures against dramatic performance, see Edmund S. Morgan, "Puritan Hostility to the Theatre," *Proceedings of the American Philosophical Society* 110, no. 5 (October 27, 1966):

340–47. For more on thematic elements of Warren's satiric plays, see Jeffrey H. Richards, *Mercy Otis Warren* (New York: Twayne, 1995).

5. MOW to "A Very Young Lady," November 1791, MOWP. On MOW's views of gender roles, writing, and family values in general, see especially Rosemarie Zagarri, *Woman's Dilemma: Mercy Otis Warren and the American Revolution,* 2nd ed. (1995; Hoboken, NJ: Wiley, 2015), chap. 3.
6. On republican motherhood, see Linda K. Kerber, *Women of the Republic: Intellect and Ideology in Revolutionary America* (Chapel Hill: University of North Carolina Press, 1980), and Kerber, "The Republican Mother: Women and the Enlightenment—An American Perspective," *American Quarterly* 28, no. 2 (Summer 1976): 187–205.
7. Zagarri, *Woman's Dilemma,* 69.
8. MOW, *The Adulateur,* act 1, scene 1, in *The Plays and Poems of Mercy Otis Warren: Facsimile Reproductions,* ed. Benjamin Franklin (Delmar, NY: Scholars' Facsimiles and Reprints, 1980).
9. Ibid., act 1, scene 2.
10. Quoted in Katharine Susan Anthony, *First Lady of the Revolution: The Life of Mercy Otis Warren* (Garden City, NY: Doubleday, 1958), 84.
11. For example, Elisha Hutchinson, the governor's son, recounted "a melancholy adventure to the very sympathetic Chief Justice Hazelrod." *Boston Gazette,* January 24, 1774, quoted in Nancy Rubin Stuart, *The Muse of the Revolution: The Secret Pen of Mercy Otis Warren and the Founding of a Nation* (Boston: Beacon, 2008), 58.
12. MOW, *The Adulateur,* act 1, scene 1.
13. Ibid., act 4, scene 2; act 3, scene 1; act 5, scene 3.
14. MOW to "A Very Young Lady," November 1791, MOWP.
15. MOW to James Warren, April 22, 1772, *MOWSL,* 6.
16. James Otis Sr. to JOJ, August 1, 1772, GOFP.
17. John Adams, *DAJA,* October 27, 1772, 2:64–65.
18. MOW to Sarah Walter Hesilrige, ca. December 1773 or March 1774, *MOWSL,* 21.
19. Catharine Macaulay to JOJ, April 27, 1769, *WAL,* 7.
20. MOW to Catharine Macaulay, June 9, 1773, *MOWSL,* 15–16.
21. On the relationship and correspondence between MOW and Catharine Macaulay, see Kate Davies, *Catharine Macaulay and Mercy Otis Warren: The Revolutionary Atlantic and the Politics of Gender* (New York: Oxford University Press, 2005).
22. MOW to Winslow Warren, November 11, 1784, *MOWSL,* 192.
23. MOW to Catharine Macaulay, June 9, 1773, *MOWSL,* 16.
24. The other historians include, notably, William Gordon, *The History of the Rise, Progress, and Establishment of the Independence of the United States of America,* 3rd American ed. (New York: Samuel Campbell, 1801).

25. *HRPT,* 1:109.
26. George Bancroft, *History of the United States, from the Discovery of the American Continent* (Boston: Little Brown, 1856), 6:430, 431–32.
27. Stuart, *Muse,* 46.
28. *HRPT,* 1:109.
29. Anthony, *First Lady,* 86.
30. Thomas Hutchinson to Thomas Whately, January 20, 1769, Thomas Hutchinson, *History of the Colony and Province of Massachusetts-Bay* (Cambridge, MA: Harvard University Press, 1936), 3:293.
31. On the assembly's response to the Whately letters, see John R. Galvin, *Three Men of Boston* (New York: Crowell, 1976), 257–58.
32. MOW, *The Defeat,* act 3, scene 2, in Franklin, ed., *Plays and Poems.*
33. Ibid., act 2, scene 2.
34. Ibid.
35. *HRPT,* 1:107.
36. John Adams to James Warren, December 22, 1773, *PJA,* 2:3.
37. MOW, "The Squabble of the Sea Nymphs," *PDM,* 202–5.
38. *HRPT,* 1:108.
39. Ibid., 1:157.
40. For accounts of Hutchinson's departure, see Bernard Bailyn, *The Ordeal of Thomas Hutchinson* (Cambridge, MA: Belknap Press of Harvard University Press, 1974), 271–73, and Andrew Stephen Walmsley, *Thomas Hutchinson and the Origins of the American Revolution* (New York: New York University Press, 1999), 1–3.
41. Walmsley, *Thomas Hutchinson,* 155.
42. *HRPT,* 1:125.
43. MOW, "Female Foible Love of Dress," *Royal American Magazine,* June 1774, 233. MOW also included it in *PDM,* 208, under the title "To the Hon. J. Winthrop, Esq."
44. A detailed account of events in the spring and summer of 1774 appears in Ray Raphael, *The First American Revolution: Before Lexington and Concord* (New York: New Press, 2002).
45. On the events of September 1774 in Barnstable, see Simeon Deyo, *History of Barnstable County, Massachusetts* (New York: H. W. Blake, 1890), 68–69, and John J. Waters, *The Otis Family in Provincial and Revolutionary Massachusetts* (New York: Norton, 1975), 184–86.
46. Deyo, *History of Barnstable County,* 69–70. The original founding document, dated November 16, 1774, is contained in the James Otis Papers, box 2, MHS.
47. Waters, *The Otis Family,* 185.
48. Samuel Allyne Otis to Joseph Otis, June 4, 1774, quoted in Galvin, *Three Men,* 272.

49. Clifford K. Shipton, "James Otis," in *Sibley's Harvard Graduates,* vol. 11, *1741–1745* (Boston: Massachusetts Historical Society, 1960), 283.
50. Frederick Freeman, *The History of Cape Cod: The Annals of Barnstable County and of Its Several Towns* (Boston: Rand and Avery, 1860–62), 2:307.
51. MOW to Catharine Macaulay, December 29, 1774, *MOWSL,* 39.

## CHAPTER 10: "THERE IS NO RECEDING"

1. MOW to Abigail Adams, December 29, 1774, *MOWSL,* 41.
2. MOW to John Adams, July 14, 1774, MOWP, quoted in Nancy Rubin Stuart, *The Muse of the Revolution: The Secret Pen of Mercy Otis Warren and the Founding of a Nation* (Boston: Beacon, 2008), 64.
3. Alluding again to the line from "The Squabble of the Sea Nymphs": "None will neglect the sex's sage advice." *PDM,* 203.
4. James Warren to MOW, April 7, 1775, *WAL,* 1:44.
5. James Warren to John Adams, January 15, 1775, *WAL,* 1:36.
6. MOW, *The Group,* act 1, scene 1, in *The Plays and Poems of Mercy Otis Warren: Facsimile Reproductions,* ed. Benjamin Franklin (Delmar, NY: Scholars' Facsimiles and Reprints, 1980), act 1, stage setting/directions.
7. Ibid., act 1, scene 1.
8. Ibid.
9. Ibid., act 2, scene 3.
10. For more on the Warrens' ride, see Stuart, *Muse,* 73–74.
11. Stuart, *Muse,* 127, mentions two loyalist cousins in the area—Nathaniel Ray Winslow in Marshfield and Edward Winslow in Plymouth. On the latter, see "Winslow, Edward," in *Dictionary of Canadian Biography,* vol. 5, *1801–20,* ed. George W. Brown, David M. Hayne, and Francess G. Halpenny, http://www.biographi.ca.
12. MOW to Sarah Bowen Brown, April 1775, *MOWSL,* 47.
13. MOW to James Otis Sr., April 1775, MOWP.
14. On the mustering and march of the Barnstable militia in April 1775, see John J. Waters, *The Otis Family in Provincial and Revolutionary Massachusetts* (New York: Norton, 1975), 187, and Donald Grant Trayser, *Barnstable: Three Centuries of a Cape Cod Town* (Hyannis, MA: Goss, 1939), 448.
15. Elizabeth Ellet, *The Women of the American Revolution* (New York: Baker and Scribner, 1848–50), 1:75.
16. James Warren to MOW, June 18,1775, WAL, 1:59–61.
17. A photograph and transcription of the Proclamation of Rebellion, issued August 23, 1775, can be viewed at "By the King, a Proclamation, for Suppressing Rebellion and Sedition," MHS Collections Online, http://www.masshist.org.

18. On James Warren's election to the speakership, Mercy's reaction and migraines, see Stuart, *Muse*, 75–76.
19. MOW to Dorothy Quincy Hancock, ca. April 1776, *MOWSL*, 41.
20. Kate Davies, *Catharine Macaulay and Mercy Otis Warren: The Revolutionary Atlantic and the Politics of Gender* (New York: Oxford University Press, 2005), 13.
21. MOW to James Warren, December 2, 1775, MOWP.
22. MOW to John Adams, August 2, 1775, MOWP, quoted in Ellet, *Women*, 1:30.
23. James Warren to John Adams, addendum dictated by MOW, November 14–16, 1775, *WAL*, 1:184.
24. On smallpox, the Boston epidemic, and variolation, see Elizabeth Fenn, *Pox Americana: The Great Smallpox Epidemic of 1775–82* (New York: Hill and Wang, 2001), and Samuel Bayard Woodward, "The Story of Smallpox in Massachusetts," *New England Journal of Medicine* 206, no. 23 (1932): 1181–91.
25. Adams recounts the inoculation and follow-up care in his autobiography text for the years 1764–65, *DAJA*, 3:280.
26. James Warren to John Adams, July 17, 1776, *WAL*, 1:261.
27. MOW to James Warren, November 24, 1776, *MOWSL*, 79.
28. On Elizabeth (Betsy) Otis Brown, her marriage, and her departure to England, see William Augustus Otis, *A Genealogical and Historical Memoir of the Otis Family in America* (Chicago: W. A. Otis, 1924), 137; John Adams to Elizabeth Brown, December 10, 1785, *PJA*, 18:25; James H. Ellis, *Luminaries of Early West Barnstable: The Stories of a Cape Cod Village* (Charleston, SC: History Press, 2014), 61; and Clifford K. Shipton, "James Otis," in *Sibley's Harvard Graduates*, vol. 11, *1741–1745* (Boston: Massachusetts Historical Society, 1960), 284.
29. On James Otis III and Mary Otis Lincoln, see Otis, *Genealogical and Historical Memoir*, 137–38; Ellis, *Luminaries of Early West Barnstable*, 61; and Shipton, "James Otis," 284.
30. On the breakdown and return home of young James Warren, see *MOWSL*, editor's note, 74–75, and Stuart, *Muse*, 112–13.
31. Abigail Adams to John Adams, May 27, 1776, *The Letters of John and Abigail Adams*, ed. Frank Shuffelton (New York: Penguin, 2004), 108.
32. MOW to James Warren (son), June 1776, *MOWSL*, 76.
33. She referred to him in identical terms in letters to husband James, March 12, 1780, and Winslow himself, March 25, 1780, both *MOWSL*, 128–29.
34. MOW, *The Blockheads*, act 1, scenes 1, 2; act 3, scenes 1, 3, in Franklin, ed., *Plays and Poems of Mercy Otis Warren*.
35. James Warren to John Adams, July 17, 1776, *WAL*, 1:261–62.

36. MOW had been in Boston the previous weekend to be inoculated. Husband James's letter to John Adams was dated one day before the reading of the Constitution, for which Abigail was on hand as well. "Great attention was given to every word," Abigail wrote to her husband, John, on July 21. Abigail Adams to John Adams, July 21, 1776, L. H. Butterfield et al., *Adams Family Correspondence* (Cambridge, MA: Belknap Press of Harvard University Press, 1963–), 2:56.
37. From John Adams's abstract of the Writs of Assistance Case, ca. April 1761, *LPJA*, 3:144.
38. *HRPT,* 1:310–11.
39. Joseph Otis to Benjamin Edes, July 18, 1776, cited in Waters, *The Otis Family*, 188n14; Peter Force, ed., *American Archives: Consisting of a Collection of Authentick Records, State Papers, Debates, and Letters and Other Notices of Publick Affairs* (Washington, DC: M. St. Clair Carl and Peter Force, 1848), 1:147–48.
40. For details of local mobilization and the war effort, see Simeon Deyo, *History of Barnstable County, Massachusetts* (New York: H. W. Blake, 1890), 71–72; Frederick Freeman, *The History of Cape Cod: The Annals of Barnstable County and of Its Several Towns* (Boston: Rand and Avery, 1860–62), 1:496–518; and Waters, *The Otis Family*, 190–91.
41. Deyo, *History of Barnstable County,* 72–73.
42. MOW to James Warren, September 15, 1776, *MOWSL,* 77–78.
43. MOW to John Adams, September 19, 1776, *WAL,* 1:274.
44. MOW to John Adams, August 10, 1777, *WAL,* 1:349.
45. MOW to James Warren, June 14, 1777, *MOWSL,* 96.
46. MOW to Abigail Adams, December 1, 1776, Butterfield et al., eds., *Adams Family Correspondence,* 2:143.
47. Shipton, "James Otis," 285, citing *Diary and Letters of His Excellency Thomas Hutchinson, Esq.*, ed. Peter Orlando Hutchinson (Boston: Houghton and Mifflin, 1884–86), 2:232.
48. Shipton, "James Otis," 285, citing Elkanah Watson, *Men and Times of the Revolution* (New York: Dana, 1861), 89.
49. Shipton, "James Otis," 285, citing Benjamin Guild Diary, October 1778, MHS.
50. MOW to James Warren, n.d., quoted in Susan Anthony, *First Lady of the Revolution: The Life of Mercy Otis Warren* (Garden City, NY: Doubleday, 1958), 116.
51. MOW to Abigail Adams, January 19, 1779, Butterfield et al., eds., *Adams Family Correspondence,* 3:152.
52. James Otis Sr., will, attested copy, April 21, 1774, GOFP.
53. Ibid.

54. MOW to John Adams, December 16, 1778, *MOWSL*, 106–7.
55. Rosemarie Zagarri, *Woman's Dilemma: Mercy Otis Warren and the American Revolution*, 2nd ed. (1995; Hoboken, NJ: Wiley, 2015), 52.

## CHAPTER 11: THE FLAMING CAR

1. Reverend Shaw was the father of Lemuel Shaw (1781–1861), who served for thirty years as chief justice of the Massachusetts Supreme Judicial Court, the position James Otis Sr. coveted but never got.
2. On politics in Barnstable, Joseph's election loss, and the Otis dynasty, see John J. Waters, *The Otis Family in Provincial and Revolutionary Massachusetts* (New York: Norton, 1975), 191–96.
3. MOW to John Adams, October 15, 1778, *WAL*, 2:54.
4. MOW, "The Genius of America," *PDM*, 249n; *Boston Gazette*, October 5, 1778.
5. MOW to John Adams, [May?] 1783, *MOWSL*, 168.
6. MOW to Winslow Warren, December 4, 1779, *MOWSL*, 119.
7. MOW to James Warren, April 5, 1778, MOWP.
8. Abigail Adams to MOW, [January?] 1777, L. H. Butterfield et al., *Adams Family Correspondence* (Cambridge, MA: Belknap Press of Harvard University Press, 1963–), 2:150.
9. Susan Anthony, *First Lady of the Revolution: The Life of Mercy Otis Warren* (Garden City, NY: Doubleday, 1958), 120.
10. "In 1777, long after the evacuation of Massachusetts by the enemy, we find that 12,591, out of 68,720 troops enlisted, were from Massachusetts, being a larger number than any other state. The same lead was maintained throughout the war, except in 1779 and 1780. . . . Massachusetts soldiers marched or sailed to every colony, and bore their part of every battle, from Bunker Hill down to Yorktown." Ainsworth Rand Spofford, *Massachusetts in the American Revolution* (Washington, DC: Society of the Sons of the American Revolution, 1895), 14–15.
11. MOW to John Adams, May 8, 1780, *MOWSL*, 134.
12. MOW to Abigail Adams, March 14, 1779, *MOWSL*, 108.
13. Ibid., 107.
14. MOW to James Warren, June 1, 1779, quoted in Anthony, *First Lady*, 121.
15. James Warren to MOW, June 6, 1779, *WAL*, 2:101.
16. MOW, *The Motley Assembly*, scene 2, scene 4, coda, in *The Plays and Poems of Mercy Otis Warren*, ed. Benjamin Franklin (Delmar, NY: Scholars' Facsimiles and Reprints, 1980).
17. JOJ, *Boston Gazette*, January 11, 1762.
18. MOW to Hannah Fayerwether Winthrop, 1774, *MOWSL*, 28.
19. MOW to James Warren, March 12, 1780, *MOWSL*, 128.
20. MOW to John Adams, May 8, 1780, *MOWSL*, 133.

21. Nancy Rubin Stuart, *The Muse of the Revolution: The Secret Pen of Mercy Otis Warren and the Founding of a Nation* (Boston: Beacon, 2008), 149.
22. Waters, *The Otis Family*, 195.
23. See MOW to John Adams, May 8, 1780, *MOWSL*, 133.
24. Traditional sources refer to him as Joseph, Isaac, or Samuel Osgood, all of Andover. Modern sources, including the Andover Preservation Commission/Andover Historical Society, identify the owner of the home and Otis's host as Jacob Osgood (1752–1838), the fourth son of Captain Isaac Osgood (1713–1792).
25. MOW to Janet Livingston Montgomery, January 5, 1780, *MOWSL*, 125.
26. MOW to James Warren, January 27, 1781, quoted in Anthony, *First Lady*, 133.
27. James Warren to Winslow Warren, June 15, 1781, quoted in Stuart, *Muse*, 156.
28. Captain Barry went on to fame as the first commissioned officer in the U.S. Navy (February 22, 1797), with the title of "commodore." He shares unofficial recognition with John Paul Jones as the "Father of the American Navy."
29. James Warren to Winslow Warren, June 15, 1781, quoted in Stuart, *Muse*, 156.
30. MOW to Winslow Warren, September 28, 1781, *MOWSL*, 154.
31. Ibid., 153.
32. *HRPT*, 3:26.
33. Ibid., 1:88.
34. Quoted in William Tudor, *The Life of James Otis, of Massachusetts* (Boston: Wells and Lilly, 1823), 481.
35. On James's visit to Boston, see Harrison Gray Otis letter, n.d., quoted in Tudor, *Life*, 482–83n.
36. As recounted in Clifford K. Shipton, "James Otis," in *Sibley's Harvard Graduates*, vol. 11, *1741–1745* (Boston: Massachusetts Historical Society, 1960), 285; and John R. Galvin, *Three Men of Boston* (New York: Crowell, 1976), 299–300.
37. As recounted in Tudor, *Life*, 482; Anthony, *First Lady*, 145; and Stuart, *Muse*, 165.
38. JOJ to John Hancock, May 12, 1783, quoted in Shipton, "James Otis," 285.
39. John Adams to William Tudor, June 5, 1817, *WJA*, 10:265.
40. John Adams to MOW, September 10, 1783, *WAL*, 2:224.
41. Tudor, *Life*, 485–86.
42. James Clark Ridpath, *James Otis: The Pre-Revolutionist* (Milwaukee, WI: Campbell, 1898), 80; Francies Bowen, *Life of James Otis* (Boston: Little and Brown, 1844), 194.
43. MOW to Elizabeth Otis Lincoln, June 15, 1783, *MOWSL*, 172.
44. Ibid., 173.

45. Ridpath, *James Otis*, 80; Shipton, "James Otis," 286
46. Tudor, *Life*, 483.

### CHAPTER 12: WRESTING A FEMALE PEN

1. *HRPT*, 3:248.
2. On the comings and goings of the family, see Susan Anthony, *First Lady of the Revolution: The Life of Mercy Otis Warren* (Garden City, NY: Doubleday, 1958), 138–43; Nancy Rubin Stuart, *The Muse of the Revolution: The Secret Pen of Mercy Otis Warren and the Founding of a Nation* (Boston: Beacon, 2008), 167; and Rosemarie Zagarri, *Woman's Dilemma: Mercy Otis Warren and the American Revolution*, 2nd ed. (1995; Hoboken, NJ: Wiley, 2015), 113–14.
3. MOW, *The Ladies of Castile*, dedication, in *PDM*, 99.
4. Ibid., 144.
5. Ibid., 143, 117.
6. Ibid., 101.
7. For an insightful discussion of the two dramatic works, see Nina Baym, "Mercy Otis Warren's Gendered Melodrama of Revolution," *South Atlantic Quarterly* 90 (1991): 531–54.
8. MOW, *The Sack of Rome*, epilogue, in *PDM*, 96.
9. John Adams to MOW, December 25, 1787, *WAL*, 2:301.
10. Anthony, *First Lady*, 135–36.
11. MOW to Winslow Warren, November 11, 1784, *MOWSL*, 192.
12. MOW to Winslow Warren, November 10, 1784, MOWP.
13. David Rich Dewey, *Financial History of the United States*, 5th ed. (New York: Longmans, Green, 1915), 56.
14. John J. Waters, *The Otis Family in Provincial and Revolutionary Massachusetts* (New York: Norton, 1975), 200–201.
15. MOW to Winslow Warren, November 11, 1784, *MOWSL*, 190.
16. *Boston Gazette*, February 14, 1785, quoted in Charles Warren, "Samuel Adams and the Sans Souci Club in 1785," *Proceedings of the Massachusetts Historical Society*, 3rd series, 60 (1926–27), 341.
17. MOW to Unknown, n.d., quoted in Anthony, *First Lady*, 143.
18. Ibid.
19. Henry Jackson to Henry Knox, March 12, 1786, Henry Knox Papers, Gilder Lehrman Institute of American History, http://www.americanhistory.amdigital.co.uk.
20. *HRPT*, 3:323.
21. Zagarri, *Woman's Dilemma*, 117.
22. MOW to John Adams, December 1786, *MOWSL*, 210.
23. *HRPT*, 3:347–48.
24. MOW to John Adams, December 1786, *MOWSL*, 210.

25. MOW to Catherine Macaulay Graham, September 28, 1787, quoted in Charles Warren, "Elbridge Gerry, James Warren, Mercy Warren and the Ratification of the Federal Constitution in Massachusetts," *Proceedings of the Massachusetts Historical Society,* 3rd series, 64 (1930–32): 162.
26. The original Boston edition, 1788, carries a printer's note identifying Gerry as the author.
27. MOW to Catharine Macaulay Graham, December 18, 1787, *MOWSL,* 215–17. For more on Charles Warren's discovery of the 1787 letter and his confirmation of MOW's authorship, see Warren, "Elbridge Gerry, James Warren, Mercy Warren, and the Ratification of the Federal Constitution," 143–64, and Janis L. McDonald, "The Need for Textual Revision: Mercy Otis Warren, a Case in Point," *Yale Journal of Law and Feminism* 5, no. 1 (1992): 185n5.
28. MOW, *Observations on the New Constitution, and on the Federal and State Conventions* (Brooklyn, NY: N.p., 1788), 8, 12–13.
29. Ibid., 6, 3.
30. Ibid., 23.
31. On the influence of the pamphlet, see Warren, "Elbridge Gerry, James Warren, Mercy Warren, and the Ratification of the Federal Constitution," 143, and Zagarri, *Woman's Dilemma,* 122–23.
32. *HRPT,* 3:357.
33. Thomas Hutchinson, Diary, October 19, 1779, *Diary and Letters of His Excellency Thomas Hutchinson,* ed. Peter Orlando Hutchinson (Boston: Houghton Mifflin, 1884–86), 2:290.
34. MOW to Catharine Macaulay Graham, May 31, 1791, *MOWSL,* 231.
35. Quoted in Stuart, *Muse,* 202.
36. *PDM,* iii.
37. MOW, "Lines, Written after a Very Severe Tempest, Which Cleared Up Extremely Pleasant," *PDM,* 219.
38. MOW, "To Mrs. Montague, Author of 'Observations on the Genius and Writing of Shakespeare,'" *PDM,* 182.

## CHAPTER 13: THE LAST FRAIL REED

1. MOW to Henry Knox, June 30, 1791, MOWP.
2. MOW to Winslow Warren, Spring 1791, quoted in Susan Anthony, *First Lady of the Revolution: The Life of Mercy Otis Warren* (Garden City, NY: Doubleday, 1958), 175.
3. MOW, unpublished newspaper article, quoted in Nancy Rubin Stuart, *The Muse of the Revolution: The Secret Pen of Mercy Otis Warren and the Founding of a Nation* (Boston: Beacon, 2008), 182.
4. MOW to Janet Livingston Montgomery, April 1792, *MOWSL,* 235.

5. MOW, "Written in Deep Affliction," Edmund M. Hayes, "The Private Poems of Mercy Otis Warren," *New England Quarterly* 54, no. 2 (June 1981): 220–21.
6. Catharine Macaulay Graham, *Observations on the Reflections of the Right Hon. Edmund Burke* (London: C. Dilly, 1790).
7. MOW to Catharine Macaulay Graham, May 31, 1791, *MOWSL*, 231.
8. Thomas Jefferson, "II. The Response," February 12, 1790, *The Papers of Thomas Jefferson*, ed. Julian P. Boyd et al. (Princeton, NJ: Princeton University Press, 1950–), 16:179.
9. MOW, *Observations on the New Constitution, and on the Federal and State Conventions* (Brooklyn, NY: N.p., 1788), 14.
10. MOW to John Adams, April 2, 1789, *WAL*, 2:309.
11. John Adams to MOW, March 2, 1789, *WAL*, 2:305–6.
12. MOW to John Adams, May 8, 1789, *MOWSL*, 218–20.
13. John Adams to MOW, May 29, 1789, *WAL*, 2:314; MOW to John Adams, May 8, 1789, *MOWSL*, 218.
14. Abigail wrote about Mercy and the Warrens to sister Mary Smith Cranch on July 12, 1789: "I know no other equally ambitious, but I presume her pretensions and those of her family will fail, as I think they ought to if one quarter part is true which has been reported of them." Abigail Adams to Mary Smith Cranch, July 12, 1789, *Adams Family Correspondence*, ed. L. H. Butterfield et al. (Cambridge, MA: Belknap Press of Harvard University Press, 1963–), 8:390.
15. "Washington's Farewell Address, 1796," The Avalon Project, Yale Law School, Lillian Goldman Law Library, https://avalon.law.yale.edu. The address first appeared in the *American Daily Advertiser*, a Philadelphia newspaper, on September 19, 1796, and then in other publications around the country. There were no presidential term limits until ratification of the Twenty-Second Amendment in 1951.The modern rules and procedures for electing a president and vice president did not go into effect until 1804, under the Twelfth Amendment.
16. MOW to Samuel Allyne Otis, March 23, 1800, MOWP.
17. MOW to Sarah Gray Cary, February 7, 1802, *MOWSL*, 250.
18. Thomas Jefferson to Spencer Roane, September 6, 1819, *The Writings of Thomas Jefferson*, ed. H. A. Washington (New York: J. C. Riker, 1853–55), 10:140.
19. *HRPT*, 3:435.
20. "Thomas Jefferson's Library," Library of Congress Memory Exhibition, http://www.loc.gov.
21. *HRPT*, 1:vi.
22. This insight comes from Leonard H. Cohen in his foreword to MOW's *History* in the Online Library of Liberty (Indianapolis: Liberty Fund, 1994), vol. 1, https://oll.libertyfund.org: "History was 'philosophy teaching by

examples,' as Lord Bolingbroke had written; it 'inculcates images of virtue and vice,' and its proper task was to train people, especially young people, in 'public and private virtue.' This was the eighteenth-century version of the 'exemplary theory of history,' which swept the Revolutionary generation of historians and which accorded perfectly with Warren's understanding of her proper role." This approach to history, it might be noted, also accorded with John Locke's precept of teaching children by example and practice rather than by rule (see chapter 5).

23. *HRPT,* 1:1.
24. Ibid., 1:85.
25. Ibid., 1:85–86.
26. "Mrs. Warren's History of the Revolution," *The Panoplist* 2 (1807): 380.
27. *HRPT,* 3:392–94.
28. John Adams to MOW, July 11, 1807, "Correspondence between John Adams and Mercy Warren Relating to Her 'History of the American Revolution,' July–August, 1807," *Collections of the Massachusetts Historical Society,* 5th series, 4, part 3 (1878): 321–28.
29. Ibid., 328.
30. MOW to John Adams, July 16, 1807, ibid., 328–30.
31. John Adams to MOW, July 30, 1807, ibid., 391.
32. MOW to John Adams, August 1, 1807, ibid., 397.
33. John Adams to MOW, August 15, 1807, ibid., 463.
34. MOW to John Adams, August 27, 1807, ibid., 490–91.
35. Abigail Adams to MOW, December 30, 1812, ibid., 502. The matching handkerchief pin and ring, both with gold settings and seed pearls, are archived at the MHS.
36. MOW to John Adams, July 10, 1814, *WAL,* 2:395.
37. John Adams to MOW, August 17, 1814, *WAL,* 2:396.
38. John Adams to Elbridge Gerry, April 17, 1813, *WAL,* 2:380.
39. D. Hamilton Hurd, *History of Plymouth County, Massachusetts, with Biographical Sketches* (Philadelphia: J. W. Lewis, 1884), 154.
40. Simeon Deyo, *History of Barnstable County, Massachusetts* (New York: H. W. Blake, 1890), 78–81; Frederick Freeman, *The History of Cape Cod: The Annals of Barnstable County and of Its Several Towns* (Boston: Rand and Avery, 1860–62), 1:751.
41. Quoted in Alice Brown, *Mercy Otis Warren* (New York: Charles Scribner's Sons, 1896), 307–8.
42. MOW to Mary Gray Otis, May 24–25, 1814, *MOWSL,* 257.
43. See MOW, "A Thought in Sickness," Hayes, "The Private Poems of Mercy Otis Warren," 222.
44. Henry Warren to Maria Otis, October 19, 1814, GOFP.

## EPILOGUE

1. Simeon Deyo, *History of Barnstable County, Massachusetts* (New York: H. W. Blake, 1890), 375.
2. William Thomas Davis, *History of the Town of Plymouth: With a Sketch of the Origin and Growth of Separatism* (Philadelphia: J. W. Lewis, 1885), 100; D. Hamilton Hurd, *History of Plymouth County, Massachusetts, with Biographical Sketches* (Philadelphia: J. W. Lewis, 1884), 187, 184.
3. Jeffrey H. Richards, *Mercy Otis Warren* (New York: Twayne, 1995), 155; Thomas Warren, *A History and Genealogy of the Warren Family* (N.p.: N.p., 1902), 350; William Thomas Davis, *Plymouth Memories of an Octogenarian* (Plymouth, MA: Memorial Press, 1906), 169–70; "Necrology of Historic, Genealogical Society," *New England Historical and Genealogical Register* 29 (1875): 107.
4. William Tudor, *The Life of James Otis, of Massachusetts* (Boston: Wells and Lilly, 1823), 20.
5. J. L. Bell, "Poor Mrs. Brown, Who Was Betsy Otis," Boston 1775, April 12, 2015, http://boston1775.blogspot.com. Bell cites an English genealogical work, *Lincolnshire Pedigrees*, ed. Canon A. R. Maddison (London: N.p., 1902), 1:183.
6. John J. Waters, *The Otis Family in Provincial and Revolutionary Massachusetts* (New York: Norton, 1975), 181n75.
7. The insight of Rosemarie Zagarri, *Woman's Dilemma: Mercy Otis Warren and the American Revolution*, 2nd ed. (1995; Hoboken, NJ: Wiley, 2015), 129.
8. John Adams to Hezekiah Niles, February 13, 1818, *WJA*, 10:283.

# Index

*In this index, James Otis Jr. is abbreviated as JOJ and Mercy Otis Warren as MOW. Page numbers in italics refer to photographs and illustrations. Letters are indexed under the name of the letter's author.*